Constructing Music

Constructing Music

Musical Explorations in Creative Coding

TERESA M. NAKRA

OXFORD
UNIVERSITY PRESS

Oxford University Press is a department of the University of Oxford. It furthers
the University's objective of excellence in research, scholarship, and education
by publishing worldwide. Oxford is a registered trade mark of Oxford University
Press in the UK and certain other countries.

Published in the United States of America by Oxford University Press
198 Madison Avenue, New York, NY 10016, United States of America.

© Oxford University Press 2024

All rights reserved. No part of this publication may be reproduced, stored in
a retrieval system, or transmitted, in any form or by any means, without the
prior permission in writing of Oxford University Press, or as expressly permitted
by law, by license, or under terms agreed with the appropriate reproduction
rights organization. Inquiries concerning reproduction outside the scope of the
above should be sent to the Rights Department, Oxford University Press, at the
address above.

You must not circulate this work in any other form
and you must impose this same condition on any acquirer.

Library of Congress Cataloging-in-Publication Data
Names: Marrin Nakra, Teresa (Teresa Anne), 1970– author.
Title: Constructing music : musical explorations in creative coding / Teresa M. Nakra.
Description: New York, NY : Oxford University Press, 2024. |
Includes bibliographical references and index.
Identifiers: LCCN 2023033838 (print) | LCCN 2023033839 (ebook) |
ISBN 9780197669204 (paperback) | ISBN 9780197669198 (hardback) |
ISBN 9780197669228 (epub)
Subjects: LCSH: Max (Computer file : Cycling '74) | Computer
music—Instruction and study. | Computer composition (Music)
Classification: LCC ML74.4.M39 M38 2023 (print) | LCC ML74.4.M39 (ebook) |
DDC 781.3/45133—dc23/eng/20230719
LC record available at https://lccn.loc.gov/2023033838
LC ebook record available at https://lccn.loc.gov/2023033839

DOI: 10.1093/oso/9780197669198.001.0001

Paperback printed by Marquis Book Printing, Canada
Hardback printed by Bridgeport National Bindery, Inc., United States of America

This work is dedicated with love to Jahangir, Yezad, and Anna Nakra, for their support, camaraderie, and stimulating conversations about life and music—at tea time, and always.

Contents

Foreword ix
   Youngmoo Kim
Preface xiii
Acknowledgments xv
About the Companion Website xvii

Introduction: The Mystery of Music 1
   I.1 Goals 2
   I.2 Reasons 3
   I.3 Uses 6
   I.4 Approach 7
   I.5 How to Use This Book 13

1 Tutorials 16
   1.1 Loops 19
   1.2 Simple Arithmetic 27
   1.3 MIDI Notes and Variables 35
   1.4 MIDI Basics 43
   1.5 Digital Audio Basics 53
   1.6 Hardware Kits and Controllers 56

2 Building Blocks 62
   2.1 Silence 64
   2.2 Sound 65
   2.3 Frequency 70
   2.4 Intensity 74
   2.5 Rhythm 79
   2.6 Valence 87
   2.7 Timbre 93

3 Pitch-based Structures 96
   3.1 Make a Note 96
   3.2 Name a Note 98
   3.3 Make an Interval 101
   3.4 Name an Interval 109
   3.5 Make a Scale 114
   3.6 Make a Chord 129
   3.7 Make a Key 132

4 Time-based Structures 138
   4.1 Tempo 139
   4.2 Meter 148
   4.3 Make a Melody 152
   4.4 Make an Arpeggio 162
   4.5 Make a Harmonic Progression 166

5 Finer Granularities — 170
- 5.1 Just Intonation — 170
- 5.2 Equal Temperament — 172
- 5.3 Playing in Tune — 176

6 Reflections — 179
- 6.1 On the Role of Technology and Invention in Music — 179
- 6.2 Creative Technology Enables Access and Inclusion — 182
- 6.3 Defining Music Broadly — 183
- 6.4 Music, Coding, and Constructionism — 184
- 6.5 Looping Back; Final Thoughts on Creative Coding and Music — 185

Notes — 187
Glossary — 197
Index — 215

Foreword

The histories of music and technology are highly interconnected. For example, advances in woodworking, metallurgy and casting, materials for strings, reeds and membranes, and much more enabled the development of the traditional orchestral instruments. Musical training has been profoundly advanced by writing, notation, printing, engraving, sound recording, and most recently, digital media. I would argue that new technology has always been a driver of musical creativity and innovation.

I would further argue that a book like this is long overdue. The pedagogy of (Western) music theory has been largely stuck in the mindset of the mid-twentieth century. Although the medium may have changed (from printed scores and staff paper to digital documents and streaming), the teaching of music theory largely retains a focus on the scales, rhythms, harmonies, and practices of Western "classical" music. Of course music itself, along with its associated practices and tools, has evolved substantially since the mid-twentieth century, so an evolution (or perhaps, revolution) of pedagogy is warranted.

In this book, Dr. Teresa M. Nakra puts forth a different and novel perspective: let us use modern technology to pursue the learning of music fundamentals alongside the building blocks of computing and coding. Although computers have been part of music making for generations, most still learn about music and computing through separate and distinct pursuits: musicianship (notation, instrumental training, theory, and composition) and computer-based tools (apps and devices for recording, processing, and synthesizing sound). Even when there is overlap, curricula tend to favor one over the other: some programs emphasize the technical details of computation and signal processing, while others place technology as tools in the service of music making. I believe there are even greater rewards when following the integrated approach of this text.

In my view, there is no one better qualified to author this book. Dr. Nakra has straddled the worlds of music and technology throughout her training and career. Her groundbreaking work in the field of Affective Computing studied how the gestures, movements, and physiological changes of renowned orchestra conductors can be sensed and translated into expressive intent. She has developed interactive, public music installations that have been presented in high-profile outlets around the globe. Professor Nakra has been teaching music and technology to undergraduate students for decades, and she currently oversees the Music Technology program at The College of New Jersey. This volume embodies her deep experiences combining and connecting music, computing, and learning.

The modules of the curriculum contained within this text are interactive, practical, and epitomize "learning by doing." In the best traditions of Constructionism, Seymour Papert's groundbreaking theory of learning, it encourages students to build, test, play with, and modify initially simple creations to scaffold the next layers of learning. Music is a practice, and the approach of this book makes musical learning similarly active and exploratory. Theory does not always translate into actual music making, but these lessons make the connections explicit. Making abstract concepts concrete through sound, manipulating that sound, and reflecting upon that to alter or solidify one's understanding of the concept represents a powerful form of iteration and a way of reinforcing core concepts. Each lesson is demonstrated through interactive interfaces ("patches"). Students first copy, then remix each patch to direct learning toward their interests. We are immediately introduced to capabilities that would be difficult or impossible to implement without computing, emphasizing how the technology can be much more than a tool, but a creativity amplifier when making music.

The *Max* application environment is an approachable starting point for students embarking upon a new journey of music and technology discovery. As Dr. Nakra emphasizes, it is a mature platform with an historic tradition and lineage of its own. The application itself is a direct descendant of pioneering work in computer music, created by those with a deep understanding of both music and computing. It is a groundbreaking tool for music making, but also much more. While other applications offer powerful tools for creation and production, *Max* allows users to directly connect musical concepts (rhythm, pitch, harmony, timbre, etc.) to physical and acoustic principles through computing. Students can deeply explore both the "signal" (sound waves and their properties) and the "symbol" (note, chord, etc.) simultaneously. The ceiling of what one can accomplish in this environment is nearly unlimited (even professional music producers and engineers view *Max* as "highly advanced").

In my view, the learning of music has long been overly beholden to "legacy technologies," and the field can be particularly averse to change. Music pedagogy draws upon centuries of handwritten and printed music notation, and much instruction remains within the constraints of those traditional formats (much less the theories and practices built upon them). Even the Musical Instrument Digital Interface (MIDI) standard, one of the first widespread digital technologies for music, remains predominant today, more than forty years after its introduction (an eternity for a technology standard). It's more than a bit contradictory, given how quickly popular musical styles and sounds have evolved over the last century. Musicians, composers, and producers are expected to boldly break from tradition to make new works and spawn new genres, which keeps the art vital and vibrant.

I believe this book to be an analogous effort for musical learning, boldly breaking from past practices to establish a new path forward. It is an exciting route with many unfamiliar stops along the way. We will soon be closer to the midpoint of the twenty-first century than its beginning, and university students today will have careers that extend well into the second half of the century. What knowledge, skills, and tools will they require in their careers? What new technologies will they encounter? There seems to be so much, too much in fact, to incorporate into every class or program.

In higher education, we find it easy to add requirements, but are loath to remove any piece. Many of us believe the solution is for our pedagogies to better integrate knowledge across disciplines, and this book demonstrates the benefits of such an approach. I believe that students following this text will be inspired by the possibilities, and they will be empowered to break new ground in the future, keeping our beloved art of music evergreen.

Dr. Youngmoo Kim,
Vice Provost of University and Community Partnerships
Professor of Electrical and Computer Engineering
Drexel University

Preface

Music theory is the study of how music is constructed. It is an important discipline for those who are learning to create and perform music because it provides analytical tools and skills that help explain why certain note combinations work well and sound "right" in different contexts. However, the way we teach music theory topics has remained largely unchanged for many years, despite rapid advances in technologies, sociocultural understandings, and best practices. Our techniques have drifted out of step and become disconnected from the way that music is made and consumed in contemporary societies. Norms, expectations, and approaches have changed, and teaching materials should be updated to reflect current lived experiences and ways of thinking.

Teaching methods and materials should represent the diverse ways in which humans experience and make music, in order for musical understanding and creativity to become more accessible. In order to regain cultural relevance, music theory curricula should evolve to include a wider range of musical genres, learning styles, and modes of musical production. Standards that previously excluded large populations of learners must be revised. It's not enough simply to transfer traditional methods directly to new technologies, such as paper-and-pencil notation skills to computer software; any continued use of notation literacy prerequisites itself remains a barrier that excludes those who did not have the privilege of access to childhood musical education.

Given that music theory teaching methods historically emphasized musical notation, the idea for this book originated with a question: how might we learn music theory without using any notation at all? The answer to that question was to develop a new method for teaching music fundamentals: a step-by-step sequence of lessons and examples using computer code. The goal is that this new method will connect different forms of music making; I hope that, after engaging with the concepts in this book, students will be prepared to learn musical notation, combining traditional and digital forms of music making.

In order to connect with music learners today, one needs a skill set that is well adapted for our rapidly evolving digital culture. It helps not only to be able to play an instrument or sing, but also to be well versed as a content creator, expert software user, and coder. And that is what this book emphasizes: the application of creative technologies to music fundamentals. Harnessing the computing knowledge today's students bring with them to the classroom, this book foregrounds creative coding practices and invites readers to engage directly with the components of musical structure. This interdisciplinary combination of music and code forms the foundation on which new forms of composition and music production will be realized for years to come. Technology will likely continue to increase in importance in the lives of future generations of students. Music learning can be connected to technology in ways that don't distract or detract from but rather enhance the overall experience.

Above all, the whole point of making music is to fulfill our human capacities for creativity and connection—whether through tools made of wood, horsehair, and catgut, or today's computers, tablets, and smartphones. As long as we are engaging in a creative process, we will continue to derive lasting benefits for our mental, emotional, and physical wellness. It is my hope that this book will serve as a useful bridge connecting music learning to creative technologies, inviting students from diverse backgrounds to experience the joy of making music in ways that amplify all voices and lift our collective spirits.

Acknowledgments

This book would not have been possible without the curious and creative students at The College of New Jersey (TCNJ) who helped me refine this content over many years. During my own student years, I was fortunate to work with superb teachers who shaped my ideas in ways that continue to resonate deeply; I am especially indebted to Tod Machover, Rosalind Picard, Marvin Minsky, John Harbison, Jan Swafford, Benjamin Zander, Shreeram Devasthali, Graeme Boone, Stephen L. Mosko, David Lewin, Ivan Tcherepnin, Luise Vosgerchian, Lucia Lin, Sophie Vilker, and Richard Freitas. I am grateful to TCNJ for the sabbatical release time that enabled me to finish this work; conversations and shared experiences with valued colleagues in the Departments of Music and Design and Creative Technology also provided the impetus to address barriers to learning and seek inclusive, equitable, student-centered approaches. Heartfelt personal thanks to Maurice Hall, Kim Pearson, Ursula Wolz, Robert Young McMahan, Colleen Sears, Chris Ault, John Kuiphoff, Josh Fishburn, Warren Buckleitner, Yuri Ivanov, and my team at Immersion Music. Sarah Dash and the Trenton Makes Music project helped me understand the critical importance of music and the arts in cultivating community vitality and resiliency. This work has been strengthened by the contributions of the many distinguished scholars, anonymous reviewers, and editors who advised on its preparation, including Norman Hirschy, Rachel Ruisard, V. J. Manzo, Jan Swafford, Robert Rowe, Stanley Pelkey, Gena Greher, Marti Epstein, and Martina Vasil. V. J. Manzo, Gena Greher, Veronica Li, and students at UMass Lowell and Worcester Polytechnic Institute provided valuable feedback on the software examples. Many thanks to Cycling '74 and the worldwide community of *Max* users for their generous information and support! And to my parents, Steve and Jane Marrin, who encouraged me to pursue what I loved and trusted that I would figure out what to do with that freedom.

About the Companion Website

www.oup.com/us/ConstructingMusic

This book features a companion website containing a set of sample code "patches" referenced throughout the text.

To be able to use the patches provided, you will first need to download and install *Max* software on your computer. Instructions are provided in the Introduction and at https://cycling74.com/. Afterward, you can download example patches from the website URL listed above and run them in conjunction with the lessons in this book.

As you progress through each lesson, first read the written description and then apply the information by running the associated code example on your device. Instructions will guide your interactions and explain how each example works. As you gain confidence and facility using *Max*, you will gradually be able to independently edit and expand upon the examples. Give yourself permission to get creative as you explore the capabilities of this software tool. You are cordially invited to experiment with and remix the examples in your own unique way, reorganizing the elements and modifying the code to make it "your own."

Max code examples are provided using Creative Commons license CC BY-SA type, which allows reusers to distribute, remix, adapt, and build upon the material in any medium or format, so long as attribution is given to Teresa M. Nakra and Oxford University Press. The license allows for commercial use. If you remix, adapt, or build upon the material, you must license the modified material under identical terms. License definitions available here: https://creativecommons.org/about/cclicenses/.

Introduction

The Mystery of Music

When I was a small child, my parents kept a record player in our living room. My mom, who delighted in the joys of early childhood, encouraged me and my siblings to engage in boisterous play. One of the things she particularly enjoyed doing with us, especially on cold or rainy days when we couldn't go outside, was to run around and dance to music. This was a great way for us to work out our extra energy and stay emotionally positive while stuck at home. Mom kept a few prized records in the turntable cabinet—some classical symphonies, a few folk groups, military marches, and Disney soundtracks. One of my favorite things to do was to put on a record all by myself and dance deliriously to the music, moving my arms and legs in synchrony with the shapes of the sounds, allowing the music to move through me. It felt mysterious and magical, as if my movements were unlocking something important and profound.

Years later, after studying, performing, researching, and teaching music for decades, those memories of pure joy, transcendence, and spiritual connection with music come flooding back vividly. I remember with clarity what it felt like to spin and twist and careen around the room, completely engaged in a moment of ecstatic perfection. Music is freedom! Music is wellness! And it is also a glorious mystery.

Why does music have such a strong pull on us? How does it affect our emotions? How does it help promote inventiveness, imagination, and positive energy? How does it help us cope with the difficult parts of life? The wonderful truth is that no one really knows for sure, despite significant scientific research to map the brain regions that activate during musical experiences and measure the physiological signals of musicians. Music confounds most attempts to explain where its powers come from.

Some of that mystery is good—we don't necessarily always want to know exactly how music works or how it works on us. Some people worry that if we probe too deeply, we might lose the ability to experience that special magic—that a deeper understanding of music's construction will take away the childlike wonder it instills. In my experience, the opposite is true! For every new insight gained about how music works, another question arises. There is a wonderful sense of infinity in the search for musical meaning and the origins of musical behavior. Do not be concerned about that aspect—I can promise that you will have just as much wonder and joy in your future musical experiences after working through this book. And perhaps you might have a new appreciation for the depth and complexities involved.

Music itself is in a constant state of transformation, co-evolving alongside human cultures and technical tools. In some ways, our understanding of how music works and what it means is still somewhat dependent on earlier ways of thinking. Artificial Intelligence (AI) pioneer Marvin Minsky once said that music is "like Chemistry before the Periodic Table, and there's lots to do."[1] Prior to Mendeleev's groundbreaking discovery in 1869, chemical properties were understood in an ad hoc way—each element was understood singly, without the benefit of a systemic understanding that tied it all together. The medieval precursor to a structured understanding of chemistry was called *alchemy*: a traditional practice in which people perceived chemical processes as magical transformations of materials. In many ways, our modern approach to music is like alchemy—we have a basic understanding of the building blocks and how to put them together to make a result that feels spellbinding and produces an intended effect. But much remains to be understood about the processes that underlie music's power over us. This is not a criticism, but rather an invitation to investigate further! This book represents an attempt to make some progress on that front.

As part of this exploration, it is important for us to proceed humbly by striving to overcome challenges and engaging with disappointment about not meeting expectations. Although it's not fun to struggle, grappling with negative emotions may be a necessary part of the learning process.[2] It can help us realize important life lessons and contextualize our experiences along the way. This is especially true in music, where it helps to develop an attitude of confidence and continual self-improvement. Regardless of what raw materials we bring to the starting line, everyone can have a good experience developing their musical potential and creativity through dedicated effort and attention. Although your individual focus and commitment might wax and wane throughout the years, nonetheless musical skills transfer and accumulate through experience. So don't give up on yourself! The creative process is not easy and has many pitfalls, but can be satisfying and meaningful. I invite you to release yourself from any emotional baggage that may be holding you back from your creative potential. Take a moment to sit back, contemplate any raw fear of failure or mediocrity, acknowledge it fully, and let it go. And in that cathartic moment, enjoy the gorgeous possibilities in front of you! Let's dig in.

1.1 Goals

The aim of this book is to present a practical and fun way to explore music fundamentals that leverages the computing skills students already possess. The software examples foreground creative coding practices and invite readers to engage directly with the components of musical structure. Readers can try out accompanying code examples to reinforce each topic through simulation, modification, and experimentation. Once readers start to gain a level of comfort with the software environment, they can then start to use it as an authoring tool to modify, remix, and personalize the code examples for themselves.

This book focuses on the practical application of coding to the core musical skills that college students often encounter during first- and second-semester music theory courses. Each section presents basic information about a music theory topic and encourages readers to follow along with both guided and self-directed software explorations that reinforce the topic. While this approach does not completely replace the comprehensive music theory curriculum available in textbooks, it nonetheless maps out a new way to explore that content. This book could be an effective complement to a classic music theory textbook that fully fleshes out the topics in greater detail.[3] It could also work really well in combination with another software-based, creative approach to teaching musical fundamentals, such as Ableton's "Learning Music" website, located at https://learningmusic.ableton.com. While this book will occasionally provide "right" and "wrong" answers in certain cases, the goal is to encourage learners to apply that information toward creative outcomes. The book has not been designed for drill-and-practice work or testing, but rather to incorporate the results of that learning into projects and compositions that use musical elements in interesting ways.

We will investigate the ways in which music is constructed by engaging directly with its building blocks. After completing several basic software tutorials in Chapter 1, we will encounter the core content in Chapters 2–5. Here we will explore creative coding practices and simulate the fundamental elements of musical structure. The process of working through Chapters 1–5 will raise questions about music, creativity, and technology, which we will discuss briefly in Chapter 6.

In this book, we will also focus on the ways in which individual building blocks can be grouped together to create larger forms. Just as you can combine Lego pieces together in larger and larger configurations, recognizable structures in music can be thought of as combinations of basic sonic elements in different arrangements. And various levels of musical structure, from simple to advanced, can themselves be combined into macrostructures to form the outer architectures of a piece of music.

I.2 Reasons

The rationale for this book is to foster inclusion in college music curricula by making musical understanding and creativity accessible to greater numbers of students. The book attempts to address several long-standing barriers to studying music at the postsecondary level; these are the result of tacit limits on the musical cultures, styles, and methods that are included and taught in required music courses. Enculturation is one resulting problem: the tradition of teaching introductory music theory through the lens of the largely white, European classical music tradition has implications for how students absorb and integrate the values and norms of that culture. Students from backgrounds that don't comfortably align with those norms and values sometimes discover unwelcome obstacles that challenge their ability to progress in established programs of study.

Another problem that this book addresses is the strong emphasis placed on notation literacy in the music learning process. Music notation requirements for auditions and placement exams privilege certain students and exclude those who don't yet comfortably read music notation. Students whose families can't afford music lessons or whose K–12 schools didn't offer music programs face a distinct disadvantage in gaining admission to college-level music programs, even sometimes when they are deeply skilled, invested, and creative musicians. Notation literacy requirements have long been considered to be necessary components of music education, but they also create real obstacles to diverse and inclusive classroom environments. Ethically, it is imperative that we develop alternative approaches and evaluate their effectiveness in recruiting and retaining new populations of students. It may likely remain a standard expectation that college music graduates be able to confidently read written music notation (depending upon the style of music in which they work), but whether they need to have that skill before they begin their studies should be thoughtfully reconsidered.

There are other challenges that create barriers to music study. Many students learn music theory principles kinesthetically on an instrument—that is, they develop a physical understanding of the patterns—but sometimes struggle to conceptualize or articulate how those patterns are constructed. For example, identifying notes and counting intervals using score notation can be difficult skills for students to acquire because they first encountered those concepts when they learned to navigate the physical interfaces of their primary instruments. (These tasks may be a bit easier to pick up for those who play keyboard instruments such as the piano, because the notes are laid out in one continuous line.) Also, many students work in popular music styles where traditional staff notation is not commonly used; instead, they are able to create and produce large amounts of music on their own using software tools that provide alternate ways to visualize musical elements. For example, many students write music using software such as Logic Pro X, a commonly used digital audio workstation (DAW). Most DAWs display musical events using a graphical scheme called "piano roll notation," featuring individual notes as rectangles on a two-dimensional grid representing pitch and duration. Often in piano roll notation, additional note variables such as loudness are indicated using graphical variables such as color. (The term "piano roll" originated in the late nineteenth century with player pianos that used punched paper rolls to record and play back musical scores.) Figures I.1 and I.2 display the same musical notes two different ways—figure I.1 shows how the notes look using piano roll notation in Logic Pro X, and in figure I.2, the same notes are presented using standard music notation in software called MuseScore. It is instructive to compare the different visual formats that can be used to represent the same musical information.[4]

The reasons outlined above all point to the need for curricular change; this realization has been gaining greater acceptance among college-level music educators

Introduction: The Mystery of Music   5

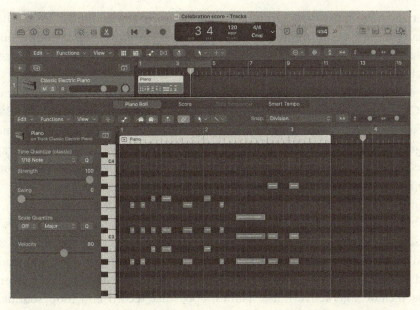

Figure I.1 MIDI piano roll notation in Logic Pro X, displaying the first three bars of Kool and the Gang's "Celebration" (1980)

Figure I.2 Standard staff notation in MuseScore software, displaying the first three bars of Kool and the Gang's "Celebration" (1980)

in recent years.[5] However, the question of *how* to change remains unresolved. This book charts a novel approach—but why learn coding to better understand music theory? This idea might at first seem far-fetched, because learning to code is a new skill that could be more difficult than learning to read and write music notation. But as STEM programs continue to gain popularity and traction in K–12 school curricula, more students are developing coding skills at younger and younger ages. These days, many students may be more comfortable with the language of code than the language of music. And as students have become accustomed to online learning formats during the Covid-19 pandemic, a computing-centered approach can provide quicker answers, inexpensive simulations, and easy access to reference materials. As with pretty much any style of course delivery, though, it helps to have a human expert to guide, reinforce, and support the learning process. Coding doesn't replace the joys of in-person music making, but it can be a useful tool to enhance and enrich the learning process.

The idea for this book emerged out of a course I have taught for many years at The College of New Jersey called *Interactive Music Programming*. Students take the course with different disciplinary backgrounds: music, creative technology, media, design, engineering, video production. As a result of their varied prior preparation, some students know music theory but have no coding experience, whereas others have coding but no music theory. Despite these challenges, things usually work out fine—we find ways to connect across our disparate fields and develop common vocabularies that help us communicate effectively. Most students who take the course learn to write both code and music well enough to create meaningful work. It can help to have a creative goal that motivates the learning process, and students build ambitious final projects to present to the public at the end of the semester. These include interactive music games, apps that record and loop sounds, ear training assistants, counterpoint generators, accompaniment systems, and music visualizers. Some projects are more formally composed, while others rely heavily on interaction and improvisation with computers. The sheer imagination and variety of outcomes is wonderful; I am proud of their work and am pleased to share a few code examples produced by students later on in this book.

1.3 Uses

Constructing Music is intended to be used in college music courses as an all-purpose introduction to music theory that supports a wide range of popular styles and technologies. It can also provide helpful professional development materials for music theory instructors who want to learn coding and seek inclusive, inviting, music-centered ways to approach that daunting task. There is increasing acceptance of students who work on laptops as their primary instruments; for them, this book can be a valuable resource. This book can also be helpful in efforts to recruit and retain students through pre-theory "bridge" or remediation courses that offer extra support before the required theory sequence begins.

Collegiate music disciplines are in the midst of a shift that started accelerating during the disruptions of the Covid-19 pandemic. Music departments are striving to adapt their offerings and attract more diverse student populations with varied backgrounds and interests. In order to recruit new music majors, many are committing to implement more responsive, student-centered approaches that connect to students' real needs and interests. These programs are accepting students who have wider interests beyond classical and jazz genres, who engage with popular music, music production, musical theater, composition, media, and other areas. The past few years have witnessed greater emphasis on interdisciplinary combinations, double majors, and multiple minors. A growing number of current students who are attracted to music study are self-taught musicians who pick it up from their family and community environments. They are deeply committed to music but don't easily fit the categories of the classical conservatory model. Nonetheless, they do interesting work and expect their voices to be included and heard.

This book may also be of interest to non-traditional students, self-directed learners, and those who have minimal formal musical training. The rise of YouTube as a platform for lifelong learning has been essential in the development of a market and critical mass for nontraditional students. YouTube and online course platforms provide informal ways to pursue self-guided learning, experimentation, and exploration of personal areas of interest and passions. Many of these learners do not expect to ask for permission from a faculty expert to begin the learning process; they understand that learning has become market-driven and self-directed.

Motivated by multiple intersecting goals, this book reframes music theory as a creative activity of constructing sound and invites readers to use code to actively investigate, simulate, and manipulate sonic structures. Creative coding provides a useful strategy for learning this content because it enables and encourages interactivity. Instead of grappling with fixed recordings or static printed scores, students are invited to engage with bits of code to learn how music is constructed and to reconstruct it for themselves. In this way, students are not expected to "reinvent the wheel" for every new topic—rather, code examples provide starting places from which they can modify, extend, reuse, and remix the structures to suit their creative goals. This aligns with the way that code is developed in the real world, keeping in mind that it is also important to acknowledge or cite one's sources when sharing work with others.

I.4 Approach

To develop a fuller understanding of how music works and how it works on us, we will first investigate how it is built from basic structural components that are not themselves musical. Like atoms that bond together to form molecules of chemical elements, the fundamental building blocks of music join together to form coherent, complex, coordinated behaviors. These are the grouping mechanisms that make music possible. Experienced music theory instructors may instead prefer that students first engage with structure at a more intermediate level of organizational complexity, such as songs, phrases, loops, and beats. This middle level of musical structure tends to be more intuitive, familiar, and compelling; therefore, it is a good pedagogical practice to begin analyzing these structures before breaking them down into their less-familiar constituent parts. Where possible, this book tries to balance both approaches—building up structures from basic components such as pitch and duration, and breaking down existing musical forms into their essential parts. The use of coding also inevitably adds some complexity to the learning process, and for that reason significant attention has been paid to the careful, step-by-step, simultaneous development of facility and confidence in both code and music.

Throughout this book, you will encounter analogies between musical structures and children's construction kits such as Lego bricks, Tinker Toys, and Lincoln Logs. These historical toys allowed children to engage in open-ended creative play, constructing objects of their own design and discovering new ways of thinking in the process. They also influenced the development of "blocks world" software tools like Scratch, Minecraft, and Roblox. The ways in which these educational, exploratory platforms have been modeled connects directly to the learning philosophy called Constructionism, which we will discuss at the end of the book.

The method employed in this book emphasizes step-by-step experimentation. First, we will explore music fundamentals by investigating the structural elements themselves. Then, we will tinker with combining them in ever-increasing levels of complexity. As needed, we will also appropriate bits from computer science, math, acoustics, statistics, circuits, design, and other non-musical topics. In Chapter 1, we will learn how to operate the *Max* software environment. In Chapters 2–5, we will address how musical structures are put together and how they function—first in structures that use pitch, then in structures that use time, and finally in smaller increments of pitch that define our tuning systems. In Chapter 6, we will reference unresolved questions and themes from earlier sections and develop new theories about how music works and how it works on us. Along the way, we will try to avoid the solipsistic definition of music as comprising elements that are themselves coherent or patterned; this can result in a loop wherefrom we cannot escape to see the larger phenomena. We will attempt to define these simpler elements from first principles.

An important note about musical style and the use of tonality: the focus throughout this book is on building and understanding the fundamental structures of tonal music, meaning that we are using a conventional system of musical organization that establishes a hierarchical structure of notes in relationship to each other. (Tonality will be further defined in section 3.7 "Make a Key.") But this focus should not be confused with the idea of a common practice period defined by music theorists and associated with European classical music written in the eighteenth and nineteenth centuries. As the story has often been told in college-level music courses, the early twentieth century brought about a shift whereby Western art music styles veered off the tonal path toward more modernist, *atonal* experiments and aesthetic movements. These new styles were said to express the angst and suffering of two world wars and subsequent social upheavals, eventually returning to a "New Tonality" by around 1990.[6] However, this interpretation leaves out many important popular and religious music traditions that developed during the twentieth century, including jazz, blues, swing, rock and roll, gospel, rhythm & blues, Motown, funk, soul, disco, rap, and hip-hop, to name just a few. Exclusion of these musical styles has often been explained by means of a distinction between the "art" and "popular" music traditions; great works from the white European classical tradition were considered acceptable source materials for academic study, whereas the commercial recordings and scores from other traditions were not. Indeed, there was a clear racial component to this lack of inclusion; all of the popular and religious traditions listed above originated in African American culture. Technologies, the music industry, and popular culture played a role in fostering the spread of these musics, but classrooms and textbooks were slow to incorporate them into the canon. Undeniably, racist social attitudes played a significant role. The topic of race, gender, and class exclusion in music education has become a topic of great interest in recent years, as institutions and instructors have sought to create new curricula and programs that more equitably represent the full range of contemporary musical experience.

Despite the complexities outlined above, popular and religious music styles do share a general tonal framework with the Western classical music tradition. This is especially true with foundational structures such as chords, keys, and scales. There are significant differences as well, which must be acknowledged: African American musical styles are widely acknowledged to emphasize greater rhythmic intricacy, timbral variety, and vocal expression, placing less priority on harmonic structures. To describe the basic framework used by all the traditions included above, we will occasionally borrow the term "everyday tonality" coined by Philip Tagg, a music theorist whose approach resolutely includes African American music and other traditions beyond the European canon.[7]

This book includes musical examples from a wide range of styles, traditions, and cultures, with the aim of weaving multiple perspectives into a unified approach for learning how tonal music works. There is a great deal of overlap between culturally white-framed Western tonal theory and BIPOC-framed musical structure. Both bodies of material exist in relationship to each other, both are worth teaching and learning, and indeed, software technologies like *Max* have vast untapped potential for those purposes. I hope this way of teaching will make music more accessible and inclusive for learners of all backgrounds.

I.4.1 The Benefits of a Scientific Perspective in Learning Music

Science and STEM fields have developed helpful tools and concepts that can be adapted and applied toward understanding and creating music. Some of these include technical processes such as statistical analysis, Machine Learning, and AI, but some are more conceptual. For example, the field of computer science uses the concept of abstraction to explain how we manage complexity by modifying the granularity of detail we use in our descriptions. This idea can be applied to learning and creating music: sometimes during the early stages, it can be helpful to emphasize the main concepts and simplify the smaller details, ensuring that we aren't initially overwhelmed by too much information. We then gradually reveal the complexities when we are ready for them.

Here is another way to think about layers of abstraction: I once asked a friend of mine to tell me about a movie she had seen so I could decide whether to go see it in the theater. She proceeded to provide a precise description of every scene in great detail. Instead of listening to her narration, it would have been better just to buy a ticket and go watch the movie! You can think about abstraction as layers of overlapping concentric circles that progressively decrease in size to ever more compressed summaries. Whereas a low-level abstraction might summarize a two-hour movie using an hour-long description, a middle level might take fifteen minutes, and a high layer of abstraction might take two minutes. When I originally asked my friend to describe the movie, I had expected a higher level of abstraction.[8]

Related to the concept of abstraction layers is the technique of limiting our knowledge of parts of complex systems in order to focus our attention on a smaller set of features. Using this method, we purposefully allow internal mechanisms to remain unknown or opaque while we permit ourselves to consider only their general inputs and outputs. My favorite way of describing this idea is "under the hood." Many of us apply this concept in our daily lives when we use complex systems, for example, if we drive cars or use mobile phones without knowing exactly how they work. While there certainly are benefits to knowing the minute inner workings of engines and electronic devices, engaging with too much detail all at once can be distracting or overwhelming. Concepts that help us simplify our area of investigation offer practical ways to support learning and problem-solving. Throughout this book, you will occasionally see the term "under the hood" used to mean that we will temporarily suspend some of the complexities and employ a higher level of abstraction as we work through the material.

Another example of adapting a STEM concept for learning music is the term "suitcase word"; you can use it to describe short words that contain multiple complex components that you may not fully understand.[9] Suitcase words exist at too high a level of abstraction, masking a jumble of interconnected but unresolved relationships of meaning that remain to be clarified one day with more precise language. Musical terms seem to frequently serve as suitcases for all kinds of complex behaviors, feelings, and thoughts, concealing webs of entangled ideas that could benefit from some extra attention to sort out.

Throughout this book you will occasionally encounter the use of concepts adapted from science and STEM fields (such as abstraction layers, "under the hood," and suitcase words) in order to explain complex topics from music or coding. This approach is intended to make things more manageable for those who don't have much experience in those areas. I encourage readers to further engage with the complexities through open-ended prompts at the end of each chapter. In music and coding, there are so many wonderful rabbit holes to explore! Some of them go very deep.

I.4.2 A Note about the Limits of This Approach

There are a great many aspects of music that are quantifiable and knowable in a systematic way. Musical signals can be recorded, measured, and analyzed. However, music is also a social activity, and as such it is deeply influenced by the messy, unstructured, arbitrary, but often rational ways in which humans think and behave. For that reason, while this book will occasionally refer to scientific techniques to explain musical phenomena, sometimes we will instead just use the standard definitions of terms from the world of musical practice. For example: why is the piano keyboard laid out the way it is? Why are the keys black and white?[10] Why do we use certain tuning systems? We may have ways to explain these phenomena, but ultimately they were design decisions that served a specific purpose. Although research can inform practice in the dialectic conversation between art and science, science nonetheless cannot answer all the important artistic questions. Sometimes, musical terms are just slippery, elusive, and self-referential. The answers will not always be very satisfying, but we are going to adopt a practical stance and accept a certain amount of vagueness so that we can function with a shared foundation.

It should also be acknowledged that there are limits on one author's ability to capture the rich musical diversity of human musical expression in all its forms. While this book represents a serious attempt to bridge multiple approaches (traditional vs. modern, classical vs. popular, notation literacy vs. creative coding, etc.), there is so much more to be done! One weakness of this book is that it pays more attention overall to pitch than to rhythm. I sincerely hope that readers will take this on as a creative challenge and build lots of code examples to fill in the missing gaps.

I.4.3 *Max* Software by Cycling '74

In this book, we will use software simulation and experimentation to explore how music is put together. Our platform will be *Max*, a visual coding environment for interactive music, audio, and media that has been commercially available for more than thirty years. You do not need prior programming or computer science experience in order to enjoy learning *Max*. However, it is slightly more complicated to learn than programs like Scratch, which is widely used in K–12 STEM (Science, Technology, Engineering, and Math) and STEAM (STEM plus arts) classrooms.

I must acknowledge that not all students have access to high-quality technology instruction in school, and coding may genuinely present a daunting challenge! This book has been written for students who are new to coding; the step-by-step descriptions should provide a straightforward and user-friendly way to follow along. (And, if this book helps you discover that you like coding, you can try out further initiatives afterward such as Hour of Code and Girls Who Code.) While coding may seem disconnected from music theory, it is likely that future music students will benefit from having these skills.

Ongoing development and upgrades for *Max* have been stably supported since 1998 by Cycling '74, a company headquartered in San Francisco that is now owned by Ableton. *Max* is regularly maintained, and version 8 was released in 2018. Generally, software updates in *Max* are backwards-compatible, so the instructions in this book should function reasonably well for quite some time. For this reason, software examples throughout the book will reference just the "*Max*" name itself, without any version numbers such as *Max* 7, *Max* 8, or eventually *Max* 9 and beyond.

Max can be thought of as a shared music development tool. Although it's not technically an open-source environment, Cycling '74 encourages its worldwide community to share projects in ways that resemble open-source ideas. Third parties are welcome to use a free application programming interface (API) to develop and share "external objects"; a few external objects are used in the software patches in this book. An international community of developers and creative technologists contribute their projects, libraries, extensions, and tutorials on websites including https://cycling74.com/projects/. As you work through the content in this book, it can be fun to peruse popular *Max* online venues and share your own work with others.

Max is not the only interactive software development or prototyping platform of its kind. It exists in an ecosystem of construction-based sound synthesis languages that have evolved since the 1960s, including MUSIC I-V, GROOVE, Csound, SuperCollider, Pd, ChucK, and Sonic Pi.[11] The predecessor to *Max* was an editor called *Patcher*, first created by Miller S. Puckette in the mid-1980s at the Institute for Research and Coordination in Acoustics/Music (IRCAM) in Paris. *Patcher* initially allowed computers to control Giuseppe Di Giugno's 4X synthesizer.[12] Eventually, *Max* was named for Max V. Mathews, a pioneer of computer music. It was ported to the NeXT operating system in 1989 for the IRCAM Signal Processing Workstation and was first released commercially by Opcode Systems in 1990.

Max was chosen as the platform for this book because it is well supported, easy to use, and has a strong worldwide user base. In combination with several add-on packages (*MSP*, *Jitter*, *Gen*, *Mira*, *Max4Live*, *RNBO*, etc.), *Max* comprises an integrated development environment that supports creativity, experimentation, and invention. It is well known as a platform for creating live electronic music performances and installations, and it has been widely adopted by composers, performers, software designers, researchers, and artists. Another useful benefit is that *Max* files tend to be small in size, and when integrated with Ableton are able to smoothly interact with the capabilities of modern digital music production.

Although *Max* is usually thought of as a platform for expert practitioners, it can also be an effective tool for learners. Its features are terrific for simulating how music is put together. *Max* functions as a prototyping environment that allows the user to interact directly with code blocks on the screen in the form of objects that can be connected together. *Max* does not use a conventional command-line or text-based programming paradigm; rather, it uses a broad array of visual interface elements.

All these items are arranged using the metaphor of a blank canvas in a file called a patch or patcher. Items placed inside the patch have inlets and outlets, enabling connections between items using patch cords. Patch cords allow data to flow from one object to another; they connect outlets to inlets in only one direction. *Max* also provides a large library of predesigned modular building blocks ("objects") that can be connected together to create complex structures. Most routines exist as built-in functions, but there are also many available external objects created by outside developers.

Finally, despite their often dizzying visual and quantitative complexities, *Max* patches can provide important opportunities for artistic expression. As described by Dan Derks, "A bit of code can act very much like a score—it is not only an individual expression of an idea, but it encapsulates the possibilities of that idea. It's both an expression of self, like any piece of art, and a tool that can be repurposed, remixed, and reframed to fit the unique needs of a wide range of artists."[13]

I.5 How to Use This Book

This book can serve as a textbook for a one- or two-semester college course, a digital supplement for a traditional music course, or in a self-guided, self-paced format. The topics have been organized into individual lessons that are accompanied by interactive sample patches in *Max*. As you progress through the lessons, I encourage you to first read each text description and then apply it by running the patch on your computer. Instructions will be there to guide you as you interact with the example, learn how it works, and then edit, modify, and expand it on your own as you gain confidence and facility in *Max*. Give yourself permission to get creative as you explore the capabilities of this software tool. Much like practicing musical improvisation, you are welcome to experiment with and remix the code in your own unique style, repurposing and reorganizing the elements in a way that you find pleasing. Learning to code is more fun when you allow yourself to play with things and make them your own. *Max* can be challenging to learn! But we will approach each step gradually and explain the process along the way.

One challenge with learning music is that even some of the most basic concepts have long and complicated histories. Explaining why something is called the way it is or why it is defined a particular way can launch an unexpected detour into a deep rabbit hole of information. You might find such excursions pleasurable, but they can sometimes open up more questions than they answer and exhaust you before you even get to the point of the lesson. For this reason, when technical or musical jargon is used, we will highlight those words in italics and invite you to look up their definitions in the Glossary at the back of the book.

To begin, you'll need a computer running either Windows or Mac operating systems; *Max* has been designed to run on both platforms. (Throughout the book, instructions will be provided for both macOS and Windows support.) Next, download and install the current version of *Max* following the directions on the website at https://cycling74.com/downloads. (You will need to create a free account as part of this process.) This *Max* installation will be free to use for thirty days with the full feature set. Thereafter, you will be able to open and run *Max* patch files, but not edit or save them. To continue using the fully featured version after thirty days, you must purchase a license. Licenses are available as monthly or annual subscriptions, or through a onetime fee. (Academic discounts are available for students and instructors.)

After installing *Max* on your computer, go ahead and download the interactive sample code files provided with this book. Please navigate to the companion website and resources provided by Oxford University Press: www.oup.com/us/ConstructingMusic. There, you will find instructions on how to download and run these examples as you progress through the book. To keep your files organized, it will help to place them together in one folder. I recommend saving the folder on your computer's desktop for easy access. If you are using a Mac computer, click once on your desktop to pull up the Finder menu. Then navigate to File → New Folder, which will place an empty folder on your desktop. Click once on the folder's default name ("untitled folder") and give it a new name that could help you locate it later; something like "Constructing Music files" should work well. Once you have named your folder, double-click to open it up, and copy your downloaded sample code files here. It may also help to create a new folder here as well in which to save any unique modifications or versions of the code that you make along the way.

As you progress through the lessons, you will frequently be invited to modify the sample code files that have been provided with the book and "make them your own." When you take up that creative challenge, it's a good habit to give each version of the file its own unique name. Promising candidate filenames preserve something from the original version as well as a few words about the creative changes you made. By applying a principled approach to descriptive filenames, you will be able to safely retain the fruits of your labors, quickly locate them later on, and easily distinguish between the original files you downloaded and your new creative versions. (One final note about filenames: it can be helpful to use a numbering scheme to keep track of versions of files in order; this approach is called "version control." For example, different drafts of a file might benefit from version numbers, such as "tutorial 1 v.1" or "tutorial 1 v.2." This provides a record of the sequence of changes, accounting for the fact that timestamps might be accidentally overwritten.)

While we are reviewing best practices for managing the files and folders that accompany this book, we should also talk about how to properly back them up. As a general rule, it is a good idea to store important files in at least two different physical locations to ensure that they are not lost or corrupted. One copy can be retained on your local computer, and another copy can be saved either on a portable hard drive or cloud storage system such as Google Drive, Dropbox, or other options. It's important to establish a regular routine around backing up data to avoid heartbreaking losses down the line.

While you set up your computer files, it may also be a good time to pay attention to your physical workspace and supporting "peripheral devices" that could be handy while working on music. It will be necessary to have decent-quality speakers or headphones so that you can listen to the sound output from your computer. If you are using headphones, it might be worth a small investment in models that completely cover your ears for better fidelity. It is not necessary to buy expensive headphones; good-quality models are available from audio equipment manufacturers at reasonable prices. And although the built-in microphone on your computer is likely sufficient for basic recording, it can help to have a USB digital audio interface and good general-purpose microphone as part of your desktop studio. Make sure to read the reviews and compare prices online. A simple audio recording setup will be needed for sections 2.1 "Silence," 2.2 "Sound," and 5.3 "Playing in tune" later on.

If you have some experience using a piano keyboard, it could also be useful to connect an electronic, MIDI-enabled keyboard to your computer. This will allow you to play independently alongside the code examples. (Keyboards are not required and not necessary to have a good experience with this book, but can provide helpful supplements for the music theory content.) If you are looking to obtain a portable keyboard that fits within a modest budget and doesn't take up too much space, I recommend looking at twenty-five-key MIDI keyboard controllers. Many manufacturers offer good models in this category with assignable knobs, buttons, sliders, and pads in addition to the standard piano-style keyboard. Most MIDI keyboards connect to computers using a USB port and are automatically recognized by both the computer and *Max* software. In some cases, you may need to manually configure a keyboard or other MIDI device; please follow the manual or setup instructions that came along with it. (Further instructions are provided in section 1.4 "MIDI Basics.") After setting up your computer studio workspace with *Max*, downloading and organizing the sample code files, and configuring any peripheral devices such as speakers, headphones, or a MIDI keyboard, you should be ready to proceed!

1
Tutorials

The purpose of this chapter is to present a step-by-step introduction to *Max* and interactive music coding. Chapter 1 consists of six tutorials that provide critical startup information for beginners. While it can help to have some background experience with coding, the tutorials have been designed to aid those without any prior preparation to quickly ramp up to a sufficient level of comfort in the software environment. The tutorials will also introduce some basic musical terms and concepts that will be further explained in the chapters that follow. Any reader who already has a solid understanding of the details of music technology and *Max* programming can skim this chapter or skip directly to Chapter 2.

Taking the time to work through the tutorial content will ensure that readers have a good experience navigating the technical and musical topics in the book. Especially if you haven't explored coding, MIDI, or digital audio before, I recommend reviewing the sections in this chapter before proceeding on to subsequent chapters. You can think of this section as a primer for the skills that will allow you to progress through the content in the book. Although these tutorials might initially seem like the broccoli one has to finish first to get to the dessert, they are all included here for a specific reason: they serve as necessary steps toward the eventual goal of creating music in *Max*. To help motivate learning, each tutorial will begin with a short explanation about why it is valuable and relevant.

It is important to acknowledge that the tutorials in this chapter take some strategic shortcuts. We will devote time later on in the book to backfill basic details when needed. This approach leverages efficiencies that I have refined over years of experience in the classroom. One of the most important insights about developing software skills is that you don't have to be an expert in an entire tool in order to be effective in using a portion of it. As you work through the steps, you will progressively encounter new pieces of information, learning what you need to know just in time as each new topic arrives.

Additional Resources for Learning *Max*

A motivated reader may also wish to explore additional sources of information about *Max* and music technology in parallel with the somewhat minimalist (as-needed) approach taken throughout this book. If you prefer a more structured approach, I recommend the excellent materials built into the program itself. Cycling '74's *Max* tutorials provide a thorough overview that familiarizes beginners with how the *Max* programming environment works. A list of contents can be found here: https://docs.cycling74.com/max8/tutorials/00_maxindex. To access the tutorial files directly within the program itself, launch *Max* and then navigate to File → Show File Browser. From there, click on "Cycling '74 Content" on the left-side toolbar, and then select Tutorials → Max Tutorials. Start with "Max Basic Tutorial 1: Hello," and then gradually proceed through the entire set of thirty-seven topics, organized into different categories including MIDI, Interface, and Data. I recommend tackling only three or four at a time, spreading out the content over several weeks. Each tutorial comes along with its own *Max* patch, which can be helpful to keep around in your sample code folder. Cycling '74 also maintains a YouTube channel with informational videos located at https://www.youtube.com/@cycling74com.

There are several other high-quality resources on topics related to this book. An introductory tutorial on MIDI produced by the nonprofit MIDI Association can be found here: https://www.midi.org/midi-articles/about-midi-part-1-overview. Two books that provide excellent materials and examples for learning *Max* include *Max/MSP/Jitter for Music* by V. J. Manzo[1] and *Composing Interactive Music* by Todd Winkler.[2] Additional recommended resources for exploring *Max* include specific pages on the DIY website "Instructables"[3] and an online course called "Structuring Interactive Software for Digital Arts," taught by Matt Wright on the Kadenze platform.[4] Cycling '74 maintains a list of workshops, online classes, and certified trainers here: https://cycling74.com/places-to-learn-max. If you are interested in music production, you might also want to investigate *Max for Live*, which provides a useful way to embed a *Max* patch inside Ableton, an industry-standard Digital Audio Workstation (DAW).[5]

Coding Basics

Before we jump into our first tutorial, it is important to introduce a few foundational concepts about programming. The most important is that creative coding environments like *Max* share similarities with spoken and written languages. Just as written words take on specific roles within sentences (serving as nouns, verbs, adjectives, and other lexical categories), elements of a *Max* patch are defined by the types of tasks they perform. The five basic components of a patch include:

- *objects*: like verbs, they perform actions and functions[6]
- *messages*: like nouns, they store and send alphanumeric data (text)
- *comments*: they display helpful written notes, labels, and instructions
- *interface objects*: a subcategory of objects that allow user input and control via specialized interactive interfaces
- *patch cords*: they connect objects and messages together and enable information (data and commands) to flow between them

The next important concept to establish is that order matters. That is, the sequence in which components are connected to each other determines how a patch behaves. Just as verbal languages use *syntax* rules to group words together in sentences and create meaning, items in a *Max* patch are grouped together and connected by patch cords to create a clear *order of operations*—a deterministic pathway through which commands move around and are interpreted. You can think about this as a form of *signal flow*, where audio data passes from object to object via patch cords, often being modified at each step.

A critical detail to observe here is that instructions in a *Max* patch are processed in a specific direction, from right to left and then from bottom to top. This feature can affect the exact times at which messages are received.[7] To a new *Max* user, this may seem strangely inverted from the normal expectation; we are accustomed to read English prose in the opposite direction. However, there is a technical reason why it is done this way: this order of operations ensures that all necessary data are received before commands get sent. By long-standing convention going back to the early days of *Max*, the leftmost *inlet* for any object is assigned to be active ("hot"). When hot inlets receive messages, they initiate actions. The other inlets receive and retain messages but do not process them; these inlets are described as "cold." Typically, values are first received in the cold inlets on the right side of an object, and then the hot inlets on the left side trigger actions; this is why instructions are processed from right to left. In addition, the bottom-to-top convention exists because of a characteristic of the two-dimensional computer display system: horizontal (x) values increase toward the right, and vertical (y) values increase in a downward direction. Patches are read and interpreted by the computer after it sorts the display window in descending order along both axes. I promise that you will become accustomed to these unusual quirks as you gain experience using *Max*, although it can take some time to get used to the way things work. The particular order in which things happen will become more important as you encounter patches of increasing complexity.

And thirdly, this book relies on the creation of musical structures from *algorithms*. Algorithms can be thought of as step-by-step procedures, or recipes, for handling data. Similar to the recipes we use for cooking, algorithms are sets of instructions that prescribe how a set of actions should be performed. Most of us rely on algorithms in our daily lives without even thinking about them, and the design of algorithms is a focal point for computer programmers. One of the most important concepts in algorithmic design is the idea of a *variable*, or a representation of a piece of data that has a changeable value. Variables allow us to store quantities and change them over time. For example, in a cooking recipe, variables might be assigned to the amounts of each item—on a particular day, the cook might want to add a bit less salt or more milk.

We can apply step-by-step recipes to music as well, with the same flexibility, improvisation, and whimsy that an experienced chef might use in the kitchen. For example, the loudness of a sound can be thought of as a variable: a cellist might start playing a sound with a high *volume*, leaning in with the weight of her arm to increase friction at the point of contact between the bow and the string. After a few seconds, she might then gradually reduce the force and steadily taper the volume down to silence. In this example, the cellist's changing use of arm weight is also a variable. This description demonstrates how we might begin to think about the characteristics of musical sounds as variables and treat them as data that we can incorporate into musical *algorithms* in our *Max* patches.

In addition to developing a few foundational concepts to rely on for creative coding, it can also help to anticipate some common challenges. (Getting ahead of these as early as possible will maximize your chances of having a good experience.) The first challenge is to quickly build a sufficient vocabulary (lexicon) of objects that enable you to "read" a patch and understand how the objects and signals interact with each other. The second is to learn how to break down complicated behaviors into smaller tasks and sequence them into step-by-step procedures. To develop fluency using *Max*, it is important to quickly gain a level of comfort with using and modifying patches. It can also help to learn the shortcuts and key commands that speed up the process of adding and connecting objects; these can be useful in accelerating your coding skills.

As you prepare to approach the process of learning to code in *Max*, one of the best things you can do is to cultivate a sense of fearlessness, curiosity, and experimentation. Pretty soon, with some regular practice, you will gain familiarity with a core set of objects; this will increase your functionality, expertise, and self-confidence within the environment. Initially, *Max* users should aim to develop a sense of how to "read" a patch and follow the signal paths; then, they can learn to modify and manipulate existing code. Finally, the goal is to get to the point where they can create their own! Along the way, it's important to try things out and directly manipulate the code yourself. Even if something breaks, you can always just go back and re-download the sample code from the book's companion website, so the risk is quite low. And things do generally start to become more fun when you can build structures that you find interesting or meaningful (or ideally, both).

1.1 Loops

Now we are ready to start our first tutorial! Loops are fundamental coding structures used in all aspects of musical creation with software. By the end of this tutorial, we will use a looped network of objects to create a visual metronome. Be forewarned that we will not immediately make music in this section. We need a little bit of time to get situated in the programming environment and learn the basics that will help us get there. You will be able to play along with a recorded musical track at the end of this first tutorial, to accompany and support your first coding effort.

To create your first patch, go ahead and launch the *Max* application. (This step will open a window called "*Max* Console," which you can disregard and close for now.) Then, select *File* → *New Patcher* to open a brand new, blank patch. Alternately, you can use a keyboard shortcut to achieve the same purpose: on macOS, hold down the *command* key (⌘) while typing the letter "n"; on Windows, use the *control* key instead by holding down *control* or *ctrl* while typing the letter "n."

A blank *Max* patch resembles a painter's canvas, and it invites creativity in similar ways. You will shortly learn how to place objects on your blank patch and draw patch cord connections between them. But before we jump in and start slinging objects around, let's take a moment to situate ourselves and visually navigate around the patch interface. Helpful toolbars are located around the outer periphery of the blank patch window. We won't delve into them right now; even after using *Max* for many years, there are still tools that I rarely use. However, I invite you to take a few minutes to hover your mouse over each icon and move around the outer frame of your patch. Familiarize yourself with some of the tool names, especially those along the top and on the right-hand side. Click on and informally explore any that catch your interest. Some of the particularly useful ones include Search, Inspector, Reference, and *Max* Console; they may open up side panels or new floating windows, which you can close when you are done. We will return to use some of these tools later on in the book.

Next, let's establish a method for organizing and managing *Max* patches on your computer. Inside the "Constructing Music files" sample code folder that you created in section I.5 "How to Use This Book," create a new folder called "My Patches." Then, click once on the empty canvas of your new blank patch to ensure that it is selected, and select *File → Save*. When the dialog box appears, type the filename "tutorial #1" in the "Save As" field. In the "Where" field located in the same dialog box, navigate to the "My Patches" folder and click on the "Save" option in the bottom right-hand corner.

Now that you have named and saved your first *Max* patch, let's explore some simple interface objects. Open your new patch and add your first object into it by clicking once inside the patch window and then pressing the letter "n" key to create a new object box. Type the word "button" into the empty box; as you type, the object will autofill with related object names. Double-click on the word "button" to select it from the list below the object, and then press enter/return. Alternatively, you can use a shortcut key to place a new button object in the patch window by pressing the letter "b." (To see a list of all the built-in shortcut key commands while working in *Max*, press the letter "x"; click on any object name to add it to your patch.) Here is yet another way to add a button: locate the "Buttons" tool near the midpoint of the toolbar at the top of the patch, click it once, and then select the *button* object on the left. There are often multiple routes to accomplish tasks in *Max*, and you now have several ways to add a button object to your patch.

You should now see a small square with a circle inscribed in the middle; this is the button object, which serves as a user-clickable interface object. Click on it once, and "handles" should appear that allow you to resize it. Go ahead and make it as large as you wish. Your patch should now look something like the image shown in figure 1.1.

Like other interface objects, "button" takes on a visual shape and form that enables direct user input. It performs a simple function: sending and receiving commands

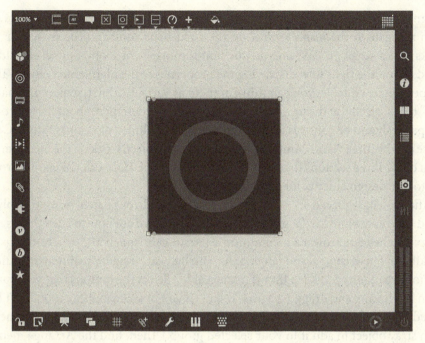

Figure 1.1 Add a button

called *bang messages* that start and stop things. (The circle in its center also "blinks" or lights up when it is activated.) Instantaneously upon receiving a mouse-click, *button* triggers a *bang message*. Please note that the button object itself does not make sound, although later on it can be used to trigger a sound to play.

To allow your button object to behave as expected, you must first "lock" the patch by clicking once on the lock icon in the lower left corner of the patch window. Locking and unlocking patches is the visual metaphor that *Max* uses to indicate when you can run (execute) or edit (modify) your code. When the patch is unlocked (*edit mode*), you can move objects around and make changes. When the patch is locked (*patching mode*), objects perform their functions as intended. To save time and work more efficiently, use a shortcut to lock and unlock your patch and toggle between the two modes of operation: press the command key (⌘) and, while holding it down, press the letter "e." (We will call this step *command+e* for short; on Windows, use *control+e*.). While the patch is locked, go ahead and click on the button to see what happens: it should blink once for every click, similar to user interface selection mechanisms in other software applications.

Next, we are going to edit this patch, so go ahead and unlock it (command+e or control+e). Then, using the letter "b" shortcut, go ahead and place several more buttons around the screen. (Notice that the button will be created wherever your mouse cursor is located. If you keep your cursor in the same spot, multiple "b" commands will cause buttons to be piled one on top of the other. Just click and drag them away from the pileup of buttons as needed.) Move and resize the buttons as you wish. Be whimsical! Add color by clicking once on individual buttons to highlight them, and then navigate to the *Inspector tool* on the right-hand toolbar. (The Inspector icon looks like a script "i.") When you click on the Inspector icon, a panel should expand out on the right side, displaying the properties of the highlighted object. These properties are editable; you can think of them as variables. First, make sure that the "All" tab is selected at the top, displaying all the properties; then, about halfway down the panel should be controls for Background Color, Blink Color, and Outline Color; these are the three visual components of the button object. Click on the color bars for each of the three sections to display a color palette tool. Have fun navigating around the tool to design fancy color combinations.

After you have placed several button objects around your patch, now probably is a good time to explore the "alignment" feature and figure out how to keep things neat. (*Max* patches tend toward a condition I like to call "spaghetti," where things can rapidly get out of control and tangled. As with hair care, regular maintenance and attention are required to keep things manageable.) Select the buttons that you want to align by clicking and dragging across them. (If you miss any buttons, you don't have to redo the click-and-drag action; instead, hold down the shift key and click once on each stray object to add it to your selected group.) Then, find the Arrange menu in the Application menu bar at the top of your screen. Experiment with the Auto Align, Align, and Distribute functions. If you don't like any updated locations for the buttons on the screen, you can undo your changes by pressing command+z on macOS or control+z on Windows.

Next, we will connect the button objects together and explore how data flows. All objects have inlets and outlets that allow them to send and receive information. Inlets are located on the top of an object; outlets are at the bottom. (It can help to make a visual analogy here with a funnel, where you pour liquid in through the top and it flows out through the bottom.) Some objects have multiple inlets and outlets, but buttons only have one of each. One way to quickly determine what kind of data is being sent and received by an object is to hover with your mouse over the inlets and outlets. This will cause a small window to pop up and display a short text description. To find out exactly how the object's functions are defined, view its "Help file": right-click with your mouse on the object (or control-click in macOS) to launch a small floating menu, and then select the top item on the list: "open [object name] Help." This will open a built-in patch file that explains and demonstrates how the object is designed to be used.

Patch cords allow data to flow between objects by connecting outlets to inlets in one direction: the outlet on the bottom of a sending object connects to the inlet on the top of a receiving object. To create your first patch cord, hover your mouse over the outlet at the bottom of a button object. Then, click and drag toward the inlet of another button; when you arrive at the inlet, hover over it and release your mouse. (On macOS, you may need to click once on the inlet for the patch cord to "attach" to it; the attachment happens automatically in Windows.) Notice that right after a connection is made, the patch cord is highlighted (bolded) and has a green dot at the outlet end and a red dot at the inlet end. You can use your mouse to grab these dots like "handles" by clicking once and dragging them to the inlets of other objects. (This feature may become particularly handy later on, when you start to work on patches of greater complexity.)

Go ahead and attach patch cords from button to button around your patch. If you wish, create a network of buttons! Experiment with different network configurations: stars (one in the center connected to many around it), trees (multiple branching connections), rings (circles), etc. Notice that when you hover over any inlet or outlet, *Max* opens a small floating window indicating the type of data or function that it handles.

As you create your button network, now is a good time to explore different types of patch cord connections. Patch cords can be generated in a few different styles. The default setting creates straight line segments from object to object, with just enough of a curve at the end to reach the inlets and outlets gracefully. Sometimes it can be helpful to "align" or "route" patch cords around other objects to avoid the visual mess of overlapping lines. You can accomplish this by clicking on a patch cord once to select it, and then either right-clicking to pop up a menu with align/route options, or by navigating to the Arrange menu on the Application menu bar at the top of the patch window and selecting "Route Patch Cords." *Max* will automatically pick a reasonable path for you. If you prefer, you can determine the exact trajectory your patch cords will take by selecting (checking) "Segmented Patch Cords" in the Options menu on the top menu bar. Then, begin the patching process normally, drawing a cord down and away from the outlet of an object. At the point where you want the cord to bend, click to create a pivot point in the cord and then continue in the new direction; the cord will bend as directed by your mouse clicks. Occasionally, patch cords can become confused while you are drawing from one object to another. You can fix this problem by clicking once outside of the patch window; this will cause the cord to disappear. Patch cords can also be removed by clicking on them once to highlight them and then pressing the delete key (the delete and backspace keys both work for this purpose on Windows).

Now lock up your patch, click on one button, and see what happens. Observe that when you click on a button, the bang message gets passed through the patch cords to other buttons down the chain. It acts as a trigger that moves from button to button through the patch cords. This activity illustrates how data flows between objects in *Max*. Next, try this variation: create a long chain by connecting several buttons together with patch cords, linking it together at the end by drawing a patch cord from the outlet of the last one back to the inlet of the first. Lock up your patch, click on one of the buttons, and observe what happens.[8] A yellow error message should appear at the top of the patch window, reporting a "stack overflow," meaning that the patch is attempting to use more space than has been allocated for it. Your patch might now look something like figure 1.2.

This stack overflow is problematic because the chain of buttons has formed an "infinite loop." If left to progress, the loop could quickly fill up your computer's working

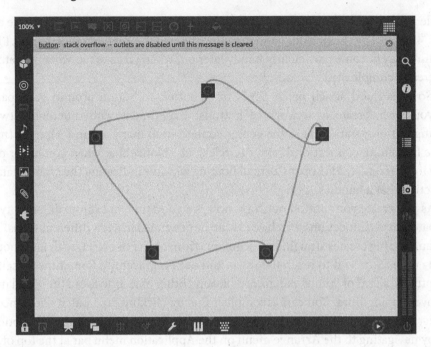

Figure 1.2 Button loop error

memory and overwhelm the processor. Clear the error message by clicking on the "x" on the right-hand side of the error message. In addition, the underlying issue should be addressed to avoid having the error message continue to appear every time the loop runs.

One way to fix this infinite loop error is simply to remove one patch cord from the loop, thereby breaking the chain and stopping the uncontrolled flow of data. However, a better solution preserves the loop by inserting a fixed amount of delay time in between any two consecutive buttons. This brief stoppage of time sufficiently slows down the infinite recursion of the loop and prevents any bad memory overflows from happening to the computer. To implement this solution, first make sure that you have cleared the error message as described above. Then, press "n" to add a new object, type the text "pipe 500" into the text box, and press enter. The *pipe* object will cause a delay by holding any message it receives for a fixed amount of time and then releasing it. Delay time is a variable value that is defined in increments called *milliseconds*. Each millisecond lasts for one-thousandth of a second; to compare this with the clock time units we are used to, 1000 milliseconds equal one second and a duration of 500 milliseconds is equivalent to one-half of a second. (One aspect to notice here is that in *Max*, time is used in very specific ways.)

Use patch cords to connect your "pipe 500" object between any two adjacent buttons in the chain. If you wish, go ahead and add other *pipe* objects with different delay times in between each pair of button neighbors to create a fun animated effect. To save time with this task, copy and paste your pipe object a few times instead of typing it out each time: click once to highlight a pipe object, and then type command+c to copy and command+v to paste (on Windows: ctrl+c to copy, ctrl+v to paste). To copy multiple objects, first select them all by holding down the shift key while clicking each one successively, or click and hold while dragging the mouse across all the objects you wish to select. Then, copy and paste the entire group together. (If you accidentally grab more objects than you wanted, hold down the shift key again and click on any objects that you wish to de-select. This will keep the group of objects highlighted but allow you to remove individual items one at a time.)

Enjoy the process of creating your own loop, alternating button and pipe objects. Once you are done with it, open up the example patch that has been provided with the sample code files for this book: "1.1 Loops." Compare your version with the sample file. While there is no single right way to create this looping structure, you can refer to the sample code for helpful debugging assistance. The *Max* patch for this first tutorial is shown in figure 1.3.

In this patch, the amount of delay time in milliseconds serves as an *argument*, a special type of variable for the pipe object.[9] Go ahead and experiment with delay values of various amounts. For ambitious coders who enjoy a creative challenge, I recommend timing the buttons to flash in synchrony with your favorite musical track. I personally enjoy listening to classic R&B recordings such as "Respect," written in 1965 by Otis Redding and later recorded in 1967 by Aretha Franklin and

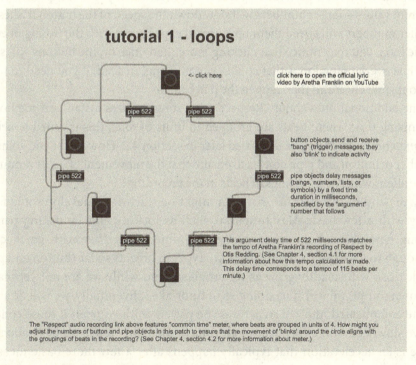

Figure 1.3 Tutorial #1 loop with button and pipe objects

released by Atlantic Records. This song won two Grammy awards in 1968 and is widely considered to be one of the most popular songs of all time. The pipe arguments in patch 1.1 have been preset to wait exactly 522 milliseconds before sending bang messages on to the next button; this causes the buttons to flash at a speed of approximately 115 beats per minute, which closely matches the speed in the song. Click on the YouTube link located at the top right of the patch and press play to listen to the official lyric video of "Respect." Then, click on one of the buttons in the patch to synchronize your loop with the beats in the song.

If you accurately timed that first button click, the alignment between your loop and "Respect" should correspond well for about half a minute. The tempo in "Respect" drifts very slightly over time, although it is extraordinarily steady due to the incredible musicianship of the Muscle Shoals Rhythm Section. R&B music of that period did not usually make use of a *click track* to lock the beats in exact precision, like a *metronome*. Instead, music in that style gave the vocalist freedom to add slight emphases and adjust the timings of words so as to enhance the meaning and emotional expression.

Once you have tried out the initial "Respect" setting for the patch, select your own favorite tune and see if you can adjust the pipe arguments to match the speed of the new song. Contemporary recordings that feature a metronomic beat work well for this activity; you can choose an EDM, Synth-pop, or hip-hop track where the speed remains perfectly steady and synchronizes with the button-loop metronome. (Chapter 4, section 4.1 "Tempo" provides information about how to calculate pipe arguments to match a particular speed; in the meantime, you can experiment with different values—larger numbers will slow down the speed of the button flashes, and smaller numbers will speed them up.) As you experiment with the timing of events in the loop, you may notice that clicking more than once on the buttons will set off multiple overlapping loops that could get confusing. Instead, if you need to restart the loop, first close and then reopen the patch.

One additional note about "Respect": this song features a standard method for organizing time where beats are grouped in units of four; this is called a *meter* of *common time*, which will be discussed later in section 4.2. How might you adjust the number of button and pipe objects to ensure that the movement of lights around the circle aligns with the groupings of beats in the recording?

By the end of this first tutorial, you might be starting to develop some familiarity with a few basic *Max* functions such as locking and unlocking patches, adding new object boxes, and connecting objects together with patch cords. Although we have only directly used two types of objects so far (button and pipe), our lexicon will steadily grow as we progress. And while we are not yet making our own sound, we will start doing so in tutorial #3. Eventually, we will be able to create complicated musical structures! Be patient with yourself if these concepts arrive slowly or with effort. Although your initial baby steps may be challenging, there is an acceleration that typically happens after a few more basic ideas and skills are introduced.

1.1.1 These Topics, Skills, and Objects Were Introduced in Tutorial #1

- creating, naming, and saving new patches
- exploring toolbars
- placing new objects in a patch (shortcut key: "n"), using autofill to select the object name
- using *button* objects (shortcut key: "b") to send/receive *bang* messages and blink to indicate activity
- modifying the size of *button* objects using "handles," and changing color using the Inspector tool
- *bang* messages as triggers that initiate functions
- locking to run or unlocking to edit (modify) your code (shortcut keys: command+e)
- aligning and distributing items in a patch to keep things neat
- drawing patch cords between objects by connecting outlets to inlets
- routing, segmenting, and deleting patch cords
- infinite loops and clearing error messages
- using *pipe* objects to delay messages (bangs, numbers, lists, symbols) by a fixed time duration
- including "arguments" (variables) in an object box
- millisecond (1/1000th of a second) values for precise timing control
- copying and pasting objects to save time
- *comment* objects are used to provide useful information in the patch; this will be explained further in tutorial #2.
- a *ubutton* object can be connected to a special command ("launchbrowser") to open a web link such as a YouTube recording; this idea will be explored further in tutorial #3.
- the "launchbrowser" command has been hidden from view using the "hide on lock" feature; this will be explained further in tutorial #4.

1.2 Simple Arithmetic

The goal of this second tutorial is to introduce the concept of different *types* of numbers and how they can be used in *Max* patches. Facility with processing numbers is a crucial skill for creating sound on computers. This tutorial will take you through the basic steps of arithmetic computation in *Max*. At the end of the tutorial, you will apply your new knowledge toward adding a new feature (loop counting) to your patch from tutorial #1.

Programming languages (including *Max*) generally must establish systems to define numerical *data types* because different sizes and representations require various storage considerations. The size of a number is determined by its number of characters, which, in turn, controls the amount of computer memory that is needed to store it. Declaring (identifying) the type and size of a number at the moment of its creation allows for more efficient allocation of storage by constraining the values it can have.

Max allows for two basic number types: *integers*, which can be thought of as "whole numbers," and *floating-point numbers*, which are functionally equivalent to "real numbers." For the time being, we will defer some of the complexities for another time and just observe that the main difference between these two types of numbers is that floating-point numbers use decimal places—incremental values in between whole numbers—and integers do not.

Let's get started using integers and floating-point numbers in *Max*! Create a new patch called something like "tutorial #2." Add a "number" object into the patch by pressing the letter "i" for integer. (Here are two alternate ways to add an integer: [1] press the letter "n" for new object, type the word "number" into the empty object box, and press enter/return; [2] locate the "Numbers" tool near the midpoint of the toolbar at the top of the patch, click it once, and then select the "number" object on the left.) Then, lock your patch. To input a value, click once inside the number object; when the triangle turns yellow, type a number and press enter. To change the value displayed in your number object, repeat the process above or click and drag the number up and down with your mouse. Just as we used the Inspector tool to select colors for our button objects in the last tutorial, you can customize certain variables here as well. Unlock the patch, click once on the number to highlight it, and then click on the Inspector tool icon on the right-hand toolbar. A panel should expand out to the right side, displaying the properties of your number object. Go ahead and set maximum and minimum values for your number object and change how it looks by adjusting its Font Name and Font Size controls. Play around with this for a few minutes to get a sense of how it works. Click once more on the Inspector tool icon to close the side panel.

Next, let's explore decimal-place numbers by adding a floating-point number object ("flonum" object) to your patch. Press the letter "f" or type the word "flonum" into an empty object box, followed by enter/return. (Or, on the toolbar at the top of the patch, select the Numbers icon and then click on the "flonum" object in the middle.) Once the "flonum" object is placed on your patch, lock the patch and try it out. Notice that it functions similarly to "number": you can click on it, type in numerical values, and press enter/return. You can also click and drag to adjust the values. The "flonum" object has an additional feature: you can align your cursor to adjust any particular decimal place. (That is, if you only want to modify the value in the "hundredths" or "tenths" place, you can do so.) If you run out of room and can't see all your decimal places, just unlock the patch, click on flonum once, and "handles" will appear that allow you to resize it horizontally. You can also use the Inspector to specify the exact number of decimal places you want your flonum object to display.

Once you are able to generate a few integers and floating-point numbers, you can apply them toward basic computation. Let's explore a few simple arithmetic operations, starting with addition. Inside your tutorial #2 patch, near where you have been working, click in a new spot and press the letter "i" to create a number object. Click nearby in another spot and press "i" again. You should now have two number boxes; move them close together so they are side by side. Just below them, press "n" to create a new object and type "+" into it; then, press enter/return to create an addition object. Now, drag a patch cord from the left outlet of the left-side number object to the left inlet on the "+" object. Drag a second patch cord from the left outlet of the right-side number object to the right inlet on the "+" object. Finally, add one more number object beneath the "+" object and draw a patch cord to it from the output of the "+" object. This bottom object will display the *sum*; the result of the addition calculation. Your code should resemble the excerpt displayed in figure 1.4.

Next, lock up the patch and click around to experiment with the addition process. Test it out and see how it works! One aspect to observe is that the "+" object retains the most recent values it receives in each inlet until those values are updated. But perhaps the most important thing to notice is that the addition calculation in the "+" object will only happen when the left-side input is updated; changing the right-side number object will not trigger a response. Thus, the way to add two numbers together is to first input a value in the right side, and then update the left side. This is directly related to the detail described above in the "coding basics" section: *Max* processes patch contents from right to left, and therefore *Max* objects receive data in

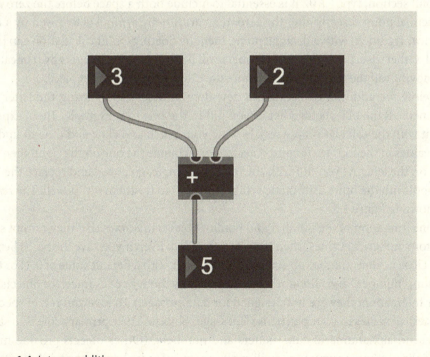

Figure 1.4 Integer addition

the right inlet before they receive data in their left inlet. For this reason, most *Max* objects are set to trigger events when they receive updates in the left inlet. As you hover your mouse over an object's inlets, you may notice that some are highlighted in blue and others in red. Blue inlets are described as "cold" inlets; they do not produce any direct output. Red inlets are known as "hot" inlets and produce an output when they receive a message.[10]

Now, let's explore the related process of subtraction, which is handled similarly. Unlock the patch, double-click inside the "+" object box to highlight the "+" addition symbol, and press "−" to replace it with a subtraction symbol. This will reset the previous numerical inputs to 0, and you will need to update new values in the number boxes. As with addition, subtraction requires that you first input the right number and then the left. Updating the left-hand number will prompt the subtraction object to initiate its calculation and subtract the right number from the left. Multiplication and division function in similar ways; to explore those objects, unlock the patch, double-click inside the object box, and type either "*" for the multiplication object or "/" for division.

Now that you have explored four basic arithmetic calculations using integers, let's run through a new set of examples—this time, using floating-point numbers. In another corner of the same patch, add the following objects: press the letter "f" twice to create two floating-point number ("flonum") objects. This will cause the second object to be created on top of (occluding) the first one; just click and drag the top one off to the side to reveal the other one underneath. In the empty space below the two flonum objects, press the letter "n" to create a blank object box, and inside the autofill section, type "+ 0." It is essential to include both a space before the zero and a decimal point directly after the zero. If an arithmetic symbol is followed by a numerical argument with a decimal point, then the floating-point calculation can proceed. Otherwise, floating-point numbers will be converted to integers by truncating (removing) all the decimal places before the calculation even takes place.

Below the addition object, add a new flonum object by pressing the letter "f." Connect all the objects together as you did in the previous example. Then, experiment with the calculation process: lock up your patch and click and drag to update the values in the top two flonum objects. (First change the one on the right, then the one on the left.) As you did with the integer example, go ahead and replace the "+" symbol with the other arithmetic symbols (−, *, /) to try them out as well. The result is shown in figure 1.5.

One limitation of the number and flonum objects in *Max* is that they cannot save or store numerical values when the patch is closed. Even if you save the patch before you close it, your number objects will reopen later with a default value of 0. (For this reason, "number" and "flonum" objects should be thought of as interface objects for user interaction; they are not designed for data storage.) To save and retain specific numerical values in your patch, use "message" objects. Their primary role is to store and send alphanumeric data—letters and numbers. (Other objects provide more specialized storage features; we will explore some of these later in the book.)

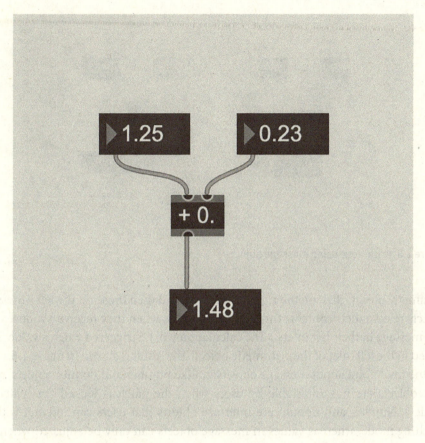

Figure 1.5 Floating-point addition

Next, add a few message objects into your patch: press the letter "m" or navigate to the toolbar at the top of the patch and select the Message object type, located on the left side. Create a few new message objects and connect them to your arithmetic symbol object with patch cords. If you wish to bypass the number or flonum objects currently in place, you can draw patch cords directly from your message objects to the arithmetic symbol objects. Or, you can copy one message objects and then use the "Paste Replace" function to overwrite the previous number objects with your new message objects. You can accomplish this by clicking once on the object you wish to replace, and then right-clicking with your mouse on that object (or control-clicking in macOS); this will launch a small floating menu from which you can select "Paste Replace." Taking this helpful step will preserve your patch cords and save you the effort of redrawing them when you swap one object for another.

To use your new message objects for basic arithmetic computations (i.e., as addends for addition, or as dividends or divisors in division), first unlock your patch and double-click inside each message object. Type numerical values into the message objects and then save your patch—message objects will store data after the patch is saved and closed. Once you have numbers in message objects connected to an

32 Constructing Music

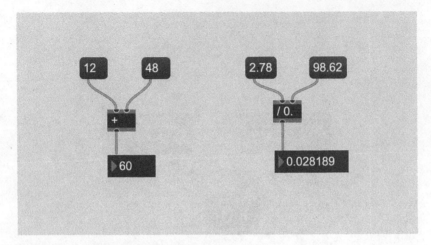

Figure 1.6 Arithmetic using message objects

arithmetic object, click on the right inputs first, and then those on the left. (Message objects release their contents through their outlets when they receive a mouse click or a message in their left inlets.) The calculation will be triggered when a value is received in the left inlet of the arithmetic object. The result is shown in figure 1.6.

One final point about message objects: unlike number and flonum objects, message objects are not adjustable by users when the patch is locked (in "patching mode"). Number and flonum are interface objects that users can interact with in patching mode, whereas values in message objects can only be adjusted when the patch is in "edit mode" (unlocked).

The *toggle* object is a special numerical object that outputs only *Boolean* values of 0 or 1. (Boolean data types are binary variables that have only two possible values: true and false, often represented in code using 1 and 0.) These values can be used like regular integers, or they can be applied in a variety of contexts to simulate conditions such as "true" and "false." For now, we will explore the numerical aspect: in your current patch, press the letter "t" to create a toggle object. (Like the button interface object, toggle will automatically take on a shape that allows for user interaction.)

To explore how toggle works, create a number object below and connect the output of toggle to the input of the number. Click repeatedly on the "x" in the center of the toggle object to output alternating values of 0 or 1. Unlike the button object, toggle retains its *state* after every click; in computing, "state" refers to a system's preceding settings or values. (You can think about state in this context like a light switch—once you turn a switch on, it normally stays on until you turn it off. This is different from the button object in *Max*, which is only "on" for an instant and then reverts back to its default "off" state.) The "toggle on" state lights up the "x" and outputs a 1, whereas the "toggle off" state turns off the "x" indicator and outputs a 0. Values of 0 and 1 can be sent from toggle to an arithmetic object, in just the same way that numerical values can be sent out from number and message objects. Go ahead and experiment

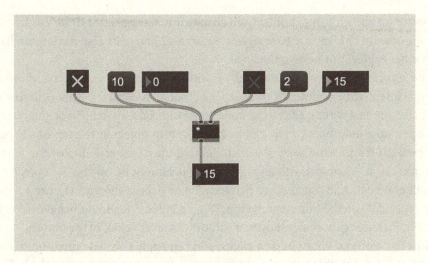

Figure 1.7 Arithmetic calculations with toggle objects

with using toggle objects alongside number and message objects in simple arithmetic calculations, as shown in figure 1.7.

As you become more familiar with the way objects are handled in *Max* and encounter new objects you haven't seen before, I recommend that you start to deepen your knowledge by seeking out the complete object definitions and usage descriptions. *Max* offers a useful way to explore and develop a fuller understanding on your own. To access this feature, unlock the patch, hover over an object, right-click on it (or control-click on macOS), and select "Open [object name] Help" from the top of the menu. This will open up a "help" file containing useful information and sample code that you can copy and use in your patch.

As an additional component for this tutorial, we will learn how to use "comment" objects to add helpful text boxes that enhance our patches. Comment objects are useful for explaining how things work to others or reminding yourself what you did! I use them all the time to write little notes to myself about what remains to be finished up in a patch. They can also provide instructions to help guide future users around your patch. (Well-placed screen text signage can be a large contributing factor in ensuring a positive user experience with the graphical interface of your patch.) To add a small block of explanatory text or a title to your patch, press "c" or type the word "comment" into an empty object box. Use the Inspector tool to change font, size, style, and color to enhance the visibility and design of your text comments.

Once you are done with the steps above, go ahead and open up example patch "1.2 Simple Arithmetic" in the Tutorials sample code files. Compare your tutorial #2 patch with the sample patch. There is no one right way to work through arithmetic in *Max*, but perhaps the sample code can provide some support. Note that the sample code is neat and orderly, including "aligned" patch cords (see above), comment object text descriptions for the different sections, and even some comment objects that feature color. (To apply color to comment objects in your own patch, navigate to the

Inspector for each comment object and change the "Background Color" settings, including opacity.) Make sure to save your tutorial #2 patch, in case it comes in handy for further explorations down the line.

And, as one last step in this tutorial, we will apply our new arithmetic knowledge to experiment with counting button clicks ("bang" messages). This will give us a useful feature that we can add to our code in the tutorial #1 patch. To begin, go ahead and open up a new, blank *Max* patch. Add a button object at the top of the patch, and beneath it add a message object containing the number 1. Below the message object, create a "+" object with an argument of 0. Finally, below the "+" object, place a number object. Add patch cords between the objects as shown in figure 1.8. Now, click repeatedly on the button at the top. What happens? It should behave like a tally counter, increasing incrementally by a value of 1 at every click of the button.

Now that you can count button clicks, you can apply this new function to create a loop counter. For this purpose, we will reuse the patch from tutorial #1. To get started, copy all the objects in your loop counting code (also available in patch 1.2a among the Tutorials sample code files). Then, paste them into your tutorial #1 patch, near the button labeled "click here." Draw a patch cord connecting the outlet of that start button to the top of your new code snippet, and observe what happens. Your

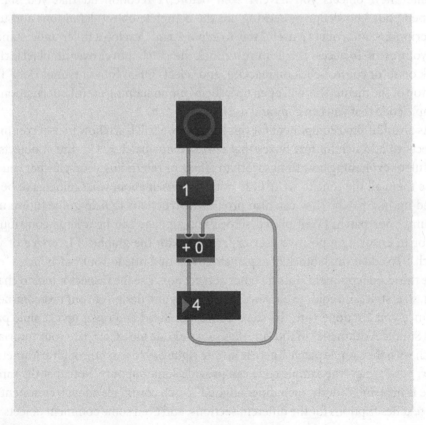

Figure 1.8 Simple loop counter

loop counter should increase by a value of 1 every time the loop restarts. You can think about this loop counting capability in the same way that you might count beats or measures in music. We can explore this idea again further when we encounter time-based musical structures in Chapter 4.

1.2.1 These Topics, Skills, and Objects Were Introduced in Tutorial #2

- types and sizes of numbers
- integer *number* objects (shortcut key: "i")
- floating-point *flonum* number objects (shortcut key: "f")
- adjusting maximum and minimum values, numbers of decimal places, and font controls for number objects using the Inspector tool
- resizing objects using "handles"
- arithmetic objects (+, –, *, /)
- objects perform functions when they receive new values in the left inlet
- *message* objects store and send alphanumeric data (shortcut key: "m")
- using "paste replace" to overwrite existing objects with new ones while preserving patch cords
- *toggle* interface objects are user-clickable and output Boolean values (0 or 1) (shortcut key: "t")
- "help" files for object definitions
- *comment* objects for text labels and instructions (shortcut key: "c")

1.3 MIDI Notes and Variables

Now that you have gained some familiarity with navigating around *Max* and accomplishing basic tasks such as adding objects to a patch, connecting them together with patch cords, and computing simple arithmetic, it is time to start making some music! The purpose of this tutorial is to provide detailed information about how to play notes using MIDI. This tutorial will function as a brief primer to quickly and efficiently build the knowledge we will need to enjoy our forays into musical coding. Let's get started.

Musicians often interact with MIDI by using familiar-looking devices such as electronic keyboards and wind controllers that resemble clarinets or saxophones. However, these digital devices work very differently from traditional instruments: they require synthesizers and speakers in order to make sound. The usual way to make sound with a MIDI controller is to connect it to MIDI software on a computer; then, when you play a note on the controller, you are sending a "note on" message to the computer. Each message is a small packet of data containing control variables for musical actions.

We use MIDI messages to pass musical data between devices, computers, and software applications. Message contents must adhere to specific formatting rules; for example, they must consist of status bytes followed by data bytes. Most MIDI variables are encoded with 128 values of precision using seven *bits*. (Bits are the smallest data values that computers can process; they represent individual binary values of 1 or 0, and their name comes from "binary digit.") Because bits can switch between two states of 1 or 0, the total number of possible values that can be expressed with seven bits is 2^7, or 128.) These variable values are typically given a numerical range of 0–127, due to the standard convention in computing where counting begins with a first number of 0.

Some special MIDI messages are encoded with 14 bits in order to provide a much finer *degree of resolution*, or detail, in the signal. ($2^{14} = 16{,}384$, a much greater "bit depth" than the standard MIDI value of 128, encoded using seven bits.) It deserves to be mentioned that when MIDI was invented in 1981, computer memory was expensive to purchase. Therefore, at that time, allocating seven bits for each variable was a reasonable decision to make—a range of 128 values gave a decent amount of precision without using too many costly computing resources such as memory or processing time. These days, since data storage is much more available and much less expensive, some of the original constraints around resolution and memory allocation in MIDI are less imperative.[11]

There are many different types of MIDI messages! Common types represent musical decisions and actions such as aftertouch, channel volume, pitch bend, control change,[12] and system-exclusive (manufacturer-specific) messages. We will use some of these message types later in the book and explain them as needed. For the time being, we are going to limit ourselves to exploring only the most basic type: the "note on" message.

Simply put, MIDI "note on" messages cause notes to play. Notes are defined as individual musical sounds or the symbols that represent them. In MIDI, notes are initiated at a particular moment in time and have four variables: note number, volume, duration, and timbre. These variables will be explored in Chapter 2 and section 3.1 "Make a Note," but in the meantime we will use simple descriptions to get started.

A MIDI "note on" message contains three bytes: a status byte to identify its type and MIDI channel number, and two data bytes—one for note number and one for velocity. Numbers are used in MIDI to identify notes according to their *pitch*. Pitch is the perceived "height" of a musical sound, or its placement within the range of possible note values. You may be familiar with the common way of identifying pitch by name using letters (as in A, B, C, etc.). In MIDI, we identify pitch by number, and there are 128 individual pitch values to choose from.

Volume is the perceived loudness of a sound. For technical reasons, the volume variable in MIDI is called "velocity." This is because MIDI keyboards determine volume by measuring the speed of each downward keystroke. MIDI velocity has a range of 128 values from soft to loud. When a note has a velocity of 0, no sound is heard. (There is also a separate message type called "note off," which causes a note to stop playing. A "note off" message is very similar to a "note on" message, except that in place of a velocity value it identifies a *release velocity* value, determined by measuring the speed of the upward keystroke at the end of the note.)

Duration is measured in units of time. Typically, we count these units in *Max* using milliseconds. As with the argument to the "pipe" object that we used in tutorial #1, note durations are treated as variables.

And finally, *timbre* is defined as the specific tone quality or "color" of a sound, usually associated with a specific instrument or synthesis algorithm that created the sound. Timbre is usually assigned in MIDI using a "program change" message that is specified for each MIDI channel. MIDI messages are received by software and devices that are listening on those individual channels. A MIDI channel can only be assigned to one timbre at a time, in the same way that a track on a mixing board can only handle one microphone input at a time. MIDI channels are grouped together in units of sixteen per MIDI "port," which could mean a wired connection to a physical device or a virtual port in software. (If more than sixteen channels are needed, additional ports can be added. Usually, numbers of MIDI ports are only limited for hardware devices; software applications can keep adding arbitrary numbers of channels.)

To begin creating MIDI "note on" and "note off" messages in *Max*, create a new patcher and call it something like "tutorial #3." Into your blank patch, press the letter "n" to add a new object, and in the text box, type "makenote" followed by enter/return. As its name suggests, the purpose of the makenote object is to create a note—it sends out a note on message, and then when the appropriate duration has elapsed, it sends a corresponding note off message. The makenote object has three required variables: note number, volume, and duration. Either these values can be received in the inlets at the top of the makenote object, or volume and duration can be listed as arguments in the object itself. For the time being, let's provide the volume and duration values as arguments: double-click on the makenote object to edit the text, and following the word "makenote" add in the numbers 100 and 1000 (make sure to leave exactly one space between each item). The first argument is a variable for volume; its value is 100 out of a maximum of 127, which is fairly loud. The second argument is a variable for duration; its value is 1000 milliseconds, equal to one second—a moderate length.

Next, press the letter "m" to create a message object, and place it just above the makenote object. Into the message object, type a number between 36 and 96. This will serve as your pitch value. For now, any value in that range should work equally well. Draw a patch cord from the message object to the left inlet of the makenote object, and then lock the patch. When you click on the note number in the message object, makenote will receive that value and send out a MIDI note on message. However, the makenote object cannot actually make the note audible—it is not empowered to do that. To sonify this note, we will need to add one more object: unlock your patch, press the letter "n" to create a new object below makenote, and into the new object box type the word "noteout." Draw a patch cord from the left outlet of makenote to the left inlet of noteout. Then, draw a patch cord from the right outlet of makenote to the middle inlet of noteout. (You can leave the right inlet of noteout empty and unconnected.) Lock up your patch, click on the message object, and voilà! You should hear a note play. The noteout object received the "note on" message and successfully sent it to a software synthesizer on your computer. (Just as a MIDI controller will not output sound until it is connected to MIDI software on the computer, the makenote object will also not make a sound unless it is connected to a noteout object.)

Congratulations! You just performed your first solo note using MIDI. You may wonder what name to call your note, aside from its number. There is a way to sort this out. However, for the time being, we will leave this aspect "under the hood" and return to it later when we learn the conventions for naming notes in section 3.1 "Make a Note." For now, listen to the quality of the note that you made and direct your attention to its individual components. Go ahead and modify the variables for pitch, velocity, and duration by unlocking the patch and editing the numbers. Enjoy experimenting with different values for all three variables. Your patch should look something like the code shown in figure 1.9.

Next, let's enable this note generator to more nimbly adjust the note number. Unlock your patch, press the letter "n" to add a new object to your patch, type the

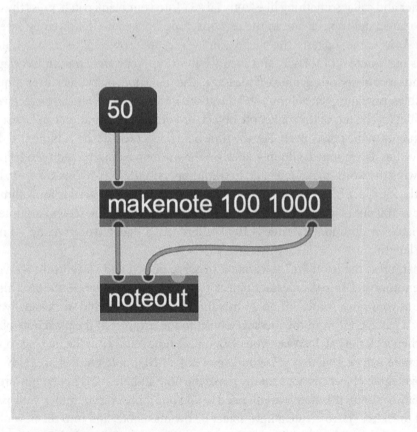

Figure 1.9 Simple *Max* code to play a MIDI note

word "number" to create a number object, and press enter/return. Draw a patch cord from your new number object into the left inlet of makenote. Lock up your patch, click once and hold inside the number object, and then roll your mouse up and down. The result should sound as if you are quickly sliding the tip of your finger up and down a piano keyboard; this is called a *glissando*.

Finally, this patch will help us explore how to change timbre. Up until now, your notes have probably been sounding like a piano, because *Max* typically defaults to the first sound ("Acoustic Grand Piano") on the first channel when not specified. However, one fun feature of the *General MIDI* specification is that it reserves an entire channel exclusively for (unpitched) percussion sounds; these can only be found on MIDI channel 10. (The "key map" list of these sounds is located at the bottom of this page: https://www.midi.org/specifications-old/item/gm-level-1-sound-set.)

To access these built-in General MIDI percussion sounds, set your "noteout" object to send notes on MIDI channel 10 by embedding an argument of "10" after the object name. Then, in the same message object that you were previously using for pitch number, replace your current value with "56." Save your patch, lock it up, and then click on the message object. You should now hear a new sound: in the General MIDI percussion map, note number 56 is assigned to the cowbell. Since one can *never* have enough cowbell, I now invite you now to locate a track for "(Don't Fear) The Reaper" by Blue Öyster Cult. (Here is a good version: https://youtu.be/oF7m P2LASCo.) Listen for the beats that start up after the guitar solo (at around 0:09), and match that speed as closely as you can with your *Max* cowbell. To crank up the volume on your cowbell, go ahead and change its velocity value (currently 100) to the maximum of 127. Notice that it actually takes a fair amount of focus and dexterity to click your mouse in time with the original recording, requiring a quick response time of 143 clicks per minute. Your patch should now look something like the image shown in figure 1.10.

Hopefully, that was a fun way to explore timbre change! Now let's switch gears. Go ahead and save your tutorial #3 patch so that you can refer back to it later. Then, please open up patch 1.3 ("MIDI Notes and Variables") in the Tutorials sample code files. This patch will allow us to explore the set of MIDI note-making variables in a different way.

Start by pressing the blue button on the top left side of patch 1.3, shown in figure 1.11, to hear a note that has been predefined for you. The three initial variables of pitch, volume, and duration have each been given fixed values with message objects. When you click on the button, you will hear a note with a pitch of "middle C" (MIDI note number 60) performed with a medium-loud volume (MIDI velocity 100 out of a maximum of 127) and a duration of 5 seconds (5000 milliseconds). Middle C is named that way because it lies in the middle of the piano keyboard. In musical notation, it exists exactly in between the treble and bass clefs, defining a common boundary between the right and left hands. It is also frequently called C4, because it is the fourth C when you count from the left-hand side—the bottom—of a piano keyboard. This idea of specifying the relative location of a note within the full range

40 Constructing Music

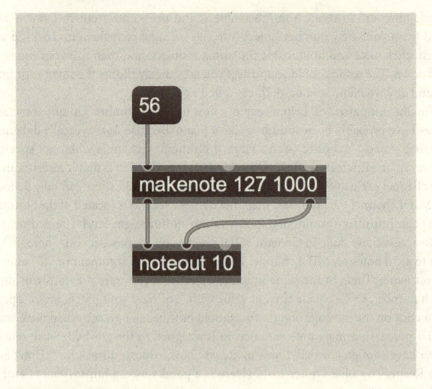

Figure 1.10 MIDI cowbell

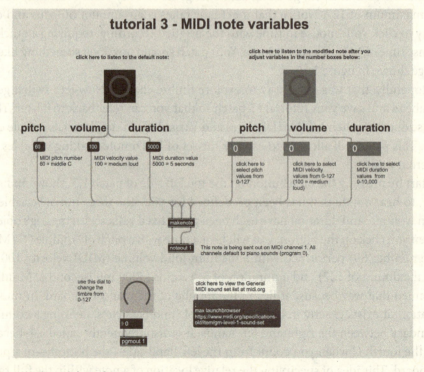

Figure 1.11 Tutorial patch 1.3

of all pitch options is called "register," will be explored further in section 3.2 "Name a Note."

Now that you have listened to the predefined middle C note, go ahead and adjust the values for pitch, volume, and duration by clicking and dragging the values in the green number objects. Alternately, you can manually type new values into the number boxes: 0–127 for pitch and volume, and 1–10,000 for durations up to ten seconds long. (Notes with pitch numbers below 25 may be hard to hear on laptop speakers; this is because the tiny drivers in laptop speakers can't reproduce the long wavelengths of low notes. Also, sending a volume value of 0 will generate silence.) Generally, you might want to change the volume and duration variables first, and then update the pitch variable to hear the note; the order in which inputs are handled here resembles what we encountered in the second tutorial on simple arithmetic. As is the case with arithmetic objects (+, −, *, /), many *Max* objects are set to trigger their outputs upon receiving updated values in their left inlets. Once you have the variables set just the way you want them, you can click on the green button to repeat the result as many times as you wish.

As you experienced a bit earlier in this section, clicking inside the pitch number object and dragging rapidly up or down will cause glissandos to slide over the large range of 128 available notes. The extent of possible values in each number object has been constrained using the "maximum" variable in the object's Inspector tool. (To change these maximum values, go ahead and unlock the patch, click once on the number object, select the Inspector icon on the right, and scroll down to the very bottom item. Double-click to highlight the value and type in a new number.)

Once you have experimented a bit with the three variables of pitch, volume, and duration, it is time to explore the fourth and final variable of timbre. To do this, locate the yellow *dial* object on the bottom of the patch. Typically, all sounds initially play out using the default timbre of Acoustic Grand Piano, the first instrument in the General MIDI sound set. But this variable is changeable, just like the others, and it can be fun to explore the range of sounds that are available. Timbral control is implemented in MIDI using "program change" messages. MIDI program change messages have two variables: program (timbre) and channel number. As with many other MIDI variables, program values have a numerical range of 0–127, whereas the channel variable is usually numbered 1–16. To send a program change message, first make sure that your patch is locked. Then use the yellow dial object on the bottom of the patch to explore new timbres. Click and drag in an upward direction to rotate the dial in a clockwise motion; click and drag downward to rotate the dial counterclockwise. Please note that as with previous examples, you must first change the timbre variable before selecting a pitch number to send the note. Typically, timbre cannot be changed in midstream after a MIDI note has been initiated.

Program change messages are implemented in *Max* using the *pgmout* object with variable values for program (timbre) and MIDI channel. In this patch, the instrument (timbre) number is directly controlled by the dial, and the MIDI channel number is listed as an *argument* for the pgmout object. (If no *argument* is present,

Max defaults to channel 1.) To change the MIDI channel number, all you have to do is either edit the *argument* value there or input a new number in the right inlet of pgmout. Program change messages belong to a special category called "channel messages," and therefore, like noteout objects, pgmout objects do not need to send their data anywhere with patch cords—they output directly to the MIDI driver for sonification.

This particular dial object has been limited to a maximum value of 128, specified in the Inspector tool under the "Number of Steps / Range" setting. The number object below will display its value. At the bottom of this patch, we also introduce another new interface object: *ubutton*. Ubutton is a transparent version of the button object; it defines a clickable region on the screen. You can place a ubutton object over text, images, or any other elements, and it will delineate the area within which you can generate a bang message to trigger or select something. Click on the ubutton object on the bottom right side of this patch to pull up the online list of sounds on the webpage of the MIDI Association. The message object below ubutton contains special text instructions that open a web link on your computer. Locate the "General MIDI Level 1 Instrument Patch Map" on the website to call up favorite instrumental sounds, such as Orchestral Harp or Drawbar Organ. (General MIDI sounds are sometimes called "patches" or "programs" or even "instruments"; yes, this is confusing.) Play and have fun listening to the sounds that are available on your system.

Once you have a good sense about how the different parts of this patch work, I encourage you to make any changes or modifications that you see fit. You can use comment objects to write notes to yourself about the different parts of the patch, change object colors, or even create a few more preset note values that you can trigger in a particular order. Experimenting with or modifying ("modding") patches can help you quickly gain facility and start to feel confident and creative in the environment.

1.3.1 These Topics, Skills, and Objects Were Introduced in Tutorial #3

- *makenote* objects send out note on messages and, after the appropriate duration, send corresponding note off messages
- *noteout* objects transmit note on and note off messages to specific MIDI ports on the computer
- constraining the range of a number object using the Inspector tool
- *pgmout* objects send MIDI program change messages, with one variable for the timbre selection and one for the MIDI channel number
- *dial* is an interface object that outputs numbers based on rotations of the dial interface (with range, offset, multiplier, and various visual modifications that can be specified using the Inspector tool)
- *ubutton* is a transparent button that defines an active region; it is an interface object that can be placed over other objects and clicked on to send a bang message

- special percussion sounds can be found on General MIDI channel 10; a key map is available online at https://www.midi.org/specifications-old/item/gm-level-1-sound-set

1.4 MIDI Basics

Now that we have had some fun making sound using MIDI in *Max*, it's probably time to learn a bit about how it actually works "under the hood." The purpose of this tutorial is to provide just enough technical information so that a beginner can understand generally what MIDI is, why it is useful, how it runs on computers, and how to play MIDI files. Most of the more complicated aspects of MIDI implementation will be revealed later on when needed. However, be prepared that this section will be a bit technical; while it may feel like a slog at times, hang in there! The value of this knowledge will become clearer later on. Interested readers are encouraged to explore MIDI in even greater detail after completing this book.[13]

Let's acquaint ourselves with information about MIDI data, drivers, and files, so we know what we are doing when we use them to make music. In order to create musical sounds on a computer, you need to use a *digital music protocol*. The purpose of a digital music protocol is to convert musical score information from a traditional representation, such as written notation on a five-line staff, to a *symbolic* digital representation: encoded data that can be manipulated on a computer. MIDI is one of the available protocols that format musical data so we can hear and view it with software. MIDI allows us to convert musical information into numbers that we can plug into *algorithms* to create musical sound, and allows us to record, shape, and control music created by synthesizers and samplers—in ways that resemble the flexibility and convenience of traditional instruments.

So, what is MIDI? It is an acronym that stands for *Musical Instrument Digital Interface*. It is also a technical standard that was created in 1981 by a consortium of musical instrument manufacturers and computer music researchers. Technical standards are also known as protocols or specifications; they are detailed agreements that ensure consistent implementation of technologies by manufacturers, so users can expect equivalent operation across products and national borders. A widely known recent example is *5G*, the fifth-generation technology standard for broadband cellular networks. In its most straightforward formulation, the MIDI specification is a serial communications protocol that handles musical data. It ensures the *interoperability* of MIDI devices—that pressing a key on a MIDI keyboard will cause a corresponding sound to play on a MIDI synthesizer, for example, and that both devices understand the same controls. MIDI is designed to work either through a cable connection or over digital networks. Its asynchronous transmission speed is 31,250 bits per second; this is a slow data rate compared with modern network speeds these days—standard wired ethernet generally transmits at a rate of ten million bits per second. But despite its limitations, MIDI continues to enable musicians to play and record musical information on digital devices without a perceivable delay.

MIDI was invented in response to the proliferation of digital synthesizers throughout the 1970s. By 1980, it had become commonplace for professional keyboard musicians to use multiple synthesizers in live performances. Each synth contributed useful sound qualities to the mix, but also came along with its own bulky keyboard and built-in speakers. Stage setups started to become elaborate, perhaps most noticeably in genres like progressive rock.[14] As a result, equipment became cumbersome to transport, set up, and maintain. A solution was urgently needed! Dave Smith of Sequential Circuits and Ikutaru Kakehashi, who had founded Roland and Boss, convened a group of manufacturers to study the problem. Their consensus was to replace large racks of keyboard synthesizers with single keyboard "controllers" that connected to smaller synth modules mounted in portable rack cases. These consolidated systems included a central controller (either a keyboard or a computer) that could communicate with synth modules over a synchronized network.

Many instrument manufacturers agreed to the MIDI standard and supported its introduction to the public at the National Association of Music Merchants (NAMM) trade show in 1983. The new MIDI system proved to be effective in live performances as well as in recording studios, and it integrated well with new personal computers that were emerging on the consumer market at that time. To this day, MIDI is maintained and updated by the MIDI Association (https://www.midi.org/), a nonprofit trade organization that ensures the compatibility and quality of MIDI products. MIDI has been quite stable over the past forty years and remains the de facto protocol despite promising alternatives that have emerged over the intervening years, including Open Sound Control, MusicXML, and music21.

1.4.1 MIDI Settings on Your Computer

These days, MIDI is a mature technology that is built directly into most computer operating systems. *Device drivers* (usually shortened to "drivers") are small software files that communicate with operating systems; they automatically handle the setup and implementation of MIDI on most computers. Usually, MIDI "just works" and does not require active intervention. For this reason, it may seem opaque, mysterious, or "under the hood." However, as computer communications protocols go, it's not very complicated. MIDI drivers simply provide a way to route music data signals between computers, software, and external devices like keyboards and synthesizers.

If you have an Apple computer, you can view the MIDI driver information on your macOS operating system by launching an application called "Audio MIDI Setup" (▓) that is typically located under Applications → Utilities. After double-clicking to open it, navigate to its Window Menu and select "Show MIDI Studio," shown in figure 1.12. (Usually, Audio MIDI Setup displays only its "Audio Devices" window by default; you have to manually open the MIDI Studio.) Any MIDI devices

Tutorials 45

Figure 1.12 Audio MIDI setup driver

that have been connected to your computer should be listed here; the icons for any prior devices that are not currently connected will be dimmed. Even if no MIDI devices have ever been connected to your computer before, there should still be a driver that allows MIDI applications to route MIDI data to each other internally within the computer. On some computers, it is called the IAC (Inter-Application Communication) driver; on others, it might have a different name.

On macOS, the Audio MIDI Setup driver can help you add a MIDI keyboard or other MIDI device to your workspace. (You do not need to have a MIDI keyboard to use the patches in this book, but you still may occasionally use the Audio MIDI Setup to debug issues or send your MIDI data to other software programs outside of *Max*.) First, install any required software provided by the device manufacturer, and follow their instructions before connecting the MIDI device to your computer (typically, with a USB cable). The default MIDI Configuration menu is displayed within the MIDI Studio window in Audio MIDI Setup. (If you wish, you can create and save alternate configurations.) To configure your new MIDI device on the computer, click on the "+" button in the MIDI Studio toolbar. This will create a new icon; double-click on it to view the device's Properties window, where you can input information such as the device name, manufacturer/model, icon, color, transmit/receive channels, and port numbers. (Once you are done editing these details, click "Apply" to save your information and close the Properties window.) Drag the In and Out connectors at the top of your new device icon to the corresponding connectors on any devices that are currently displayed, replicating the cable connections in your physical workspace.[15] If your computer runs Windows 10 or 11, your operating system may already have built-in MIDI and audio drivers. (Standard options include "midi_mme" and "Microsoft GS Wavetable Synthesizer.") However, if you want to use an external MIDI keyboard or other MIDI device with your Windows computer, you may need to first install drivers provided by the device manufacturer. Read the manufacturer's instructions to connect your MIDI device to your Windows computer and determine whether additional MIDI drivers are needed; download and install the drivers as directed. Access your device settings on the computer by going to Start → Settings → Device Manager. (When installed correctly, your MIDI device should appear under "Sound, video and game controllers" or "Sounds and Audio Devices.")

In addition to the drivers that connect physical MIDI devices and software applications, Mac and Windows operating systems also have built-in General MIDI ("GM") synthesizers that play sounds when they receive MIDI data. *Max* relies on these built-in synthesizers to play MIDI notes on your computer. General MIDI is a version of the MIDI specification that defines a specific set of features for participating devices. GM devices, including many early videogame consoles, all use the same General MIDI Sound Set (https://www.midi.org/specifications-old/item/gm-level-1-sound-set), a list of 128 specific sounds that ensure consistent playback across different equipment. (GM devices also must follow other requirements regarding numbers of channels, simultaneous sounds, and continuous controllers.)

On many computers using the macOS operating system, there is a built-in General MIDI synthesizer called Audio Unit Downloadable Sounds ("AU DLS"). (Your computer may have a different built-in synth; to determine which MIDI synth is on your computer, navigate within *Max* to Options → MIDI Setup. It should appear at the top of the list of Outputs.) AU DLS contains a bank of internal General MIDI sounds and SoundFont files, which use recorded audio samples to generate sound. If you have a Windows computer, your operating system probably has automatically installed a default MIDI synthesizer; it should show up as the default MIDI output device. One common example is called Microsoft GS Wavetable synth; there are other options as well. To determine which MIDI synth is on your computer, right-click on Start in the lower left-hand corner of your desktop, and select Device Manager. Click on the View menu and then select Show hidden devices. Expand Software devices, right-click on Microsoft GS Wavetable Synth (or alternate option), and select Properties to view its information. (Don't update, disable, or uninstall it!) In case your computer does not have a MIDI synth installed, you will need to install one yourself; see online resources for help.[16]

Max communicates directly with the MIDI driver (Audio MIDI Setup on macOS) and the General MIDI synthesizer (possibly AU DLS synthesizer, Microsoft GS Wavetable synth, or other) through internal controls. Some of these settings can be viewed and modified from within *Max*. To access the MIDI settings, locate the Options menu in the Application Menu above your patch window and navigate to MIDI Setup. Here, you can view the names of the MIDI drivers and MIDI synths on your computer, and change their input and output MIDI mappings. For example, if you recently added a MIDI keyboard or controller to your setup, you should probably double-check that it is showing up correctly in the MIDI Setup window, with the Inputs boxes properly selected. In the MIDI Setup window, shown in figure 1.13,

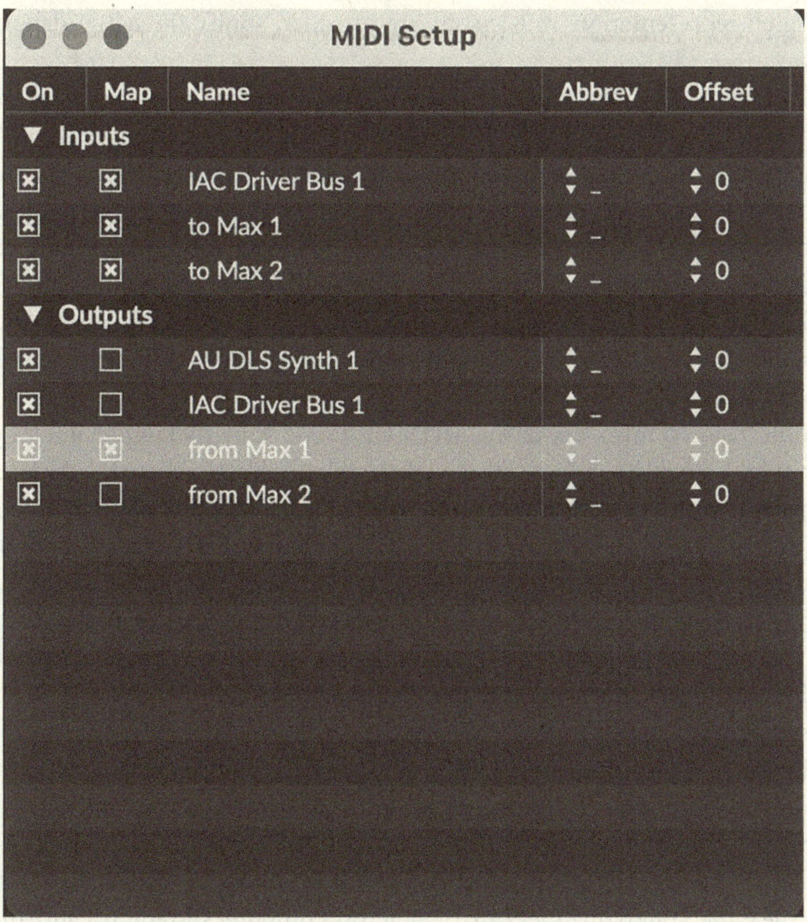

On	Map	Name	Abbrev	Offset
▼ Inputs				
☒	☒	IAC Driver Bus 1	_	0
☒	☒	to Max 1	_	0
☒	☒	to Max 2	_	0
▼ Outputs				
☒	☐	AU DLS Synth 1	_	0
☒	☐	IAC Driver Bus 1	_	0
☒	☒	from Max 1	_	0
☒	☐	from Max 2	_	0

Figure 1.13 MIDI Setup window in *Max*

you can also verify that *Max* is sending MIDI data to outputs such as built-in GM synths, MIDI drivers, from *Max* 1, and from *Max* 2. This will ensure that your MIDI data can be heard through other audio software on your computer.

1.4.2 Playing MIDI Files on Your Computer

There are many types of MIDI-compatible music software! MIDI applications are differentiated by function such as music production, notation, playback, music education, and interactive systems. In order for these applications to be able to play and modify digital sound, the information must first be encoded in MIDI format. There are a few different ways to convert music from conventional representations (i.e., sheet music notation) to MIDI format—for example, you can transcribe sheet music scores using notation software or record notes in music production software (also known as a Digital Audio Workstation, or "DAW"). Once your notes are stored in a digital representation, music software can then sonify the MIDI data in various ways.

One of the coolest parts about using MIDI software is the option to share data across multiple applications. I sometimes describe this as utilizing a common "MIDI backbone." MIDI serves as a shared protocol that allows musical data to be shuttled in between different software packages, in much the same way that text data can be copied and pasted among different applications like Microsoft Word, Adobe Acrobat PDF, and Google docs. The American Standard Code for Information Interchange (ASCII) technical standard encodes individual letters into characters and text data that can be shared, and the MIDI technical standard allows note/expression data to be shared.

Another way to think about the MIDI backbone is by making an analogy with player pianos. Pneumatically controlled player pianos were invented in the late nineteenth century; they operated as forms of musical automata that could read punched holes in a roll of paper. As the paper rolls scrolled down across a set of motorized valves, pressurized air flowed through the holes and was detected by sensors. Another component connected sensor outputs to the actions of individual piano keys. You could carry a paper roll from one player piano to another, and the music would sound nearly the same, with slight differences in playback speed and tuning between the two instruments.[17]

MIDI offers a similar way to transport musical data between devices: like paper piano rolls, MIDI data can be recorded and saved in digital files that are easily transported from one computer to another. (MIDI files are formatted text files and therefore are quite compact and small in size.) Even when the data in a MIDI file remains the same, sound qualities can differ across computer systems because they use different software and sound synthesis methods.

These days, common reasons to use the MIDI backbone might be to notate an arrangement of a song in MuseScore and then export it in MIDI format to a DAW such as Logic Pro X. Within Logic, you can produce a multitrack project that incorporates effects plugins by Waves and instrumental sample libraries from Spitfire Audio. In addition to using MIDI applications one at a time you can also use them simultaneously, where one application generates and passes MIDI data to another one for sonification in real time. For example, *Max* patches can receive incoming data from game controllers and send out MIDI data to play sound through other audio systems. Professional game developers sometimes use this approach: Eran Egozy, former CTO and VP of Engineering at Harmonix Music Systems, once told me that his engineers liked to use *Max* patches to test out sections of code while they were developing popular games like Guitar Hero and Rock Band. They used MIDI data to simulate player behavior, sending out game controller data in real time to their proprietary game engine for audio/visual playback.

Tutorial #4 illustrates the idea that MIDI provides a "backbone" that connects multiple sound-generating parts together. We will explore how to play a MIDI file in *Max* and how to send those notes to other MIDI applications on your computer. To begin the tutorial, open up sample patch 1.4 ("MIDIBasics"), located in the Tutorials sample code files. To start playing a MIDI file, click on the green button to the left. This will launch a brief excerpt of Koji Kondo's well-loved main theme for the Super Mario Bros. game series by Nintendo.[18]

Playback controls are governed by the object called "seq," which can play and record MIDI files. Its name derives from the term "sequencer," which was coined in the early days of sound synthesizers. (Sequencers are electronic devices that can record and play back *sequences* of notes in a particular order.) This MIDI file is set to loop indefinitely; click on the red button to stop playback. The red button sends a bang trigger to a message object containing the word "stop." The seq object receives that text and interprets it as a command; it stops instantaneously. The argument in the seq object is "Mario.mid," the name of the MIDI file located with the Tutorials sound files. The "Mario" MIDI file must be placed in the same folder as patch 1.4 for *Max* to be able to easily find it; it may be moved to an alternate location on your computer's hard drive, but only if you specify the "search path" in Options → File Preferences. (Further discussion of search paths will be left "under the hood" for now. If you are motivated to learn more, a summary is available here: https://docs.cycling74.com/max8/vignettes/search_path.)

Adjust the speed of MIDI playback by clicking on the orange, yellow, or blue buttons on the patch. (Speed changes will only take effect at the next restart of the loop.) The orange button triggers a message that instructs seq to play two times slower than the original, the yellow button instructs it to play twice as fast as the original, and the blue button returns the file back to its original speed. After stopping the "Mario.mid" file, you can restart playback by clicking on the green button; it will start the file from the beginning using the most recent speed value it received.

The purple object is a slider, which we are encountering for the first time. The slider is an interface object that resembles other sliding controls you might see in the real world, such as lighting dimmers or faders on sound mixing boards. Slider objects output numbers within a specific numerical range, shaped by a bottom number ("output minimum") and a scaling factor ("output multiplier"). The settings for this slider object are specified in its object Inspector. This particular slider object will allow you to select any speed between 0 and 2999; 0 will stop playback, values around 1024 will return the file to its original speed, and values approaching 2999 will get close to three times the file's original speed.

This slider object outputs its current value to the right inlet of the message object located below it, replacing the previous message contents. Because instructions in *Max* patches are processed from right to left, the updated message object then receives a bang trigger in its left inlet that causes it to release its contents through its outlet. The "prepend" object then receives that message and adds its argument ("start") in front of the incoming new alphanumeric text. The result is that the message sent to seq from the purple slider is formatted in the exact same way as the messages sent from the yellow, orange, and blue buttons.

Each of the speed controls in this patch, whether originating from a button or slider, works by triggering a message object containing "start" followed by a speed variable. Here, the message object is being used in a new way that you haven't seen before: instead of storing a single numerical value as we did in tutorial #2, each message object here stores a line of alphanumeric text that can be interpreted as a command by another object. All of the speed control changes only take effect at the point when the file restarts (the "loop point"); they cannot be changed in the middle of the file. This is because the seq object is not able to change its speed in midstream. (It is a bit brittle in this regard.) However, when seq finishes playing a file, it sends a bang trigger out of its right outlet. In this patch, a patch cord connects that bang command from the right outlet of seq back up to the green start button, automatically restarting the file every time it stops. Any change to the speed variable is updated at the moment when the MIDI file starts playing, either because the loop restarts or because the green button has been pressed.

Tutorial patch 1.4 also introduces a few other new objects: midiout, midiflush, midiparse, and unpack. The *midiout* object sends MIDI data from *Max* to a specified MIDI port on your computer. Typically, it defaults to sending MIDI data to the internal General MIDI synthesizer on the computer; on macOS, this may be called "AU DLS Synth 1," and on Windows it might be "Microsoft GS Wavetable Synth" (or similar).

Stopping MIDI playback with seq can occasionally result in "hung notes," notes that have started playing but not reached their stopping point yet. The *midiflush* object provides a solution to this problem: when it receives a bang message, it turns off all MIDI notes that have previously passed through it. Its placement right after seq allows it to monitor all notes that seq sends out and ensure that they are properly concluded. A *midiparse* object is also displayed at the bottom of the patch; it provides a visual output of a portion of the raw MIDI data being sent out by the seq object. The "unpack" object is also used here to split out a list of MIDI data into its individual component parts. The MIDI data types displayed in this section of the patch are variable values for pitch, volume, and channel, which we learned about previously in tutorial #3.

It's hard to imagine that anyone would get tired of such an iconic musical theme! However, it is possible to read in a new MIDI file if you need a change of pace. There are many places where you can find MIDI files online; https://musescore.com is one place where you can register for an account and then download song files in MIDI format. Regardless of the location from which you obtain your MIDI file, you will need to ensure that it is copied to your local hard drive. To load it into patch 1.4, click on the message object called "read." This will open up a navigation menu to help you locate a MIDI file on your local computer. Once you locate the file, click once to select it and then click on "Open" to load it into the seq object. From then on, you can play the new file with the same speed controls. Please note that some software applications embed control and program messages at the beginning of MIDI files.

These messages must be removed before the seq object can read them; you can remove them using editor functions in a DAW (such as the Event List window in Logic Pro X), and then re-export the file in MIDI format. It may take a bit of experimentation to find a MIDI file that seq can read.

Another new aspect to observe in this patch is that if you unlock it, you will see a few additional items that have been hidden from view using the "hide on lock" feature. "Hide on lock" can be a simple and helpful way to hide objects "under the hood." This removes unnecessary complexity from your user's field of view, so they can focus on only the information that is needed for the patch. Access this feature by unlocking the patch, selecting the desired objects, and navigating to Object → Hide on Lock (command+k to hide, command+l to show; ctrl+k and ctrl+l on Windows). Taking this step can help reduce visual clutter and confusion.

Some of the objects that have been hidden include "loadbang" and "pgmout" objects. Loadbang objects provide preset values by sending out bang messages when the patch opens up. In patch 1.4, loadbang objects trigger a starting playback speed and a program change message. As we saw earlier in tutorial #3, the pgmout object sends program change messages that assign MIDI channels to specific General MIDI sounds (in this case, GM instrument #5, "Electric Piano 1"). In this patch, the fact that the pgmout object has been hidden makes it more difficult for users to change the GM sound. These objects will be further explored in the next two tutorials.

Now that you have learned how to play a prerecorded MIDI file, it is time to experiment with the real-time aspect of the MIDI backbone. Make sure that patch 1.4 is locked, and then double-click on the midiout object. The default GM MIDI synth port should be currently selected. Instead, change it to send data out using your computer's built-in MIDI driver; if you use macOS, this option might be called something like "IAC Driver Bus 1" or "from Max 1." Then, open up patch 1.4a "Receive MIDI Data," double-click on its green "midiin" object, and select the MIDI port with the same name. (In some cases, this option might be called "to Max 1," which should receive data sent by "from Max 1.") Click on the green start button in patch 1.4, and you should hear the same MIDI data sent over the driver bus, played through the second *Max* patch using different sounds. This idea can also be tried with other types of MIDI software such as notation packages and DAWs. One reason to explore this option is that DAWs are usually optimized for sound quality and contain high-quality sampled instruments. By sending MIDI data in real time from *Max* to a DAW, you get the dual benefit of the interactive features of *Max* combined with the music production features of a DAW. In some cases, you may need to ensure that the external software is set to receive MIDI data on all channels, but most should launch with that selected as a default option.

If you have the desktop version of MuseScore on your computer, go ahead and launch it. It should open up with a blank new file. Make sure that MIDI input functions are enabled; the button on the top toolbar should be highlighted in blue, as shown here: 🔵 . In *Max*, with patch 1.4 locked, double-click on the midiout object and select one of the other MIDI ports: IAC Driver Bus 1 (or similar), from *Max* 1, or from *Max* 2. (This will send all MIDI data out from *Max* to other MIDI software on the computer.) Then press the green start button. You should now hear the Mario MIDI file playing through MuseScore on a piano sound. If you switch the midiout port back to AU DLS Synth 1, you should hear the same MIDI data played on a different MIDI synthesizer. You can switch back and forth to listen to the qualities of the different software sonifications.

If you use Logic, make sure to open up a new project with a Software Instrument track. (Under the Track inspector for your tracks, the MIDI in Port and MIDI in Channel should both default to either to "All" or 1.) Then press start from your *Max* patch. If you use Ableton, go to Preferences (under the "Live" menu), select the "Link Tempo MIDI" tab, and locate "from Max 1" under the available MIDI in Ports. Click on the "Track" checkbox to enable input from *Max*. Then, add a new MIDI track to your set by selecting "Insert MIDI track" under the Insert menu. Assign your new MIDI track to a sound by clicking on the Sounds menu on the left side, and drag any sound to the new track. Then press start in your *Max* patch.

1.4.3 These Topics, Skills, and Objects Were Introduced in Tutorial #4

- using the MIDI protocol to represent musical information as numerical data.
- built-in MIDI device drivers and General MIDI synthesizers on Mac and Windows operating systems.
- utilizing the MIDI "backbone" to pass MIDI data between programs.
- using the *seq* object to play MIDI files.
- message objects can send text instructions as well as alphanumeric values.
- the *midiout* object sends MIDI data to any available MIDI port on the computer.
- the *midiflush* object stops any hanging note-on messages.
- the *midiparse* object interprets raw MIDI data and separates it into message types.
- the *prepend* object inserts the contents of its argument in front of any incoming alphanumeric message.
- the *unpack* object breaks a list into individual elements and sends each item out a separate outlet.
- the *slider* is an interface object that can output values restricted to a specific range, offset, and multiplier.
- The "hide on lock" function causes individual objects and patch cords to become invisible when the patch is locked; this allows areas of the patch to be treated as "under the hood."

1.5 Digital Audio Basics

Now that we have learned about MIDI and used it to play notes and MIDI files, this might be an opportune time to take a moment and acknowledge that MIDI is not the only way to produce sound on a computer. Although it is an important protocol that will help us explore the properties of musical sound in this book, lots of musical applications instead use *digital audio* specifications to play files or streams of recorded sound data. The purpose of this fifth tutorial is to provide just enough technical information about digital audio so that a beginner can comfortably interact with the audio features in the patches that accompany this book.[19] Although the majority of *Max* content in this book relies on MIDI, there are some places where we will use audio files instead. Therefore, it could help to pick up a few salient pointers here before launching into the audio content in future chapters.

The audio engine in earlier versions of *Max* was originally called "MSP." Depending on whom you talk to, these three letters either stand for *Max Signal Processing* or the initials of Miller S. Puckette, inventor of the original predecessor to the *Max* language. For this reason, you may sometimes see earlier versions of *Max* software referred to as "Max/MSP," reflecting the established understanding that *Max* provides MIDI support and the MSP component provides digital audio support.

MIDI specializes in transmitting low-bandwidth, symbolic note events and musical actions; MIDI data include a small set of features (pitch, volume, duration, channel, etc.) that tell synthesizers how to produce sound. On the other side, digital audio data provide direct representations of signals that can be used to convincingly recreate the actual sounds themselves. (There is a concomitant increase in data usage as well; whereas MIDI files usually require no more than a few hundred bytes, audio files typically have much larger file sizes on the order of tens of megabytes—a difference representing five orders of magnitude.)

Digital audio systems record sounds using microphones and store the signals in computer-readable files. These files are sometimes called "samples" if they capture a short duration of time. Audio production tools (DAWs) help us edit those recordings, process or filter the sounds, mix them together, and stream them out. Digital audio is useful for all sorts of day-to-day reasons: we use streams of digital audio data on phone calls, Zoom sessions, voice memos, podcasts, Spotify playlists, etc. Many of us are comfortable and familiar with using digital audio on our devices, but we may be somewhat unaware of how it works. The next section will go "under the hood," exploring some of the finer details related to the playback and processing of audio signals.

Several widely used digital audio standards specify formatting requirements for the digital representation of sound, including sampling rate and bit depth values for common file formats such as WAV, AIFF, and MP3. This tutorial will focus on the playback of these sound file formats in *Max*. To proceed, please open up the patch for tutorial #5, called "1.5 Digital Audio Basics." Before using the patch, please verify that your audio system is enabled by clicking on the power button icon in the bottom right-hand corner of the *Max* window. The power button should be blue when the audio system is functioning properly. Next, the section on the left labeled "simple sound playback" provides a bit of *Max* code that allows you to play a digital audio recording. A sample has already been preloaded for you to listen to. To hear it, click on the "x" in the blue toggle object at the top. As we observed in tutorial #2, the toggle object alternately outputs values of 0 or 1. Clicking once will send a 1 to start playing back the audio file, while clicking again will generate a 0 to stop it. Go ahead and click a few times and observe how it works.

The sig~ object receives a 0 or 1 from toggle and converts those numbers into audio-rate signals. This detail is important because, unlike MIDI, where individual messages have a maximum transmission rate of approximately 31,250 bits per second, audio signals in MSP require much faster speeds of 44,100 samples per second. Since digital audio is usually encoded using 16-bit samples, its transmission speed is approximately 705,600 bits per channel, times two for stereo.[20] The MSP patch cords that carry the faster audio rate signals can be distinguished from regular *Max* patch cords by their yellow and black stripes. The objects that handle audio-rate data are also differentiated from other objects by a tilde ("~") at the end of their object name.

The groove~ object receives an audio-rate signal from the sig~ object; a value of 1 tells it to play a sound forward at normal speed. The loadbang object located above groove~ sends a bang automatically when the patch is opened; this causes groove~ to repeat continuously by triggering the "loop 1" (loop on) instruction to be sent from the message object. Because groove~ is set to loop, a value of 0 tells it to pause; the next 1 from sig~ will start playback from where it left off. (If looping had not been enabled, a value of 0 from sig~ would stop playback and reset the sample back to the beginning. To experiment with the different settings, change the message object to "loop 0," lock up your patch, and click on the "loop 0" message.)

The groove~ object plays audio files by referencing samples stored in an object called "buffer~" that is located in the upper right area of the patch. Buffers are computer memory locations that are allocated to store data for short time periods, typically using random access memory (RAM). The term "buffer" came into common parlance in recent years due to the popularity of streaming services such as YouTube; computers will often "buffer" (preload) portions of video and audio files in advance to minimize the impact of Internet traffic disruptions on playback quality. The buffer~ object in *Max* functions in a similar way, storing audio data for quick, uninterrupted access within the patch itself.

Just above the buffer~ object are a few objects that will allow you to choose between different audio files to play. Just as in tutorial #4, when the "read" message enabled users to load a different MIDI file, these objects swap out the current audio file with a new one. The object at the top is called *umenu*; its interface allows you to select from a list of available items. The middle outlet of the umenu object outputs the name of the selected item. As we saw earlier in patch 1.4, the *prepend* object receives the text filename and adds its argument ("read") in front of it. Two patch cords are sent out from the prepend object to the message object below: the right inlet sets the new message content ("read [filename]"), and the left inlet subsequently triggers that text instruction to be sent out. When buffer~ receives the instruction to read a new audio file, it locates that file in its search path.

Audio files listed in the umenu object belong to a built-in library of sounds that are automatically included with the *Max* software installation. To explore these audio files, navigate to the "Audio" icon (♪) located halfway down the left-side toolbar of your patch. Click once on the Audio icon to open a list of audio samples; you can limit this list to only examples of a particular duration using the green slider on the left. Browse and listen to however many you wish. (Sounds with a "vs" prefix are so named because they belong to the Virtual Sound Macros library in *Max*.) To add any of these sound files to your patch, navigate to the umenu's object Inspector. Then, scroll down to the "Menu Items" option and click on "edit" to add the filenames of the audio samples you want to make available in your patch. Make sure to use commas to separate each filename, and click "OK" to save your changes. To load any other sound file from your computer, return back to the patch, click on the message object called "replace," locate the file on your hard drive, and select "Open." The buffer~ object is able to read audio file formats including AIFF, WAV, AU, and RAW.

Both groove~ and buffer~ use arguments to identify the buffer locations where their audio data is stored. Both objects must use exactly the same buffer name to reference the correct audio file. In this patch, a sound file called "drums" has been preloaded in a buffer called "sample." The groove~ object doesn't need to know the name of the sound file; it only needs to correctly reference the name of the buffer in which that sound file is stored. To confirm that the correct sound is indeed stored in the buffer, lock up the patch and double-click on the buffer~ object. A small floating window should open up, displaying the audio data in the buffer.

When groove~ starts playing the sample located in the buffer~ object, it sends a pair of audio signals down two audio-formatted (yellow and black) patch cords. (The argument of "2" located in groove~'s object box directs it to use two channels for playback in stereo format.) The two audio signals are received by special sliders called "gain~," located below groove~. "Gain~" sliders are interface objects that allow users to multiply the power in audio signals and adjust the output levels for headphones or speakers. These two gain~ sliders are connected together with a patch cord that passes the slider value from one to the other. This ensures that slider adjustments made on the left channel also simultaneously modify the right channel. Outputs from the gain~ objects then split in two directions: one side branches off to a pair of meter~ objects on the right that display the peak audio level; the other branch passes the audio signals down to the "dac~" object. "Dac~" converts audio signals from digital to analog and outputs them to speakers or headphones via your Audio MIDI Setup driver.

To the left side of the gain~ sliders is a loadbang object that accomplishes two things: it turns on audio processing by sending a message of "1" to dac~, and it sets a moderate level of 100 for the gain~ sliders. Double-click on the dac~ object to open the Audio Status panel and configure audio settings on your computer; this window provides information on audio drivers, input/output audio devices, and sampling rates. You can select which driver is currently running, connect directly to the Audio Devices panel in Audio MIDI Setup, and manage the audio "I/O Mappings" on your computer. (As described above in tutorial #4, the routing of audio signals on macOS computers is determined by the Audio MIDI Setup driver.)

Now that you have an introductory understanding of how to load samples in buffers and play them on your computer's audio system using groove~ and dac~, you will know how to use these objects when you see them again in future patches, such as in sections 2.1 "Silence" and 2.4 "Intensity." For fun, experiment with loading different sound files into the buffer~ object and adjusting the loudness levels using the left gain~ slider. (Because the two gain~ objects are connected together with a patch cord, moving the left slider will also move the one on the right.)

1.5.1 These Topics, Skills, and Objects Were Introduced in Tutorial #5

- the *groove~* object plays audio samples stored in a corresponding *buffer~* object located in the same patch; groove~ can be set to loop indefinitely.
- the *buffer~* object stores audio samples in memory for quick access in the patch.
- the *loadbang* object sends a bang message automatically when a patch is opened; it can be used to preset starting values for objects.
- the *umenu* is an interface object that allows users to select from a list of available items.

1.6 Hardware Kits and Controllers

Some of the sample patches in this book have been designed to work with a *Makey Makey* kit. This sixth and final tutorial will introduce the practice of integrating *Max* software with hardware interfaces and provide a starting place for those investigations. Although we are at an early stage on this journey, it's not too soon to develop an appreciation for the affordances that physical devices can contribute to live musical interaction. As with traditional musical instruments, digital music making can be greatly enhanced by physical devices that respond to signals and movements from our bodies—finger taps, breathing, etc. Physical controls also allow for more intuitive, gestural interactions than what a regular computer mouse or keyboard can offer.[21]

Makey Makey is a commercially available educational product that was designed in 2012 by two students at the MIT Media Lab, Jay Silver and Eric Rosenbaum. Their goal was to promote kids' invention and creativity through experimentation and play. Makey Makey developed alongside the Maker, DIY, and STEAM educational movements, inspired by the same Constructionist learning philosophy that is infused throughout this book. A brief video deftly explains what you can do with a Makey Makey: https://youtu.be/rfQqh7iCcOU.

Makey Makey kits have been robustly road-tested by students in K–12 educational programs for ten years now. Each kit consists of a circuit board, alligator clip cables, tinned jumper wires, and a USB cable. The circuit board serves as a "keyboard emulator" by allowing electrical connections to directly generate computer keystrokes and mouse commands. Kits can be purchased for about $50 at https://makeymakey.com and elsewhere online. The Makey Makey website offers high-quality instructions, lesson plans, resources, and ideas for educators. Their materials encourage K–12 students to explore principles of electrical conductivity through whimsical combinations of craft projects and code. The magical aspect of a Makey Makey project happens when students devise elegant mappings between everyday objects and rich audio/visual responses. Perhaps the most beloved Makey Makey project is the "banana piano"; this video provides an overview: https://youtu.be/70Ykn2k5LOg.

Many Makey Makey projects use the Scratch coding language to facilitate mappings between circuit connections and digital media outputs. I prefer to use *Max* instead, because it was designed to simulate more sophisticated musical structures. (The p5.js coding environment offers another more advanced coding option as well.)

If you haven't previously heard about Makey Makey or experimented with other physical computing hardware platforms (Arduino, Raspberry Pi, Particle's Photon board, etc.), it might be helpful to see an example of one of these kits being used in combination with *Max* software. Having developed the content in this book for college courses, I have mentored many students as they created compelling hardware prototypes for class assignments and projects. Although singling out individual students is a little bit like picking favorites among one's own children, perhaps the one project that most represents what is possible with *Max* and a Makey Makey controller was the Rose Quartet project that students presented in a Spring 2015 concert at The College of New Jersey: https://youtu.be/Oj4q_z7_xG8?t=1645 (starting at 27:25). To create this memorable performance, undergraduate students Dan Malloy, Rebecca Roberts, Kyle Sheehan, and Jonathan Wang used custom *Max* software and a Makey Makey kit to adapt a twelve-part arrangement by Jan Sandström of a well-known sixteenth-century German chorale by Michael Praetorius: "Lo, How a Rose E'er Blooming." The students each sang one line from the standard four-part hymn, accompanied by an eight-part digital choir whose beautiful chord clusters expanded the sonic landscape. In this performance, the human singers each controlled two additional digital vocal parts using actual roses as sensors connected to a Makey Makey. Touching a rose cued the next note in the vocal part with which it was associated; each performer had to carefully keep track of three lines of music simultaneously. Extensive rehearsal time was needed! The students created a custom *Max* patch that played the eight digital parts, synthesizing vocal sounds using wavetables made from recordings of their own actual voices, adding to the haunting effect of the digital choir. The samples were looped and pitch-shifted to create the harmonic background of the eight voices in the second choir.

Throughout the sample code files for this book, you will find *Max* patches that invite Makey Makey input. It is not necessary to use the Makey Makey functions in those sections, but it can be fun! For those who already have a Makey Makey and would like to try it out with *Max*, official setup instructions can be found here: https://makeymakey.com/blogs/how-to-instructions/first-time-set-up-basic-how-to-guide. A short tutorial is also included below.

Here is how to set up the Makey Makey and get started: plug the small side of the USB cable into the corresponding port on the Makey Makey, and plug the larger side into a USB port on your computer. Close any computer windows that prompt you to install software or set up your new hardware. Connect an alligator clip to the panel marked "Earth" on the bottom of the Makey Makey. Hold the metal clip on the opposite end of the wire; this will connect you to electrical "ground." (You can connect yourself to ground in different ways to free up your hands: copper tape or cellophane tape can be very useful.) While continuing to hold the alligator clip connecting you to ground, touch the area called "Space" on the Makey Makey board. A green LED should light up and the computer should receive a "space bar" command. Next, insert a few white jumper wires into the connectors marked "WASDFG" on the underside of the circuit board. Open up an application that can receive keyboard input from your computer, such as an email window or Microsoft Word. While maintaining your connection to ground, touch the individual jumper wires. Your computer should receive a letter every time you touch a jumper wire; a different letter for each wire. Once you get this simple connection mechanism working and triggering discrete symbolic data, you can start to imagine the possibilities. Any electrically conductive materials can be connected to the jumper wires and used as contact sensors: aluminum foil, fruit, water, graphite, copper tape, moist Play-Doh, etc. Experiment with different types of conductive materials to trigger sounds!

For this tutorial, we will need to establish eight separate contact points on the Makey Makey. We already have six points with the WASDFG connectors; for the remaining two spots, we can use the "Space" connection point and one of the Arrow/Mouse inputs on the right side of the circuit board. (The top one—up arrow—should work pretty well. This will bounce the mouse around but should not cause any problems. Also, be careful not to touch the back of the circuit board; this can affect the circuit, and contacts can fall out.) Using the handy alligator clips provided with the kit, attach eight conductive objects to your eight connectors. It can be tricky to keep all the wires and objects separate and secure; take some time to place your Makey Makey inside a box or tape it to the table to ensure that things don't slide around or fall apart.

Once the hardware is ready, go ahead and open up *Max* patch 1.6 "Hardware Kits and Controllers." (A software note: if you recently used patch 1.5, you may need to first quit and restart *Max*. Sometimes after the digital audio functions have been activated, the MIDI driver needs to be relaunched.) Let's start right at the top: the "key" object reports incoming key presses on the computer keyboard and identifies them by number. Because the Makey Makey functions as an ASCII keyboard emulator, it outputs the same numbers as your keyboard does when you type on it. The number object located below the key object displays the most recent key number. Below it is an object called "select"; it reads in numbers and compares them with its list of arguments. If there are any matching numbers, it sends a bang out the appropriate outlet corresponding with the order of the arguments.

Currently, the numbers in the argument list for "select" include 49–56; these match the ASCII characters for numbers 1–8 on a standard Mac computer keyboard. The ASCII character numbers can vary based on the model of your particular Makey Makey or computer and may need to be adjusted. Those who don't have a Makey Makey or Mac can use this patch by changing the arguments to match the values on your computer. To do this, first press the number keys on your computer and observe the values displayed in the number object located in between *key* and *select*. Then, unlock your patch and type those exact numbers into the "select" object, taking care to ensure that you leave exactly one space between each.

Next to the key object at the top of the patch is a similar object called "keyup." It reports any key releases from the computer keyboard and outputs their ASCII number. We use it here to turn notes off; rather than waiting the full duration specified in the makenote object, we can perform a real-time note off instead, in much the same way that a pianist might lift their finger to stop a note. The button object sends a bang whenever a key is released, and that message is received by an object called "flush." Flush is related to the midiflush object that we encountered in tutorial #4. When triggered by a bang message, it outputs note off messages for any notes it has received that have not yet been turned off.

Go ahead and touch each of your eight connection points to see what number the "key" object reports. Observe the values displayed in the number object; if the numbers on your system don't match the arguments listed in the *select* object, then unlock the patch and edit the *arguments* in the select object accordingly (taking care to ensure one space between each). Once you get the values to match, go ahead and play the eight notes of this scale. For fun, go ahead and experiment with modifying note numbers, as you did in tutorial #3. You can also add message and number objects to modify the volume and duration values, using code from patch 1.3. The pgmout object also offers timbral control here.

Enjoy experimenting with notes and playing around with sound! We will see a version of this scale again in Chapter 3, section 3.5 "Make a Scale," but for now let's just enjoy the pleasure of open-ended exploration and improvisation. Feel free to experiment with different timbres and pitch numbers. You can connect each alligator clip to larger conductive objects so you have a larger surface area to work with. See if you can figure out how to play a specific piece or melody that you have in mind. Continue to develop this *Max* patch as you progress through the book and use it to power novel versions of popular projects such as the Banana Piano. I encourage you to explore your own creative ideas for interacting with music using physical objects.

In addition to Makey Makey, there are many other types of hardware interfaces and alternative input mechanisms that can be used with *Max*. As was mentioned before, you might have a MIDI keyboard that you would like to use with *Max*. It could provide a helpful supplement as you work through the music content in this book. Go to Options → MIDI Setup to ensure that *Max* recognizes your keyboard connection. If *Max* can "see" your keyboard, then open patch 1.6a in the Tutorials sample code files. As you touch the keys on your MIDI keyboard, you should see updated values in the number objects and the *kslider* (keyboard slider) object in this patch. Other types of MIDI controllers can serve as popular alternatives to keyboards, such as the Akai APC40 and other light-up DJ-style interfaces that are designed to support live performances. A variety of game controllers, cameras, virtual reality wands, and novel gestural interfaces such as Imogen Heap's "Mi.Mu" gloves can all be used with *Max*. In some cases, specialized *Max* objects called "external objects" have been created and generously shared by enterprising innovators; I encourage you to explore all the available online resources for integrating your favorite devices with *Max*. (And make sure to acknowledge the source where you obtained the helpful external object; those folks don't get enough credit!)

1.6.1 These Topics, Skills, and Objects Were Introduced in Tutorial #6

- Makey Makey kit
- the *key* object reports key presses received from a computer keyboard or Makey Makey and identifies them by number
- the *keyup* object reports key releases received from a computer keyboard or Makey Makey, identified by number
- the *flush* object outputs note off messages for any notes that have passed through it but not yet been turned off
- The *select* object reads in numbers and compares them with its list of arguments. If there are any matching numbers, it sends a bang out the appropriate outlet corresponding with the order of the arguments.
- integrating MIDI keyboards, MIDI controllers, game controllers, cameras, virtual reality wands, and novel gestural interfaces with *Max*
- The *kslider* object functions like an onscreen keyboard, converting mouse clicks to pitch and velocity values.

Having reviewed the six tutorials in Chapter 1, you might be starting to develop a level of comfort and familiarity with the basic aspects of *Max*, MIDI, digital audio, and hardware integration. I invite you to jump headlong into Chapter 2. You don't have to feel confident yet—just familiar enough with *Max* to navigate the landscape of a patch, run it, unlock it, and tinker with it a little bit. Take things one page at a time, first reading the text in each section and then running the patches to experiment with how they work. Let's proceed!

2
Building Blocks

In Chapter 2, we will explore the fundamental building blocks of musical sound—the "Lego bricks" with which music is constructed. In this first full content chapter of the book, we will engage with the most basic elements of sound—the large and obvious features that people often experience viscerally. It can be helpful to think about these aspects through pairs of opposites: sound versus silence, music versus noise, loud versus quiet, beats versus durations, consonance versus dissonance, tension versus resolution. We will learn how to modify the qualities of these sound elements by changing their variables. We will also learn about overtones and how they impact our culturally constructed perceptions of "harmonious" or "discordant" qualities of sound. In later chapters, we will proceed to some of the more conventional topics covered in introductory music theory courses such as intervals, scales, chords, melodies, and harmonic progressions.

A useful way to begin thinking about the basic building blocks of music is to explore the idea that sounds contain both "vertical" and "horizontal" components. In music, the vertical dimension is associated with pitch, and the horizontal dimension is associated with time. We often visualize pitch as rising up from low to high, and time as progressing from left to right. This conception of the directional flow of pitch and time is also frequently reflected in music software (**as well as in traditional music notation**), where two-dimensional visual representations of sound flow along as the music plays.

Thinking about music as a function that can be plotted on a grid with two orthogonal axes (x and y) gives us the opportunity to visually separate out its different components and reveal its inherent structure through visual analogies. In the field of audio signal processing, a similar concept is used to describe characteristics of audio signals: the vertical dimension is often described as the frequency domain (associated with pitch), and the horizontal dimension is described as the time domain. Figure 2.1 shows two ways of viewing a digital audio recording using Audacity® software: the top image shows an audio file in time domain representation as a waveform, with the vertical axis representing amplitude and the horizontal axis representing time.[1] (We will temporarily leave the definition of amplitude "under the hood" and return to define it in section 2.4 "Intensity.") The bottom image shows the same audio data displayed in frequency domain format as a spectrogram, with the vertical axis representing frequency and the horizontal axis representing time. Spectrograms are visual depictions of frequencies in audio signals, displaying the amount of energy contained at individual frequency values over specific intervals of time. They allow you to observe how frequencies change as the music flows by.

Building Blocks 63

Figure 2.1 Time and frequency domain representations

(The definition of frequency will be reviewed in section 2.3.) The spectrogram on the bottom of figure 2.1 displays greater sonic energy at the lower end of the frequency range.

Google's Chrome Music Lab also features a real-time spectrogram tool; it displays sonic frequencies in vibrant rainbow colors. You can use its rich visual imagery to gain a better understanding of audio frequency components.[2] Figure 2.2 displays a spectrogram image of a harp sound; red colors indicate the loudest frequencies, while frequencies with softer volumes are represented on the blue and purple range of the color spectrum (You can view these colors in the eBook and online editions, but they will appear black and white in the print edition. Please follow the web link in the footnote to access the spectrogram tool yourself and experience its full color display.)

Ideas about how to handle pitch and time inform the ways we think about constructing music. Once you start to investigate these components in detail, new issues will emerge for consideration. We have a lot of ground to cover! But, as stated in the venerable Chinese proverb, "a journey of a thousand miles begins with a single step." Every piece of music must begin with one sound followed by another, establishing the special logic by which the composition will be organized. And so it goes with learning as well. Let's begin.

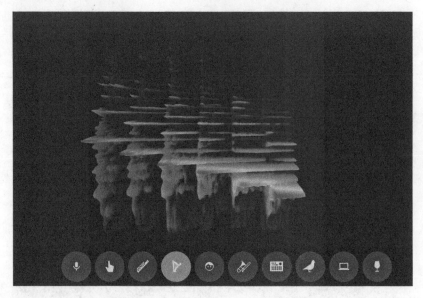

Figure 2.2 Spectrogram in Chrome Music Lab

2.1 Silence

Silence. Stillness. The absence of sound. A blank canvas housing the empty space in which our sonic creations will take shape. The negative space against which sounds seek meaning. Why is it, then, that we don't usually include silence when we think about the components of music?

American composer John Cage noticed silence and gave it special attention. In 1951, he visited an anechoic chamber—a space that was especially designed to minimize and absorb as many ambient noises and acoustical reverberations as possible, from both inside and outside the room. Cage was surprised that he could hear sounds coming from his body that he had never noticed before, such as high-pitched sounds of his nervous system and lower-pitched sounds of his blood circulating.[3] In reflecting on that visit, he arrived at the insight that there is no such thing as pure silence.

This realization ultimately led Cage to create a piece called 4′33″ in 1952. As the first known composition entirely without sound, 4′33″ attracted much controversy. Cage later described creating the piece through a gradual and painstaking process of responding to his experiences in the anechoic chamber: it took a few days to write the piece using chance operations, it took a few years to decide to release it, and he lost friends over that decision. He was also deeply influenced and encouraged by seeing Robert Rauschenberg's 1951 series of White Paintings, which Cage called "airports for shadows and for dust . . . mirrors of the air."[4] Cage's silent piece stands today as a commentary on the complexities that emerge when you make a work of art in which the most basic, expected components—those that would ordinarily define it—are absent. What emerges can be a rich source of new discoveries.

Inspired by the pioneering ideas of John Cage, let's reflect on our own versions of silence. Take a minute or two to sit back, close your eyes, and fully attend to the quietude of the space around you. What do you hear when you listen to silence? You might sink into a meditative reverie, or you might notice that the ambient sonic environment blossoms in your consciousness when you stop tuning it out.

While this experience is fresh on your mind, go ahead and open up patch 2.1 from the Chapter 2 sample code files. Unlock the patch and type into the comment object your thoughts and reflections on the experience of attending to silence. What things did you notice? What sounds did you hear? What sounds might you have imagined? (Sometimes it's hard to tell what is real and what is imaginary when you focus your attention on the subtle, almost-imperceptible levels of near-silence.) Patch 2.1 is set up to automatically play a very quiet simulation of John Cage's experience of silence in the anechoic chamber. (Please note: it may be difficult to hear these sounds if you are in a noisy environment; headphones should help. In case you are not certain whether your audio system is working, check the audio meter on the bottom right corner of your patch window; if the audio is playing, there should be a low volume level displayed there.) Listen carefully to the subtle recordings of heartbeats and breathing and think about the sound that your blood makes when it courses through your veins. If you wish, record your own heartbeat and breathing sounds and load them into the buffer~ objects using the "replace" message object. Breathe in. Breathe out. Ahhhhh.

2.1.1 These Topics, Skills, and Objects Were Introduced in Section 2.1 "Silence"

- Multiple groove~ objects can run in parallel, each with its own buffer~ object, to allow simultaneous playback of different audio files; these can be "mixed" together by adjusting the levels on the gain~ sliders, combining the various audio components into one unified sonic output.

2.2 Sound

Sound waves are invisible, which can cause them to seem magical or inscrutable. They are also *ephemeral*: they tend to exist for a short time and fade away pretty quickly, leaving no tangible trace. If we're not paying attention to sound, it can wash over us like warm water without impacting our conscious thoughts; this makes it hard to hold on to sound in our memories. The ability to "tune out" sound is a related capacity that probably evolved because we don't have "ear-lids" to block out auditory signals.

It can be deeply satisfying to develop a high degree of sensitivity and discernment about sound. In order to get there, you will need to undertake a deliberate, conscientious, iterative approach to listening. As with many things, steady practice can help you gain skill and confidence. The process of ear training aims to instill the skill of careful listening for students; this is a valuable tool for a developing musician. Sound recording engineers extend that idea through training programs sometimes called "golden ears" that are designed to hone their analytical listening skills. Composer Pauline Oliveros coined the term "Deep Listening" and pursued the holistic practice of increasing the awareness of sound in our daily lives.[5]

But what exactly *is* sound? Let's first establish a few important fundamentals. Sound is the physical transmission of energy from one place to another by pressure waves that move through a medium such as air. (Sound also travels through solid and liquid materials—e.g., you can hear sounds when swimming under water, although they tend to be a bit garbled.) Sound waves do not permanently change the materials they travel through; they just temporarily displace (move) the molecules by a very small amount. Our ears are remarkably sensitive to the subtle signals that are conveyed through these pressure waves. The capacity to hear and perceive sound allows us to receive important information from the world and also enjoy the rich sonic tapestries of music that we create for aesthetic pleasure, social connection, and mental, emotional, and physical wellness.

A useful way to think about how sound works is to compare it with water: when you drop a pebble into a small pool of water, what happens? Usually, you see small ripples emanate out from the center of the impact point in concentric rings. Sound behaves in a similar way: when you make a sound, waves emanate out from the source in concentric rings that move out through the three-dimensional space around the source. (Whereas the waves in a pool of water move in two dimensions across its surface, sound waves move in three dimensions through the volume of air around us.) When sound waves hit a wall or other hard surface, they bounce off it and head back the other way. Each bounce of a sound wave is called a reflection, and multiple reflections jointly contribute to the overall reverberation of an acoustic space.

Sound waves are composed of quick alternations of positive and negative pressure that temporarily displace molecules of air. High-pressure areas are caused by compression, or the tight packing together of molecules; low-pressure areas are caused by rarefaction, or the spreading out of molecules as they return back to their previous positions after the moment of high pressure passes. These oscillations between positive and negative pressure can be captured by microphones, transmitted as electrical voltages down a wire, digitized, and recorded into software. They can then be viewed by opening an audio file and zooming in on a time domain representation of sound at a very tiny time scale. Figure 2.3 depicts a waveform using Audacity® software at a high level of zoom. This segment comprises nearly eight one-hundredths of a second, and contains almost twenty-seven complete pressure-wave oscillations.

Looking at figure 2.3, you can see that there are two nearly identical-looking waveforms; this file has been recorded in stereo format with one waveform for each ear (right and left channels). The top waveform displays the left channel and the bottom waveform displays the right channel. Within each waveform, you might notice that the top half and the bottom half are roughly balanced around

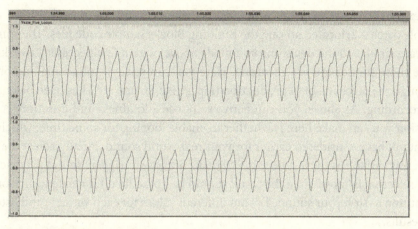

Figure 2.3 Sound pressure oscillations

a center line, although they are not perfect mirror images of each other. The top half of each signal represents the positive pressure component, and the bottom half represents the negative pressure component. The horizontal middle line that passes through the whole waveform represents a fixed sound pressure level of 0. The number of pressure-wave oscillations per second determines this sound's frequency of vibration, which is used to establish its pitch. We will leave the frequency-pitch relationship "under the hood" for the time being and return to it in section 2.3 "Frequency."

2.2.1 Make a Sound

Having been introduced to a few basics, let's now start to experiment with making sound! Our goal at this stage is not to make music, but just to explore raw sound and start to investigate its properties. Our first sonic experiment will make its debut in the "real" world. Take a moment to look around your immediate environment and select an object—it could be a pen, a cup, a tabletop, a "fidget toy," or an instrument. (Try to avoid picking noisemakers that could break or make a mess!) Then carefully tap or strike or strum it, and listen attentively to the result. Describe how it sounded. Did you find it pleasing? What were its sonic qualities? How did those qualities depend upon the way you interacted with the object? Notice that the action of producing a sound requires making four decisions: picking the sound-making object itself, selecting the mechanism of production (tap, strike, strum, etc.), determining the loudness through your use of force, and resolving when to start. If you actively stopped the sound, then you can also count duration as a fifth decision. If you wish, record your sonic experiment in a sound file and save it on your computer so you can access and use it at a later date.

Next, switch over to your computer to make a sound using *Max*. Please open sample patch 2.2, located among the Building Blocks sample code files. The controls here are similar to the decisions you made above, with a few necessary tweaks because these sounds are pre-recorded. Here you can select a sound-making object, although the mechanism of production (tap, strike, strum, etc.) has been baked into the recording. As above, you can actively choose a loudness and duration. A new decision you can make here is whether to enable looping for some time, which you might not have considered earlier for your real-world sound. Finally, select the start time: this variable is the last decision to make because it triggers sound playback. (If your selection is "now," then the result should be immediate.) If needed, click on the red button to stop your sound. Try out different values for each variable and listen to the results.

Because our *Max* functions are steadily increasing in complexity, objects and patch cords are starting to proliferate! For this reason, patch 2.2 introduces a new *Max* feature: "presentation mode." Presentation mode enables a top-level viewing layer for displaying the objects in your patch. It allows you to choose where to place objects and resize them independently of their position in patching mode. This helps manage complexity by placing items "under the hood" and out of the way so they don't overly complicate the user's field of view. Patch 2.2 automatically loads in presentation mode; this option can be set for any patch by navigating to View → Inspector Window and checking the box near the bottom called "Open in Presentation." To switch out of presentation mode back to patching mode, click on the yellow icon (▨) in the bottom left corner of the patch window. (A small warning: when you hover your cursor over this icon, a pop-up text label identifies the mode that you will switch to if you click on it—not the mode you are currently in.) There are now two ways to edit your patch: if you unlock your patch while in presentation mode, your changes will be reflected only in the visual presentation layer. If you wish to edit the underlying functionality of the patch, exit presentation mode and unlock the patch to make changes in edit mode.

How do the objects work in this patch? Let's take a look: to view the code for this patch, take it out of presentation mode by clicking on the yellow icon (▨) in the bottom left corner. The interface objects probably look familiar; you might recognize the umenu, button, and toggle objects from previous sample patches. A few new objects here provide a different way to play audio files. In place of the groove~ object that we previously used, the playlist~ object organizes groups of audio files, allowing you to select and play from among several options. Its interface displays the sound waveforms, which can be helpful for identifying them. When the patch is locked, you can drag clips around within the playlist to change the playback order and right-click on individual clips to remove them or view their file locations on your computer's hard drive.

The sounds used in patch 2.2 come from the set of built-in sounds provided by Cycling '74 when it installed *Max* on your computer. Click and drag to select a

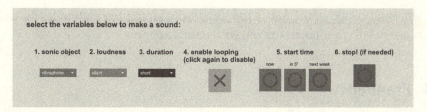

Figure 2.4 Make a sound

portion of a waveform to play. You can add different sound files to the playlist~ by first taking the patch out of presentation mode, then dragging the new files from your hard drive and releasing your mouse over the intended spot. (This should work regardless of whether the patch is locked or unlocked.) Please note that adjustments to the playlist~ may cause the "sonic object" menu to stop working correctly in presentation mode. Update the item names listed in the umenu object to ensure that they match the current contents in the playlist~.

Instead of the gain~ slider we used previously to control audio volume, this patch introduces the live.gain~ object. Live.gain~ provides similar volume control and also indicates the current audio intensity level in decibels, which will be defined below in section 2.4 "Intensity." (Objects whose names begin with "live" are also used with Ableton's Max4Live software.) This patch also features a new object called loadmess. Like loadbang, it establishes starting values for variables in the patch. The argument to loadmess is sent out as a message when the patch loads; here it is used to set values for the umenu objects on the front panel, as well as to ensure that looping is initially disabled. See figure 2.4.

Experiment with this patch by making a few modifications. To do so, take the patch out of presentation mode and unlock it. If you wish, you can include the playlist~ object in presentation mode: add new objects to the presentation mode display by highlighting them (click once) and selecting Object → Add to Presentation. (Once in presentation mode, they can be removed by selecting Object → Remove from Presentation.)

2.2.2 These Topics, Skills, and Objects Were Introduced in Section 2.2 "Sound"

- The playlist~ object organizes, displays, and plays sets of audio files.
- Presentation mode provides a viewing layer for a patch in which you can choose how to display objects and design a compelling interface for your user to interact with. To include objects in presentation mode, first make sure your patch is in edit mode. Then, select the objects you wish to display and choose "Add to Presentation" in the Object menu. Finally, click on the yellow icon in the bottom

left-hand corner of the *Max* window to switch into presentation mode, and arrange or edit your objects as you wish them to appear.

2.3 Frequency

As described in the previous section, sound is created when pressure waves move through a physical medium such as air. Sound pressure waves are composed of quick alternations between pressure levels; molecules of air "oscillate" back and forth between two opposite states of positive and negative pressure, called compression and rarefaction. The speed with which these oscillations occur is called the frequency of vibration. Sustained frequencies can be identified and associated with individual pitch values.

The concept of pitch was explained in tutorial #3 in Chapter 1 using a high layer of abstraction that allowed us to put aside the sonic complexities and focus instead on the details of MIDI implementation. On this iteration, we will take a closer look at some of the subtler aspects. Pitch is the perceived "height" of a musical sound, determined by its frequency of vibration, or the number of oscillations per second. The more oscillations (cycles) a sound has per second, the faster is its speed of vibration and the higher is its pitch. (And, as was also discussed in tutorial #3, notes are sounds that comprise a pitch value combined with values for volume, duration, and timbre.)

Musical notes generally contain one primary, steady frequency of vibration. This vibration is called a fundamental frequency: the speed of the lowest or strongest oscillation of the instrument or resonant object that is creating the sound. Usually, additional simultaneous frequencies occur when a note is produced; these are called overtones or harmonics, and will be discussed further in section 2.6 "Valence." All the frequencies present among the fundamental and overtones are measured by counting the number of oscillations per second. When naming a particular frequency, we identify it using units called Hertz (abbreviated "Hz"), representing the number of cycles per second. The higher the oscillation number in Hertz, the "higher" the note seems to us. (The name came from Heinrich Hertz, 1857–1894, a German physicist and student of Helmholtz who discovered electromagnetic waves.)

To interact directly with the variables of frequency and pitch height, go ahead and open up a blank new patch. Into it, add a slider object (press the letter "n" and then type "slider" followed by enter/return), and set its range to 2000 in the object Inspector. If you wish, you can also click once on the slider object to highlight its resizing handles and drag one of its right-hand corners further to the right. This will adjust its aspect ratio: the relationship between its width and height. If you drag the handles far enough to the right, the slider movement will shift from vertical to horizontal.

Then, below your slider object, create a new object called cycle~ and connect a patch cord from the outlet of slider to the left inlet of cycle~. (The cycle~ object generates sine wave oscillations that sound like smooth, simple, synthetic tones.) Below cycle~, add an object called "*~ 0.5"; this will set the audio output gain (volume) level at half-power to ensure that the sound is not too loud or soft. Draw a patch cord from cycle~ to *~. This should automatically create an audio-rate patch cord, indicated by distinctive yellow and black stripes. Finally, add an object called ezdac~ at the bottom of the patch. Similar to the dac~ object that you have seen before, ezdac~ sends out audio signals, with the additional feature that it functions as a user interface button object that can be clicked to actively toggle the computer's audio engine on and off.

Connect two patch cords from *~ to ezdac~; one to the left inlet, and one to the right. (This will take the single "mono" audio signal from *~ and split it into two equal signals that will be sent to the right and left channels.) Lock up your patch and click once on the ezdac~ object to turn on audio output. Set a medium level on the gain~ slider, about halfway up. Then click on the slider handle and drag it back and forth to explore the continuous frequency range of sine waves from 0 to 1999 Hertz. If you would like to know exactly what frequency values you are generating with the slider object, add a number object below it and draw a patch cord to display its output. Your resulting patch should look something like the image shown in figure 2.5.

In addition to providing some insight about frequencies of vibration, this code also demonstrates that audio frequencies are examples of continuous phenomena: you

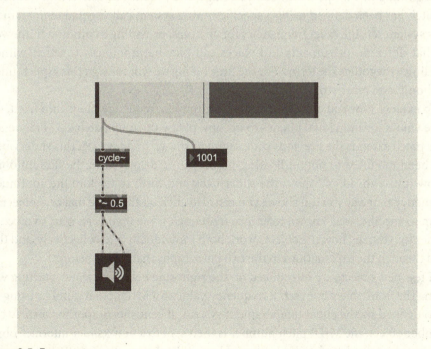

Figure 2.5 Frequency

can glide smoothly between adjacent values along the length of the slider. (For fun, mimic the behavior of this patch by sweeping through all the frequencies using your voice!) If you want to try sweeping through an even finer degree of resolution with frequencies, adjust your slider to output floating-point numbers instead of integers. To do this, go to the slider's object Inspector and check the box called "Float Output." While there, you can also experiment with different values for the Range and Output Minimum variables. Playing around with these numbers can help you start to make sense of how the slider functions and how its variables shape the way it behaves. Save your patch for further development down the line.

2.3.1 Convert Frequency to Pitch

Unlike frequency, which is a continuous variable, pitch is handled in a discrete way—meaning that it divides up the smooth sweep of frequencies into a series of countable steps. In order to treat individual pitches as distinct and separate from each other, our system carves up the continuous sound frequencies into sequential stair-steps from low to high in the audible frequency range. The smallest standard step size is called the semitone; it serves as the basic unit of pitch measurement. Semitones can be thought of as analogous to the individual colors in the visible light spectrum. Although sound frequencies do not naturally disperse into steps the way light disperses through a prism into colors, human musicians across different cultures and time periods nonetheless have taken up this task on their own.

Beginning in Europe about 400 years ago, the practice of converting frequency to pitch has been defined using a specific tuning system called equal temperament. This system sets the exact frequencies for all notes, providing a common framework so that different instruments and voices can play harmoniously together without needing to negotiate the terms. For the time being, we will consign this aspect "under the hood" and return to it in detail in Chapter 5.

To explore how you can carve up the continuous frequency range into fixed, discrete values for individual pitches to occupy, please open up patch 2.3 "Frequency." This patch extends the previous code segment shown in figure 2.5: this slider object has been modified to output floating-point values, displayed in the flonum object below it. Go ahead and move the slider back and forth to explore the continuous frequency range as you did above; you can also click on the "mile marker" objects to jump to specific, well-known reference frequencies. See if you can start to piece together for yourself how the objects work both individually and collectively, and then read through the explanations in the two paragraphs that follow below.

A few new objects are introduced on the right side below the slider, starting with ftom. The ftom object converts a frequency value to a MIDI pitch number using the ratio defined by the equal temperament system. It sends its output for display by a number object; the MIDI pitch number is then sent to a new kslider interface object that maps it to a virtual piano keyboard layout displaying the note that is currently playing. Below the kslider is a number object that has been modified using the Inspector to display its values in MIDI pitch format. Hidden from view using the hide on lock feature is a loadbang object that activates the ezdac~, ensuring that sound starts immediately. Notice that the blue slider has a finer degree of resolution than the kslider does; it allows you to slide in between semitones across the continuous frequency range, revealing some of the microtones and cents (1/100th of a semitone) that subdivide adjacent notes on the keyboard.

The blue slider has been modified using the Inspector to start at a minimum value of 66, which limits the lower range of the kslider object to a reasonable set of notes. Frequencies below 60 Hertz may be challenging to hear on a computer; depending on your speakers or headphones, these low-frequency sounds may be a bit muffled, quiet, or distorted. Similarly, you might find that very high frequencies tend to sound screechy and uncomfortably shrill. This is not uncommon; it takes specialized speakers to recreate very low and very high notes with clarity and quality.

In addition to generating audio frequencies electronically and converting them to pitch numbers as we have done here, you can also extract pitch information from audio signals using *Max* software. This can be done in real time: microphones convert sound energy to electrical voltages that flow down a wire to be digitized by an audio interface. The resulting digital signals are sent to a computer, where software applications count the number of oscillations or cycles per second. We will explore applications of pitch detection using *Max* in Chapter 3, section 3.4 "Name an Interval" and Chapter 5, section 5.3 "Playing in Tune." It should be mentioned that a small number of individuals (0.01 percent of the population) have a special ability called perfect pitch (or "absolute pitch"), which is essentially the capacity to accomplish the function displayed in patch 2.3. Perfect pitch usually develops by about age seven or so, when the brain centers for language development are most active.

2.3.2 These Topics, Skills, and Objects Were Introduced in Section 2.3 "Frequency"

- The cycle~ object generates sine wave signals with a frequency input value.
- The *~ object performs multiplication on audio-rate signals; it is used in patch 2.3 to set gain (acoustic power) levels.
- The ezdac~ interface object allows users to turn on and off the audio system.
- The ftom object receives frequency values and converts them to corresponding MIDI note numbers.
- The kslider interface object serves as a clickable on-screen keyboard that outputs and displays MIDI pitch numbers and velocity values.
- A new way to display information in a number object by converting its format to show MIDI pitch values. MIDI values can be selected using the Display Format field located in the object Inspector.

- Activity: patch 2.3 currently does not allow a user to control the loudness level in patching mode. What object might you add to enable a volume control feature in this patch? (Hint: patches 2.1 and 1.5 both use this object.)
- Activity: for fun, go ahead and change the key colors in the kslider object (upper and lower keys) as you wish, using the color palette tool in the object Inspector.

2.4 Intensity

Sound pressure waves feature a few different variables that help define the types of information they carry. In section 2.3 we investigated the variable of frequency and explored how to convert it to pitch information; another important variable of sound waves is their intensity level. When interacting earlier with patch 2.2 "Sound," you probably noticed that selecting a loudness level caused a change in the strength of the resulting sound. There are a few different ways to describe these changes of audio intensity: (1) in terms of how we perceive and interpret them with our hearing system; (2) through musical dynamic indications; (3) by measuring their acoustic power; and (4) by quantifying their signal amplitude. We will explore all four methods in the section that follows.

We often use words like "volume" and "loudness" to describe our experiences of audio intensity; these are subjective terms that convey our perception of the strength of a sound. We also have adjectives to help us describe gradations of audio intensity, such as "hushed" and "deafening," which define the general boundaries of how low and high this variable can get. The way we hear and perceive audio intensity depends upon complex interactions within our human auditory processing system and is influenced by factors such as the amount of sonic energy, the duration of the sound, the frequencies of vibration present, and other contextual clues and subjective factors.[6]

One reason why our perception of audio intensity is complicated is that the human ear is not equally sensitive to all sound frequencies. Our psychoacoustic equipment was shaped by evolution and therefore sometimes behaves in ways that do not always seem logical. Our hearing system is more sensitive to certain frequency ranges, and for that reason some sounds may seem louder to us even if they actually have a lower intensity. For example, we are especially sensitive to high-frequency sounds in the standard range where babies cry. (There may be good evolutionary explanations for this.) Our reduced sensitivity to low-frequency sounds means that in order for them to seem balanced with high ones, we often have to play them louder. Added to this unequal loudness problem is the fact that the human brain sometimes confuses pitch and loudness: above 2000 Hz, increasing the loudness of a sound seems as if the pitch is increasing; below 1000 Hz, increasing the loudness seems like the pitch is decreasing.[7]

In the context of music-making, we use another set of indications called dynamics to characterize levels of audio intensity, using Italian terms such as "forte"

Table 2.1 Dynamic (intensity) levels, listed in increasing order from left to right

pianississimo (*ppp*)	pianissimo (*pp*)	piano (*p*)	mezzo-piano (*mp*)	mezzo-forte (*mf*)	Forte (*f*)	Fortissimo (*ff*)	Fortississimo (*fff*)
very very soft	very soft	soft	medium soft	medium loud	loud	very loud	very very loud

(strong) to represent loud sounds and "piano" (floor, level) for quiet, soft sounds. The Italian language allows us to describe gradations of soft and loud using prefixes and suffixes: "mezzo" for medium, and "-issimo" for "very." As a result, you can express the range of dynamics from low to high as you move from left to right in Table 2.1 (extra uses of "-issimo" on the low and high ends are also possible, if unusual).

These terms help us communicate effectively and with specificity about varying the volume levels in our musical performances. Why do we use so many levels of dynamics? They give us greater scope to maximize the amount of variety and contrast we use, which in turn allows our music to convey more nuances. Dynamics make our music more exciting by providing a changing volume level that enables us to emphasize certain notes and minimize others. Subtle dynamic changes can give your music a sense of liveliness; these changes simulate aspects of emotional experiences by reflecting the differing activation or intensity levels of those emotions.[8] As far back as the sixteenth century, German composer Michael Praetorius (1571–1621) wrote that the purpose of using dynamics is "to express the *affectus* and move human feelings."[9]

At a high level of abstraction, intensity is a measure of acoustic energy. More specifically, intensity describes the amount of power carried by a sound wave over a defined area and direction; it is affected both by the amount of pressure in a sound wave, as well as by the speed and direction of the wave's movement. Measuring sound intensity levels (SILs) requires a special system of units because our ears are sensitive across an enormous range of variation in sound pressure intensities. We are able to detect absolutely tiny air pressure changes: 10^{-12} watts/meter^2 at the lower threshold of hearing. (Watts are not only for light bulbs! They also serve as units for different kinds of power.) Between the softest sounds we can hear and those that cause us pain (greater than 10^{-1} watts/meter^2), there are more than 100 billion quantifiable intensity levels. Our sensitivity to audio intensity is greater than any device can measure.[10] Because a huge range of numbers is needed to characterize the differences between intensity levels, we use decibels to simplify the calculations and provide a standard unit of measurement. The term decibel, frequently abbreviated dB, was named after Alexander Graham Bell, the inventor of the telephone. A difference of 1 dB in SIL between two sounds is the smallest change detectable by human hearing, and an increase of 10 dB in audio intensity level corresponds to a doubling of perceived loudness and an increase of approximately one step in dynamic level (such as going from mezzo-forte to forte).[11] Using the decibel as a unit of measure helps us accurately quantify SILs in ways that are helpful in music software and sound amplification systems.

At a lower, more detailed layer of abstraction, the decibel is a logarithmic description of the power in a sound that compares the sound pressure level (SPL) to a reference pressure level, typically 0 dB or the smallest detectable sound level. The decibel is computed as a ratio between two sound pressure levels; it is not a fixed value. It provides a relative measure of the SIL, the amount of energy that moves through a fixed area over a fixed unit of time measured in units of watts per square meter. We typically use 0 dB as the lower reference point for the threshold of hearing (the quietest sound you can possibly hear) and 120 dB for the threshold of pain (standing near an airplane engine on the tarmac). At just 10 dB, the sounds of our own hearts beating and quiet breathing are easy to tune out; at the upper end, sustained intensity levels above 85 dB are not recommended and can permanently damage our hearing. Because sonic energy spreads out in three dimensions from its source, its intensity is much higher when you are close to the source and drops off exponentially as you move away from it. This is a general property known as the distance squared law: audio intensity is inversely proportional to the square of the distance from its source.

A fourth way of thinking about audio intensity involves amplitude. Amplitude is defined as the amount of change in an audio signal over one cycle of vibration, or the maximum displacement of air molecules from their equilibrium position as the sound pressure wave passes through them. You can understand amplitude more generally as the height of the peaks in an audio waveform. The higher these peaks get, the louder they seem to us. Increases in peak amplitude correlate with increases in audio intensity.[12] Figure 2.6 demonstrates how we think about amplitude in an audio waveform, following the contour of the peak amplitudes; the image shows a waveform in Audacity with a graphical overlay highlighting the peak amplitude. (This overlay is yellow in the eBook and online editions, and appears as grayscale in the print edition.)

Figure 2.6 Amplitude following

Amplitude levels can be described for long or short segments of time, as well as for durations of individual notes. This way of describing intensity, on a note-by-note basis, is called an amplitude envelope. The envelope follows the outer contour or shape of a waveform, as if you drew a line connecting together all the positive amplitude peaks (the "peak amplitudes"). The height of these peaks corresponds with our perception of the loudness of the signal.

Amplitude envelopes typically have four phases: attack, decay, sustain, and release. Often abbreviated as ADSR, these phases correspond to the beginning, middle, and end of a note. The beginning of any note starts with an increase of amplitude from silence; this is the attack phase. This onset can be very quick, as with a percussive sounds like snare hits or piano notes. An attack is often followed by a brief decrease in amplitude (the decay phase) to a steady-state level of arbitrary length (the sustain), before finally tapering off to silence (the release). The phases that involve a changing amplitude (attack, decay, release) are examples of transients, or audio signals where major components are shifting over time.

The phases of an amplitude envelope are not always perfectly distinct or well defined; phases can merge together, be barely present, or otherwise ambiguous. Whereas instrumental envelopes are affected by the physics of the instrument and the technique of the musician, software tools in DAWs and other audio editors allow us to edit and shape our envelopes with precision. Figure 2.7 shows how you can think about amplitude envelopes for different kinds of notes. The first waveform is a long note played on a violin; it has a medium attack, an extended decay, a long sustain that is not perfectly level, and a long release. The second note is plucked on a guitar; due to the way it is generated, it has a very short attack and short decay, followed by an uneven sustain phase, and a short release. The image in figure 2.7 shows two waveforms in Audacity® with graphical overlays following the amplitude envelopes for both sounds.

In the context of instrumental and vocal music, we use another word for amplitude envelope: articulation. We can think of articulation as the way in which notes are shaped and separated from each other, as in legato (connected, elongated) or

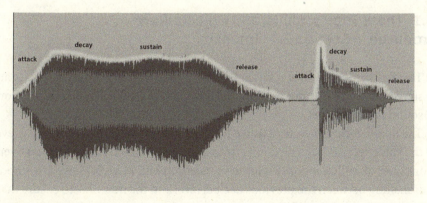

Figure 2.7 Amplitude envelopes

staccato (short).[13] Other common articulation styles include slurs, portato, tenuto, marcato, and accents. Articulation choices are important tools that musicians use to impart a piece of music with a coherent sense of identity and expression. When you make notes using MIDI, articulation choices are embedded in the sound synthesis algorithms themselves.

To experiment with the different ways of thinking about loudness described above, go ahead and open patch 2.4 "Intensity." The three panel objects shown here each display different ways to quantify intensity: as perceived loudness (on the left), as musical dynamic indications linked to acoustic power (in the center), and as peak amplitudes (on the right). The left-hand panel demonstrates how we perceive volume at different frequency ranges: click on the toggle objects to start playing two audio files. One has sounds that lie mostly in the low-frequency "bass" range, and the other has sounds in the high-frequency "treble" range. Go ahead and adjust the gain~ sliders to "mix" the two sounds together with the aim of matching their volumes as closely as possible. Typically, this will involve raising the bass level a bit so that it sounds equal to the treble level. This is due to the properties of our hearing system that are more sensitive to certain higher frequencies. There are a lot of details required to express these functions! Presentation mode here allows many of the tricky implementation details to remain "under the hood."

The middle panel in patch 2.4 displays dynamics labels that describe musical loudness levels on the left side and compares them with decibel levels on the right side. Every dynamic level is associated with a commonly used Italian term; clicking on the dynamic indications on the left side causes the decibel levels to change in increments of 10 dB, equivalent to a perceived 2× change in volume. In this section, the line~ object provides a ramp between different dB values to avoid audio clicks when the levels change.[14] The right-hand panel displays peak amplitude values using decimal values between 0 and 1, reflecting the standard units used for amplitude. The graph on the right side displays the envelope of the outer contour of these amplitude peaks, providing a real-time simulation of the highlighted lines drawn in figures 2.6 and 2.7.

2.4.1 These Topics, Skills, and Objects Were Introduced in Section 2.4 "Intensity"

- The live.gain~ object serves as a volume slider that tapers ("scales") input audio signals, indicates output levels in decibels, and provides a visual display for the sound intensity level.
- The line~ object generates a timed ramp; it changes value from a starting level to the value received in its left inlet, transitioning between the two values over the number of milliseconds displayed in its argument. Here, it is used to smoothly transition between the previous decibel level and the new one, to ensure that instantaneous changes of intensity do not cause unpleasant audio artifacts.

- The meter~ object serves as a peak amplitude level indicator, visualizing the maximum amplitude of the signal that it receives. This one is set to monitor signals in the range 0 to 1.
- The multislider object displays data either as a single slider or as a scrolling display. It is used both ways in this patch to show current peak amplitude and longitudinal amplitude flowing by over a few seconds.
- The panel object defines a background area on your patch and can use color, shape, and other attributes to highlight and visually delineate a section of the patch window.
- Here's an expert reference describing the characteristics of sound waves, including amplitude: https://www.khanacademy.org/science/physics/mechanical-waves-and-sound/sound-topic/v/sound-properties-amplitude-period-frequency-wavelength.

2.5 Rhythm

Once you can make one sound with a frequency and an intensity, you might naturally find yourself wanting to make a few more sounds. When a few sounds are played together in a sequence, we tend to hear them in relationship to each other. Musical sounds can be compared with each other using variables such as pitch and amplitude, and also in terms of rhythm: the way they relate to each other in time.

One way to approach the concept of rhythm is to start with the idea of a pulse, or its synonym, beat. In the context of music, individual pulses are single moments of strong emphasis—instants in time that are set apart from other moments around them by the delineation of short sounds with a clear attack and release. These sonic pulses are analogous to the arterial pulses that move blood throughout our cardiovascular systems. Like the pulses generated by our hearts, musical pulses provide important forces that propel the momentum forward and sustain a sonic work over a span of time.

2.5.1 Beats and Durations

Beats or pulses generally do not exist in isolation; they like to be surrounded by company! They tend to line up in stable, repeating sequences, evenly spaced apart. Their regular repetitions help us keep track of the pace of musical time. Beats serve as the basic units of time in music, akin to the way we use seconds in clock time. It might help to think about beats as mini-milestones, like the yard lines on a football field that demarcate the horizontal distances and help us keep track of how quickly our musical sounds are moving forward through time.

Although an unbroken string of regular beats might indicate a healthy heart, it is not quite yet a rhythm. A rhythm is a pattern of durations (usually, varying durations) in a group of notes. These patterns are not required to be regular or repeating, although they often are. Duration is the length of time that elapses between consecutive note onsets (attacks), measured either in clock time or in units of musical time. Varying degrees of emphasis, achieved using accents and other changes of intensity, are also associated with rhythmic patterns.

Let's undertake a simple rhythmic exercise: go ahead and tap out a sequence of beats for perhaps fifteen seconds or so on the table or desk in front of your computer. They can be of any durations you wish. Before going on much further, how might you vary these beats to keep them interesting? One thing you can do, as we explored above, is to play with levels of intensity. When you make a downward gesture to produce a beat, you can simultaneously make intensity changes by varying the amount of arm weight you apply on the table surface. Any adjustment of weight will affect the force that you use, which in turn will influence the loudness of the beat. Weight can also be thought about as heaviness or lightness. Heavy beats are strong and loud, whereas light beats are soft and weaker. Weight is a variable that can be explored on a continuum, as on a slider. Let's explore this concept by inflecting our beats with different weights, making some heavy and others light. You can do this by drumming on your desk with your hands, first heavy (with more of your palm), and then light (with more of your fingers). Try combining heavy and light beats into a coherent, repeating pattern. Then, pretend to put intensity on a slider; gradually make all of your beats louder and then softer over several beats in a row. Just for fun, try smoothly shifting from soft to loud over 4 beats, then 8, then 16. Mix things up and play around with different levels of intensity. Have fun and improvise!

Another thing you can do to keep your beats interesting is to vary the speed at which they arrive. A simple way to do this is to gradually speed up and slow down the overall pacing of your beats; this change of rate will be covered in detail in section 4.1 "Tempo." But for now, experiment with this idea by playing with the pacing of a few beats—make them flow slower and faster as if you were controlling the speed variable with a slider. Notice that when your notes get faster, the durations between them get shorter; tempo and beat duration are variables that are inversely proportional to each other. As you play around with the pacing of your beats, you may find yourself adjusting the note durations so they don't sustain too long or overlap too much.

A different way to vary the speed of your beats is to experiment with proportional divisions of time. Individual beats can be combined together into longer durations or split apart into shorter durations. The smaller chunks are called subdivisions, and they typically occur in groups of two, three, four, or sometimes more per beat. Given that a standard rhythmic duration is 1 beat, then two subdivisions per beat are each ½-beat in duration; three subdivisions per beat are each ⅓-beat in duration, and four subdivisions per beat are each ¼-beat in duration. For reasons that we will address later on (in section 4.2 "Meter"), the standard unit of beat duration is called a quarter note. When subdividing a quarter note into shorter chunks, each of two subdivisions is called an eighth note, each of three subdivisions is called an eighth-note triplet, and each of four subdivisions is called a sixteenth note. You can subdivide further into arbitrarily smaller durations; each of eight subdivisions of a quarter note is called a thirty-second note, etc. Conversely, quarter notes themselves are ½ subdivisions of longer durations called half notes and ¼ subdivisions of whole notes.

Subdivisions of a beat can be grouped together in different configurations to create interesting rhythms. The simplest way to group durations together is to fill up the length of a beat with multiples of the same type, such as two eighth notes or four sixteenth notes. However, subdivisions can also be mixed and matched together. When different types of beat subdivisions are grouped together in irregular ways that extend across beats into longer, fractional durations, that is called syncopation. There are many more interesting topics to explore with combining note durations, but we will leave those "under the hood" for now and return to untangle some of the complexities later.

Now that you have learned how to vary the weight, speed, and subdivisions of your beats, go ahead and start playing with those variables interchangeably. Try to perform beats that are heavy and fast, heavy and slow, light and fast, and light and slow. Then, start to mix and match the variables of speed, weight, and subdivisions, improvising as you wish. Allow your whimsy and imagination to carry you forward in a playful way. As you proceed, you may find yourself starting to create little rhythmic patterns. This is an exciting moment! The more creative you can be here, the more varied and interesting your beats will become. Enjoy the freedom to play.

2.5.2 Simulating Rhythmic Patterns in *Max*

One of the simplest rhythmic groups to explore is the sound pattern that your heart makes when blood moves between its chambers, often called "lub-dub." In this two-part pattern, the first sound is shorter and softer ("lub"), followed by a longer and louder sound ("dub").[15] With your hands on the table, explore a simple short-long rhythmic pattern, where the first sound is a softer eighth note, and the second sound is a louder quarter note. Next, let's simulate the lub-dub pattern in code: go ahead and open up sample patch 2.5 "Rhythm." (A software note: if you recently used patches 2.1–2.4, you may need to first quit and restart *Max*. Sometimes after the digital audio functions have been activated, the MIDI driver needs to be relaunched.) Click on the top button to hear the pattern, and then take the patch out of presentation mode to inspect how it is put together. The lub-dub pattern is located in the upper left corner in edit mode. With this simple looping construction, unequal durations are created by different arguments in the pipe objects; the first note is 400 milliseconds long, whereas the second note is twice as long: 800 milliseconds. Both notes share the same volume, but the second one seems louder because it has a slightly higher pitch. As we explored in tutorial #3, these notes are synthesized using the General MIDI (GM) Percussion Key Map on MIDI channel 10, where a pitch of 41 maps to a Low Floor Tom sound, and a pitch of 43 maps to a High Floor Tom. (The "key map" list of percussion sounds can be found at the bottom of this page: https://www.midi.org/specifications-old/item/gm-level-1-sound-set.)

The lub-dub rhythmic pattern uses gswitch, a useful object that we are encountering for the first time. Here, gswitch is being used to regulate repetition at the loop point; clicking on the toggle object controls whether the end of the pattern connects back to the beginning or not. The purpose of the gswitch object is to select between multiple pathways of incoming data. At the top of gswitch are two inlets where data can stream in, and a control inlet on the top left that determines which of the streams gets to pass through. You can think of this function as a bit like switching trains in a train yard; when one train is moving onto the track, the other train has to halt and wait.

Now that we have established a simple, repeating rhythmic group, we can build upon this structure to form larger units of increasing complexity. Returning to presentation mode, the middle section of this patch features a looping pattern of 12 beats where all beats share the same duration. These beat sounds also use the GM Percussion Key Map on channel 10, with a pitch of 46 mapping to an Open Hi-Hat sound, and a pitch of 42 mapping to a Closed Hi-Hat. Go ahead and click on the blue button to listen to this pattern for a few iterations. Then, experiment with the controls in the pink panel objects on the right side: control the speed by adjusting the duration of each beat in milliseconds, control the weight (volume) of each beat by clicking on the heavy and light options, select subdivisions to hear fractional durations, and adjust timbres using the yellow dial object or the number objects below. (The dial outputs a timbre value that also triggers the output of a second adjacent value; this ensures that two differentiated timbres are created). Click on the yellow toggle object to disconnect the loop point; the code will finish playing the current 12-beat pattern and then stop.

In the same way that you improvised above, approach the controls here whimsically by experimenting with and modifying the patterns. Explore different weights by alternating between "heavy" and "light" values to affect the MIDI velocity; if you wish, you can copy and paste the key and select objects from the top of patch 1.6 to allow you to more quickly switch between the two. There is no right or wrong way to do this; just enjoy the opportunity to play around with things. Presentation mode keeps the visual interface manageable, storing the complexities "under the hood."

After you finish exploring the front panel controls for the 12-beat pattern, click on the yellow icon in the bottom left-hand corner of the toolbar to take patch 2.5 out of presentation mode and investigate how the objects work together. Twelve beats connect from one to another here using a daisy chain configuration: a method of connecting electrical or digital objects in a chain or ring arrangement that resembles the way we tie flowers together. Here, the duration of each beat is controlled by a pipe object that directly triggers the beat that follows it. A slider provides duration values that affect all beats equally; notice here that changing the durations of individual beats in this pulse train determines the speed of the overall pattern. Two different gswitch objects regulate the flow of beats; the gswitch on the left controls the segment loop point, just as in the lub-dub pattern; the gswitch on the right allows you to select between the four different subdivision ratios. A radiogroup interface object allows you to select from among the four options; it functions much like the umenu object, with the beneficial feature that it allows a faster switching process by keeping all options available on the top level.

Also, in this section of the patch, notice that the speed slider is followed by a few objects that invert its output values. This little bit of code ensures that slow speeds are on the left and fast ones are on the right. First, the "−" object (see arithmetic symbols) subtracts 1000 from the slider's output values, yielding only negative output numbers from −1000 to 0. Then, the abs object is used to calculate an absolute value, which means that any negative values it receives will be flipped to positive values. Although these are simple steps, they accomplish the handy outcome of inverting the slider values so that the user interface is more intuitive to use.

Once you start to make sense of how the 12-beat pattern works, I encourage you to make your own version. You can save your draft efforts in a separate file and keep the original sample patch handy. Copy the existing daisy chain structure to create new notes, insert new subdivisions, and select new values for weight and speed. One thing to try might be to fix the triplet subdivision pattern—triplets are a bit tricky to discern in this section of the patch, because strong emphases (MIDI pitch number 60) occur once out of every four notes. How might you adjust the code in patch 2.5 to instead emphasize every third note for triplet subdivisions? And, can you find a way to switch between duplet, triplet, and quadruplet rhythms so they each correctly weight the strong beats? Feel free to play around with the way this loop is structured, or even create your own new loops.

A salsa-style dance rhythm has also been included in this patch as a starting place to demonstrate how you might create your own layered rhythmic patterns. This example presents one way to combine multiple individual components to build compound patterns; there are separate lines here for percussion instruments such as guiro, congas, bongos, claves, timbales, and maracas. (The interface may look simple in presentation mode, but in patching mode you will see quite a few objects grouped together at the bottom of the screen.) One problem with the approach used here is that currently all the lines are quantized, meaning that their time values are mathematically precise in a way that sounds a bit "square" or metronomic. While this approach might work well for EDM (Electronic Dance Music), it doesn't work very well for the nuances of salsa. I encourage you to experiment with ways to structure expressive rhythmic patterns so they allow for some flexibility and stylistically correct grooves.

There are several different ways to notate rhythms; these provide helpful ways to learn and remember complex beat patterns. One method for visualizing rhythm is called the time unit box system (TUBS), which uses rows of boxes to represent increments of time. Empty boxes indicate silences, whereas checked boxes show where the beats occur. Rows of toggle objects in a *Max* patch can be used to display

84   Constructing Music

this form of notation, as shown in figure 2.8. This figure displays the same salsa-style pattern featured above in patch 2.5.

To provide a point of comparison for the time unit box system, figure 2.9 presents the same rhythmic pattern in standard score notation. It is interesting to note points of similarity and difference in the ways that the timing information is visualized.

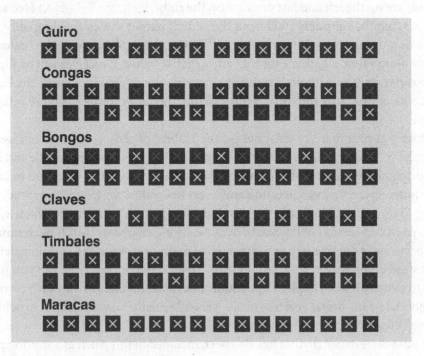

Figure 2.8 Time unit box system notation

Figure 2.9 Salsa rhythmic pattern in score notation

Figure 2.9 has been engraved using Finale software, combining the same six percussion layers as in the TUBS image above.[16]

Another novel way to notate and listen to rhythms is available using Groove Pizza, a free web application developed by Ethan Hein and distributed by the Music Experience Design Lab at New York University.[17] The app presents rhythms in a circular configuration, connecting the two ends of the looping structure together. The "slices" of the pizza serve as individual beats in a rhythmic pattern. Using this app, you can select the number of beats in your loop, assign different percussion sounds to three layers, and notate your rhythm in the TUBS boxes at the bottom of the window. Figure 2.10 displays three parts of the salsa pattern (one line each of the Congas, Bongos, and Timbales) using Groove Pizza. I encourage you to experiment with notating your own rhythmic patterns in this app; it is easy to run in a web browser and engaging to use.[18]

Rhythmic beats sometimes behave in ways that resemble embodied, physical experiences. For example, your heart might usually follow a fairly steady rate on normal days. However, on special days—for example, when you fall in love or give a speech or perform in a concert—it may speed up in unusual ways. And, as we experience in our embodied lives, beats don't like to sit around doing the

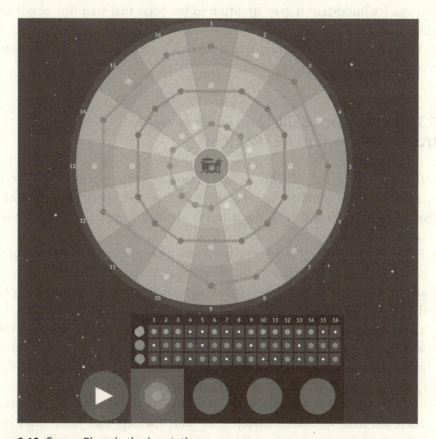

Figure 2.10 Groove Pizza rhythmic notation

same thing forever. You may have noticed by now that patterns of beats can get stale if they repeat too many times; just as with other patterns in life, sometimes things need to be varied in order to stay interesting. Research studies have shown that changes in auditory stimuli capture the attention of listeners because they thwart established expectations about the likelihood of stable outcomes. Our cognitive systems anticipate that certain patterns will continue for some time in a steady state, and when they don't, we tend to pick up and notice![19] We will return to this idea later, in sections 4.1 "Tempo" and 4.2 "Meter," when we will learn to control the speed of our beats and engage with concepts of meter and metrical groupings.

As you mess around with rhythmic patterns, you may start to notice that certain groupings feel coherent. These combinations of duration, weight, and speed sound like they belong together, perhaps because they are familiar or because you find aesthetic pleasure in the way they sound. (In the next section, we will investigate why some sound combinations work well and others less so.)

Finally, it's important to acknowledge the inherent, built-in tension in *Max* between absolute and relative units of time. For example, at certain times we assign specific millisecond values for durations, whereas at other times we use relative values for musical subdivisions: quarter notes, eighth notes, sixteenth notes, etc. It's important to pay attention to the ways that we think about units of time at different scales: sometimes we use more intuitive, informal ways of getting from note to note, and at other times we measure those distances with precision.

2.5.3 These Topics, Skills, and Objects Were Introduced in Section 2.5 "Rhythm"

- The gswitch object switches between two or more possible pathways; it receives bang or number messages in its control inlet, specifying which of the other inlets to route data through, much like switching train tracks in a train yard.
- The radiogroup object functions much like umenu as an interface object that allows the user to select from a list of options. One benefit of radiogroup is that all options are available at the top level and can be switched more quickly than they can with umenu.
- The abs object receives a number in its inlet and outputs an absolute value, which means that any negative values it receives will be converted to positive values. (In patch 2.5, the abs object is used to invert slider values so that higher speeds are on the right side and lower speeds are on the left.)
- Activity: We have just scratched the surface of rhythm-making in this section. There are some wonderful examples of "beat-making" that you can try using software environments or just on your own. Explore your own rhythmic ideas,

possibly recreating the functions of your favorite metronome or combining advanced patterns to create polyrhythmic effects. A huge range of rhythmic variety can be created with combinations of weight, speed, and duration. The types of variety that we have explored in this section can be combined together, over extended units of time, to tell a story.

2.6 Valence

Listeners sometimes find themselves attracted to certain combinations of sounds but repelled from others. They might explain their preferences by describing qualities of sound using pairs of opposites such as music and noise, consonance and dissonance, pleasantness and unpleasantness, harmoniousness and discordance, familiarity and unfamiliarity, coherence and incoherence. Sometimes it is useful to use binary distinctions in this way, but it can also be helpful to reframe opposing qualities instead as continual values distributed across a range. In order to better understand experiences of attraction and repulsion in music, we will borrow the concept of valence from the field of psychology, where it is sometimes used to quantify the relative amount of positivity or negativity in an emotional experience.[20] Applied in this context, the term "valence" can be used to expand the ways we think about qualities of pleasantness and likability in sound; we can develop a deeper understanding by conceptualizing them as variables along a continuum between positively valenced and negatively valenced responses.

When notes interact with other notes across time and frequency domains, we can't help comparing them and deciding whether we like what we hear. In order to develop a fuller understanding of how music is constructed, it can be helpful to analyze and discern exactly how notes collaborate with each other. Just as with human relationships, there are risks and rewards with sonic combinations. Things might not work out, they might clash, or a rapport might blossom in unanticipated ways. When two people meet for the first time, their social environment establishes the conditions and implicit expectations within which they behave. When individuals behave "normally" as expected, those assumptions are confirmed and a sense of comfort is reinforced. If they behave outside of those expectations, however, a feeling of unease or concern can arise in response. This feeling is sometimes described as tension, which can be characterized to different degrees. Tension can increase over time the longer or more intensely the behavior continues to deviate from standard expectations. That tension can also resolve, partially or fully, if the behavior edges back toward the "normal" range. Musical structures can also induce tension and resolution in listeners, in much the same way that human behavioral choices cause varying degrees of comfort or concern.[21] Perhaps unsurprisingly, notes get along with other notes in complex ways that resemble aspects of human relationships, and their sonic associations are governed by similar kinds of rules.

2.6.1 Noise versus Music

Let's now start to develop some techniques for describing types of valenced sonic relationships. The first aspect to consider is which sounds are musical, and which ones are un-musical? (Noise is the term that is commonly used to describe most types of non-musical sound.) How do we differentiate between the two? There are a few ways to approach this question. First, let's look at it through a subjective lens.

One might take a first step toward defining music and non-music by saying, "well, sounds that I find attractive are music, and sounds that I find repulsive are noise." Those who choose this path typically rely on culturally constructed perceptions and qualitative judgments about sounds rather than their measurable features.[22] Culture, genre, attitudes, biases, and tastes all intersect to shape our perceptions of the rightness or wrongness of sonic combinations. This is quite normal, and isn't necessarily a bad thing; rigid expectations about sound help define specific musical styles. Stylistic categories can later be exploited by innovators to remix and recombine those elements in new ways. At many points in musical history, musical composers and producers have co-opted sounds that were previously labeled "noise" and incorporated them into new forms of music.

John Cage had a lot to say on this topic; instead of limiting his definition of music to conventional ideas about pleasing combinations of notes, Cage proposed an open-ended description in 1961: the "organization of sound," which John Blacking expanded in 1973 to "humanly organized sound."[23] In advocating for broader, more inclusive interpretations of music that included noise, they were building upon earlier ideas first articulated by Luigi Russolo, the Futurists, Dadaists, and members of other early twentieth-century stylistic movements such as Musique concrète. Well-known composers of the time were influenced by those ideas: George Gershwin emulated the sounds of taxi horns and automobile traffic in the orchestral parts for *An American in Paris* (1928), and George Antheil used actual emergency sirens, alarm bells, and air horns in his futuristic *Ballet Mécanique* (1924).

In the later twentieth century, new ideas about noise started to emerge that further challenged the status quo. Groundbreaking bands like Nirvana purposefully sought to emancipate noise from its earlier non-musical associations; their signature sounds included raucous, shredded vocals and distorted guitars that were clearly meant to be interpreted as expressive musical ideas, inextricably infused with noise. The integration of different types of sound also defined the hip-hop genre, where sounds that would have previously been heard as noise were included in ways that were purposefully intended to be perceived as integral with the musical content. Beginning in the 1980s, digital technologies and sampling techniques ripped open long-simmering questions around what kinds of sounds are fair to use in a musical composition, including the copyrighted notes of another composer. These days, valence is a matter of personal taste: one person's noise could be another person's music.[24]

There is another way of thinking about qualities of sound that relies on quantifiable, measurable, objective features instead of subjective, culturally based notions. Using this approach, we analyze the components of a sound to identify or categorize it based on specific criteria. One important feature label here is harmonicity: the existence of regular, orderly, periodic patterns of vibration and acoustic components called overtones or harmonics. (Some scholarly sources describe harmonicity as "musical" and inharmonicity as "noisy"; this book aims to use more precise language and avoid where possible the more problematic, subjective terms.)

As described earlier, notes are created by sound waves whose alternating positive and negative air pressure oscillations occur at regular frequencies. The primary frequency of a note is called its fundamental frequency, which is used to determine its pitch. Notes are usually also accompanied by simultaneous sets of overtones, which are naturally occurring frequencies of vibration that occur in acoustic environments when sound waves are produced. They exist because of a fundamental principle of acoustics: when physical materials vibrate, secondary vibrations also occur along multiple modes of vibration. The resulting compound vibration consists of a fundamental frequency accompanied by a set of overtones at higher frequencies; it is this specific set of vibrations that defines the quality of harmonicity.

In harmonic sounds, overtones oscillate at frequencies related to the fundamental by whole number multiples—ratios such as 2:1, 3:1, 4:1, etc. Overtones are usually a bit softer in volume than the fundamental frequencies with which they are associated, and occur in regular sets called the overtone series or harmonic series. Referring back to the spectrogram located on the bottom of figure 2.1 earlier in this chapter, overtones are visible in the upper portion of the image as groups of darker horizontal stripes located above the brighter lines of the fundamental frequencies.

In contrast to sounds that have the quality of harmonicity, there are other types of sound that can be characterized as having the quality of inharmonicity. These are divided into two types: sounds that have "inharmonic" oscillating components, and sounds that have non-oscillating or irregular components. Inharmonic oscillations are sets of overtones that are not perfect integer multiples of the fundamental frequency; their overtones are not evenly spaced apart using whole number ratios. Some percussion instruments produce inharmonic overtones: chimes, cymbals, bells, drums, etc. The second category of inharmonic sounds are those that are composed of non-oscillating elements whose vibrations are aperiodic: their vibrations do not alternate between positive and negative air pressure in a repeating pattern. These kinds of sounds include those made by engines, flowing water, and spoken consonants. While the sounds created by musical instruments mostly contain harmonic components, they also often include inharmonic components such as breathing sounds in wind instruments, fret sounds on guitars, and the audible scraping of the bow against the strings on a violin.

To compare the features of harmonicity and inharmonicity described above, please open patch 2.6. Click on the three different icons to hear each type of sound and view its corresponding spectrogram in the spectroscope~ object on the right. Clicking on "harmonic sound" yields a spectrogram with whole numbered ratios between all the overtones; this audio file features a violin playing a fundamental frequency at 252 Hz with strong overtones at 497, 757, 1000, 1246, 1499, and 1748 Hz. (The small mathematical difference between precise integer ratios and these actual recorded numbers is considered to be within the normal range of variability.) Clicking on "inharmonic oscillations" yields a spectrogram with irregularly spaced overtones; this audio file features two simultaneous chimes playing frequencies at 2468, 3431, 4420, 5529, 7331, and 8521 Hz. Clicking on aperiodic sound yields a spectrogram with no clear sustained overtones, although a few vague horizontal stripes in the image indicate that there are some repeated frequencies here and there; this sound was recorded in the noisy environment on the International Space Station. All three audio files are available on freesound.org and are used with permission through Creative Commons licenses; full attribution information and links are included in comment objects located at the bottom of the patch.

How can we resolve the differences between traditional and quantitative approaches in the ways we think about qualities of sound? Distinguishing between music and noise is an ancient debate, and we will not be able to conclusively provide an answer here. You may find that you have strong feelings and preferences for these categories! Take a few minutes to write down your thoughts on this topic. Brainstorm a constructive way to address these ideas through a creative project. For the time being, let's temporarily put aside this controversy and now delve into a new way to think about valence: subcategories of musical sound.

2.6.2 Consonance versus Dissonance

Within the category of musical sound itself, there are some note combinations that are thought to be more pleasant (positively valenced) and others that are thought to be less pleasant (negatively valenced). Traditionally, the term "consonance" has been used to describe the more attractive or comfortable combinations, whereas the term "dissonance" has described those qualities that are more repulsive and uncomfortable. Our ideas about consonance and dissonance contribute significantly to the ways in which we experience sensations of tension and resolution in music.

There are both acoustic and psychoacoustic reasons why we hear some combinations of notes as harmonious and others as discordant. Our responses are culturally specific and nurtured; they were not provided as part of our natural equipment, but instead learned through participating in socially mediated experiences beginning in childhood. Therefore, our perceptions of consonance and dissonance are highly contingent upon the musical environment in which we developed. The field of ethnomusicology is the study of music in different cultural and social contexts; greater familiarity with musical systems from around the world can help us develop an appreciation for the wide variety of ways to perceive and interpret the sounds we hear and cultivate a better understanding of our own expectations around consonance and dissonance.

In order to develop a more quantitative understanding of how consonance and dissonance impact the ways we construct and think about music, we need to first learn about frequency ratios. As we learned in section 2.3 "Frequency," notes oscillate at more-or-less steady frequencies, measured in vibrations per second. When two notes sound simultaneously, the relationship between their frequencies can be expressed as a ratio between the two—that is, how much higher the upper one is, compared with the lower one. To calculate the ratio of two frequencies, divide the higher one by the lower one. For example, if a higher note vibrates 440 times per second and a lower one vibrates 220 times per second, the ratio of the two frequencies is 440 / 220 = 2. This is also described as a frequency ratio of 2:1 ("two to one"), where the higher note vibrates at a frequency twice as fast as the lower one.[25] Similarly, to determine the frequency ratio between a note that vibrates 660 times per second and another note that vibrates 440 times per second, calculate 660 / 440 = 1.5. We express this ratio in whole number terms as 3:2, where the frequency of the higher note is 1.5 times the speed of vibration of the lower note.[26]

Based on the early experiments of Pythagoras around 500 BCE and still observed today in traditional Western music theory, any two notes are defined to be "perfectly" consonant if the ratio between them contains numbers of four or lower. Perfect consonances feature frequency ratios of 1:1, 2:1, 2:2, 3:1, 3:2, 3:3, 4:1, 4:2, 4:3, and 4:4. These ratios correspond to intervals called unisons, octaves, fifths, and fourths, which will be covered later in section 3.3 "Make an Interval."[27] Conversely, any two notes are considered to be dissonant if the ratio between them contains numbers higher than four.[28] (In a few cases, those dissonant intervals are called imperfect consonances). This information may seem surprising to our modern ears; many of us today hear some of the higher-numbered ratios as more consonant than some of the lower-numbered ratios. Although the consensus among modern sources clearly assigns dissonance to ratios with numbers above seven (e.g., 8:7, 9:8, 10:9, etc.), labels of consonance and dissonance are particularly controversial for intervals whose ratios include numbers between four and nine. Different styles of music can also provide their own interpretations of consonance and dissonance; a chord containing an interval labeled here as dissonant might sound perfectly resolved and consonant in the context of a blues or jazz progression, for example. Two of the sample code patches in Chapter 5 (patch 5.1 and 5.2a) provide tools that you can use to listen to frequency ratios and decide for yourself which ratios are consonant and which ones are dissonant.

One of the acoustical reasons that is used to justify the Pythagorean model of consonance and dissonance is that when two notes are played simultaneously, all of their overtones are superimposed in the same frequency space. Pairs of notes with simple (lower-numbered) frequency ratios share a significant amount of alignment and coincidence in their overtones and therefore are traditionally thought to sound pleasant. But those pairs of notes that have frequency ratios with higher numbers tend to have overtones that are not well aligned, which are said to cause a feeling of unease or tension. These misaligned frequencies can cause unpleasant volume fluctuations or interference patterns called acoustic beats that conflict with each other and create a sense of "roughness." Acoustic beats are examples of phenomena that occur when multiple audio signals combine and affect each other's amplitudes, resulting in quickly alternating moments of higher intensity (constructive interference) and lower intensity (destructive interference). Patch 2.6a demonstrates a simulation of acoustic beats where one sine wave holds a frequency of 440 Hz while another sine wave moves from 440 to 430 Hz over four seconds, then returns to 440 over another four seconds. Fluttering beats occur at a rate that reflects the frequency difference between the two sounds; when the second sine wave reaches 430 Hz, the number of beats per second is 10. The more complex (higher-numbered) the frequency ratios get, the more unaligned their resonances become, and the rougher the resulting sensation is for listeners.[29]

A note about how variety can affect valence: sometimes our attraction to sounds can change over time, especially through repeated listenings. Musical patterns that repeat too much tend to be ignored or disregarded. Repeating patterns can provide comforting familiarity and recognizability, but only up to a point. Patterns are important in music because they help to establish a sense of motion (energy, activation, direction, momentum) or stasis (equilibrium, balance, calmness, resolution). Patterns that don't change imply stasis, whereas changing patterns imply movement. As listeners, although it may seem as if patterns wash over us, we nonetheless can perceive and identify (often subconsciously) qualities such as predictability, stability, repetition, and disruption. These serve as the building blocks of tension and resolution. The first time we listen to a song, it might sound great, but after 1000 repetitions, our enthusiasm might start to wane. Great musical creators keep us engaged by changing things up once in a while. They purposefully establish patterns and then change the variables so as to keep renewing and regaining our attention. Some of them specialize in the surprise fake-out, manipulating the push and pull of expectation and resolution by setting the ball perfectly and then spiking it in the exact opposite direction. They extend the shelf life of musical ideas by finding and exploiting internal variety within them. Inverting and playing with patterns is a great way to evolve an idea while delaying a resolution. For what it's worth, the Harlem Globetrotters basketball team uses these kinds of techniques to great effect as well. Thwarting expectation is an example of manipulating the standard patterns and bending the rules in order to elicit a higher-intensity response from the audience.

Ultimately, measurable features (overtones and frequency ratios) and subjective concepts (consonance, dissonance, music, and noise) all interact with each other in ways that cause us to prefer certain sonic combinations in our music, and avoid other pairings. Essentially, valence can be thought about as a cultural construct or lens that helps us make judgments about musical signals and decide what they mean to us. While there is a degree of arbitrariness and complexity to all of this, it is worth acknowledging that music, like many other human systems, contains a bit of science, a bit of art, a bit of emotion, and a bit of stubbornness all wrapped up together. It is messy and riddled with inconsistencies, biases, preferences, and cultural baggage. But if it works for you as a tool for personal expression, then it has a useful purpose. We will loop back again later to consonance, dissonance, and related topics during discussions of tuning systems in Chapter 5.[30]

2.6.3 These Topics, Skills, and Objects Were Introduced in Section 2.6 "Valence"

- Tension and resolution are human responses to music that reflect expectations shaped by subjective experiences, opinions, attitudes, cultural upbringings, etc. How does music create feelings of tension and resolution in you when you listen? Think of a few specific examples and jot them down. Describe the specific musical features (dissonance, consonance, complexity, novelty, expression, etc.) that impart those particular qualities.
- The spectroscope~ object displays a real time spectrogram, a visual depiction of audio frequencies that updates as the music flows by.
- Harmonic sounds feature equally-spaced overtones, whereas inharmonic sounds have irregularly-spaced overtones (or non-oscillating/irregular components). See if you can locate or record some examples of your own. Open patch 2.6 and load your new audio files by dragging them from your computer filesystem into the playlist~ object. View the overtones in the spectroscope~ object on the right. Attend to the distinct, special qualities of each sound.
- Explore the concept of acoustic beats further by opening up patch 2.6a and adjusting the numbers in the message object located above the line~ object. The first number in the list sets the starting frequency; it is followed by a comma and then two pairs of numbers. The first item in each pair contains the goal frequency that will be reached over a duration defined by the second number (given in milliseconds). Play around with different values and enjoy listening to the results.

2.7 Timbre

As defined in tutorial #3 in Chapter 1, timbre is a feature of sound that is often described as "tone quality" or "color." Timbre is usually associated with individual instruments or voices or synthesis algorithms. For example, when two instruments each produce a note with the exact same pitch, loudness, and duration, timbre then becomes the primary remaining difference between the sounds. Go ahead and explore this idea by opening patch 2.7 "Timbre" and listening to the different timbres produced by the four different sound sources.

Timbre represents not just one variable but rather a collection of several variables that influence the features in an acoustic signal. These properties can fluctuate over time, even within the duration of a single note. Expert musicians take great care to carefully adjust subtle qualities of timbre when they perform, emphasizing special characteristics of their instruments' sound range for expressive effect. The sheer variety of timbral features provides many opportunities to explore the richness, variety, and complexity of sound.

One important variable that significantly contributes to the timbre of a sound is its sound spectrum: the combined collection of all the frequency components it contains (fundamental plus overtones), along with their amplitude levels. Most real-world sounds contain several different frequencies; very few sounds have only one frequency. With musical sounds, we particularly focus on the relative weightings of the amplitudes for each overtone. These can be visualized using spectrum graphs that show the decomposition (breakdown) of sounds into their sinusoidal frequency components (overtones). For example, the oboe typically has a few strong overtones (especially the first and third), which at times can be louder than the fundamental; these overtone frequencies contribute to the signature "nasal" quality of the oboe sound as an unusual feature of its sound spectrum.

Timbre is also affected by the shape of the attack phase of the amplitude envelope (described in section 2.4 "Intensity"), particularly the characteristic ways in which the different overtones increase in volume during that phase. And it is also deeply affected by individual perception—our hearing systems are very good at identifying individual timbres in a complex mix and following them as a piece evolves.

Timbre is the main area of attention in orchestration, the activity of arranging notes of different sound qualities to create interesting combinations. When you mix timbres together, they tend to merge and blend with each other, synthesizing new complex textures that take on their own compound identities. In music, the term "texture" refers to the way in which different timbral elements combine to create a uniform density, much as fiber strands combine to create a woven textile. The way we perceive texture in music can be influenced by the vertical spacings between notes, the number of parts or layers, the number of simultaneous instances of pitch classes (doublings), the combined overall volume, and other factors. Monophonic music is sometimes described as having a thin texture due to its unaccompanied solo lines. When more than one layer of sound is present (in textures described as homophonic or polyphonic), those layers engage in a collaborative interplay across both time and frequency domains. In paying attention to these interactions and discerning how individual notes relate to each other, you can find lots of scope for aesthetic pleasure.

Patch 2.7 in the sample code provides a way to compare sounds and explore how the variables described above affect timbre. Open up the patch and click on each of the four toggle objects located near the top. Listen attentively to the tone quality of each sound: notice that although all of these sounds share the same pitch, they are very different from each other in timbre. These differences can be largely attributed to the variables of waveshape, sound spectrum, and attack shape. The spectroscope~

window displays a spectrogram; it is the same object that we used in patch 2.6, but here the display is set in horizontal mode. This allows it to present audio frequencies on the horizontal axis and volumes on the vertical axis. The peaks here represent the overtones; as you click between the four different sounds, notice how the overtone patterns change. For example, "timbre 2" has a strong fundamental and several noticeable overtones in the upper frequency range, whereas "timbre 3" mostly has a strong fundamental and first two overtones, with much weaker upper overtones. After listening to each sound individually, try triggering them quickly in different combinations, layering them into different unified textures.

With digital synthesis and modern music production software, it is possible to create and modify a wide range of new timbres. *Max* provides an excellent set of tools for analyzing and synthesizing sounds. Although these advanced functions are beyond the scope of this book, they are worth checking out! Below are some links to a few high-quality examples.

2.7.1 These Topics, Skills, and Objects Were Introduced in Section 2.7 "Timbre"

- We undertook some initial explorations in viewing sound spectra and learning how their features affect timbre; for additional *Max* resources on sound spectral processing, please see the tutorials and sample code available here: https://cycling74.com/tools/charles-spectral-tutorials, especially the patch called "1-record-spectrum in matrix" in the downloadable zipfile of materials: http://cycling74.com/download/Share/Jean-francoisCharles/jfc-spectral-tutorials.zip (more recent work by the same developer is also available here for $6: https://newfloremusic.gumroad.com/l/plvIn).
- Activity: watch *Deep Listening: The Story of Pauline Oliveros*, a documentary directed by Daniel Weintraub, 2022.

3
Pitch-based Structures

In Chapter 3 we will address the "vertical" dimension of music, also known as the frequency domain or "tonal pitch space."[1] In this chapter, we will primarily focus on the aspect of pitch, mostly avoiding considerations of the "horizontal" dimension of time except for a few inevitable mentions of durations and melodic intervals where one pitch follows another.

In this chapter, we will address how to create and name notes. We will also explore how notes are grouped together to form standard units of musical structure such as intervals, scales, and chords. We will investigate how to group and scaffold pitches together, learn how they function, and create them using code. We will discuss how a sense of tonality defines the complex system of relationships between notes and note groupings, governed ultimately by our perceptions of (and responses to) consonance and dissonance. And near the end of the chapter, we will engage with the concept of musical keys and how they support an overarching system and context within which notes, intervals, scales, and chords derive their meanings and functions.

3.1 Make a Note

Notes are sounds that contain a single instance of the element of pitch. We first encountered notes in tutorial #3 (section 1.3 "MIDI Notes and Variables"), when we made an initial foray into the process of making a note. We learned how to set and modify the quantities for important variables such as pitch, volume, duration, and timbre; we also learned how to send out MIDI "note on" messages and change timbre using the pgmout object and the General MIDI patch list. We further expanded our understanding of notes later during section 2.3 "Frequency," when we learned that notes are individual sounds that have steady frequencies of vibration. On this third iteration, we will expand our knowledge by taking a deeper dive into the details of constructing, modifying, and naming notes.

The idea of a note is something that one might reasonably take for granted; it's a word that gets used frequently in conversations about music. But the definition of a note turns out to be more complicated when you start to examine it in detail; it is another example of a suitcase word. When you investigate the established understanding of what a note is, you start to encounter multiple layers of assumptions—like peeling an onion. While some of those oniony layers should probably be left under the proverbial hood, we will address them wherever possible. In this section, we will unpack the familiar and comfortable concept of "note" and attempt to understand it at a lower layer of abstraction.

Notes are individual sounds that each contain a single pitch, along with the three other primary components: volume, duration, and timbre. As we first learned in tutorial #3, the four components of pitch, volume, duration, and timbre are examples of musical variables, or numerical values that can be stored and changed over time. These variables each contribute their own special qualities that may seem simple at first, but that may also serve as "suitcases" for complex physical and perceptual phenomena.

Now go ahead and open patch 3.1 to encounter new ways to make a note, combining aspects from earlier patches (1.3 and 2.3). (A software note: if you recently used patches 2.6–2.7, you may need to first quit and restart *Max*. Sometimes after the digital audio functions have been activated, the MIDI driver needs to be relaunched.) This time, we will use the kslider object to generate pitch numbers and send them out. Go ahead and click on the kslider to create individual notes or streams of glissandos! This kslider has been set to output 48 different note numbers, ranging from 36 to 83. A regular slider object is also located on the patch with the same numerical range, allowing you to compare how the two different sliders work as note generators. For fun, experiment with the numerical ranges that each slider outputs: use the Inspector tool to change variables such as Low MIDI Key Offset or Output Minimum (lowest note). This patch also includes several ubutton objects that allow you to select options for velocity, duration, and timbre. As described earlier in some of the Chapter 1 tutorials, ubuttons enable us to design more visually attractive signage that engages the attention of users and invites them to make a selection.

For those who have a MIDI keyboard, MIDI controller, or Makey Makey, how might you incorporate your hardware device into this patch? You can copy and paste bits of code from earlier patches in Chapter 1 to help you with this. Perhaps you might want your external hardware to control this virtual keyboard directly. Notice that the kslider has two inlets, one for MIDI pitch and one for velocity. Patch 3.1 is depicted in figure 3.1.

Now we have a few different ways to play MIDI notes in *Max*! Is that music? Probably not yet. Notes by themselves are just building blocks. Like individual Lego bricks, notes aren't likely to make good art by themselves. It takes time and guidance to learn how notes relate to each other through patterns and to unlock creative processes that make interesting musical sound. In the section that follows, we will begin to undertake next steps in that direction.

3.1.1 These Topics, Skills, and Objects Were Introduced in Section 3.1 "Make a Note"

- creating notes and glissandos using kslider and slider objects to generate pitch values.

98 Constructing Music

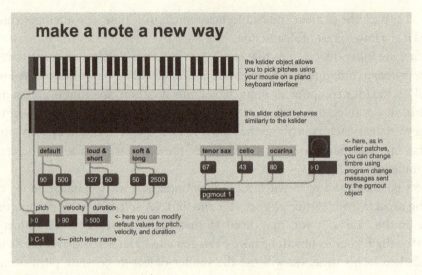

Figure 3.1 Make a note using kslider

- experimenting with the numerical ranges of kslider and slider using the Inspector tool.
- using ubutton objects to simultaneously select multiple options for velocity and duration.
- Activity: Patch 3.1 provides a few new ways to make notes, building upon concepts introduced earlier in patches 1.3 and 2.3. How might you extend patch 3.1 even further? For example, how might you use single ubutton objects to simultaneously send values for pitch, volume, duration, and timbre? Try to sequence enough of these notes together to create a simple tune.

3.2 Name a Note

Earlier, in patches 2.3 "Frequency" and 3.1 "Make a Note," we saw number objects being used to display pitch letters instead of MIDI numbers. In this section, we will learn about the system of letter notation that assigns letter names to individual notes. We sometimes call this activity "spelling" notes.

Historically, musicians have referred to notes by letter, rather than by number or frequency. (Perhaps numbers are harder to remember.) The framework we use for letter notation has a long and complex history; we can thank the ancient Greeks for developing the basic scheme. In this system, sequential pitches are associated with the first seven letter names in the Roman alphabet: A, B, C, D, E, F, and G.[2] These seven letters constitute the standard steps in a seven-note scale, which we will explore further in section 3.5 "Make a Scale." For the time being, we will use the word "step" to mean an adjacent note; we will expand our definitions of the exact distances between notes in section 3.3 "Make an Interval."

A piano keyboard layout provides a convenient way to display and learn the note letter names; we will use the kslider object for this purpose. Go ahead and open patch 3.2 "Name a Note." In this patch, individual keys in the kslider object are labeled with the standard note letter names. Clicking on individual keys highlights them and plays the note with which they are associated; presentation mode allows a few objects to be left "under the hood." A second C note sits the right side of the keyboard—this upper C is an octave higher than the lower one; we will discuss octaves later in this section.

The lower keys correspond to the seven letter names, and the five upper keys are situated in between the lettered keys. The upper keys are named using a modifier called an accidental (also called a chromatic alteration), a symbol placed after the note letter name that preserves the letter while adjusting its pitch to an adjacent piano key. Accidental symbols include the "sharp" (♯) and the "flat" (♭): "sharp" indicates that a note is raised in pitch by shifting it to the right by one key, while "flat" indicates that a note is lowered in pitch by shifting it one key to the left. We append ♯ and ♭ symbols to the letter names—for example, there is one upper key located between C and D; it can either be called C♯ (one step higher than C) or D♭ (one step lower than D).[3] There is some flexibility and ambiguity in the way that we name notes with accidentals. Selecting the correct letter and accidental to use depends on the context, which we will encounter later on. For the time being, it will be fine to use either name.

In addition to the five notes that are always named using accidentals, any note can be modified with an accidental. That is, any note can be shifted one key to the right with a sharp (♯) symbol, and any note can be shifted one key to the left using a flat (♭) symbol. You can also rename notes using accidentals. For example, the note that is one key to the right of E can be called E♯ instead of F. Similarly, the note that is one key to the left of C can be called C♭ instead of B. The natural (♮) symbol refers to an unmodified note, or erases any earlier sharp or flat and returns it back to its unmodified state. If after using A♯ for a while, you want to go back to the unmodified A, you can indicate that change by calling it A♮. You can also shift notes by two keys, using the "double sharp" (𝄪 or ♯♯) and "double flat" (𝄫) symbols. While these double accidentals are less common, they are still used for various reasons. As with single accidentals, the decision about which name to use depends on the context.

3.2.1 Mapping Letters to Numbers

In addition to letter notation, we can also refer to notes by number, as we saw in tutorial #3. Because the MIDI system assigns a seven-bit value to the variable for pitch, we have 2^7 or 128 different notes available to us, numbered from 0 at the low end to 127 at the upper end. These numbers allow for forty more notes than are included in the standard piano keyboard. They correspond to twenty notes below the range of the piano, all eighty-eight keys in the middle, and twenty notes above. These 128 notes capture nearly all the discrete pitches that are conventionally used in instrumental music composition.

The standard MIDI note numbering scheme assigns a pitch number of 60 to middle C. This association provides a convenient mile marker as we count the notes above and below it. Each neighboring note is one step away; C♯ is one step up from C (the next note to the right on the keyboard); it has a MIDI number of 61. B is the note to the left of C, and it has a MIDI number of 59. B♭/A♯ is the note just to the left of B, with a MIDI number of 58. One additional step to the left is A, which has a MIDI note number of 57.

Since there are many more than twelve notes available to use, we handle that aspect by organizing the notes A–G in sets called octaves. You can think about octaves in much the same way that you think about the days of the week. We organize the days of the week into seven days that loop in the same order over and over again, even though time itself doesn't loop; we continue to progress forward in time. Octaves work in much the same way: the same basic seven letter names loop in a cycle that repeats over and over again as you progress up and down the frequency space. Octaves are special cases of intervals and will be explained in greater detail in section 3.3 "Make an Interval" below.

In the system known as scientific pitch notation, we assign numbers to the different octaves, also called register numbers.[4] Register is defined as the relative pitch height (perceived highness or lowness) of a note, often indicated by octave number. Register is itself a variable that can be modified to create a sense of contrast in musical structure. Although the concept of register is not completely tied to the octave, the scientific pitch notation system uses a numbering scheme for each octave beginning with C to identify the register of a note. Using this system, each note is assigned both a letter name and an octave number. Middle C is named C4 because it is the fourth C from the bottom of the piano keyboard; it is the first note in the fourth full octave. The highest note on the piano is C8, and the lowest note on a piano keyboard is called A0—in the "zeroth" octave, assigned to MIDI pitch number 21. The note associated with MIDI pitch number 0 is called C_{-1}, in the octave below the zeroth octave. (We count octaves using conventions from engineering, the same way MIDI numbers start with 0 instead of 1; some music theorists also indicate octave numbers using diacritical marks (such as "'"). The pitch class of a note is its letter name, and any accidental without the octave registration number included. Pitch class also includes a notion of a note's role within a tonal structure, which we will start to investigate in section 3.5 "Make a Scale."

If you return to patch 3.2 "Name a Note" and take it out of presentation mode, you will see that there is a bit of code included there under the hood that allows you to plug in a Makey Makey and play the notes displayed on the kslider. Currently, six inputs are included as arguments in the select object; if you wish, go ahead and modify this patch to add six more inputs so you can play the full twelve semitones. (The standard six inputs on the front of each Makey Makey board are accessible with alligator clips, and there are another twelve inputs on the back: six for keyboard keys and six for mouse motion, which you can access with small jumper cables.) Have fun customizing this patch to work for you!

3.2.2 These Topics, Skills, and Objects Were Introduced in Section 3.2 "Name a Note"

- "spelling" notes using letter notation and accidentals (♯, ♭, ♮, 𝄪, 𝄫)
- Now that you are learning how to spell individual notes in multiple ways (for example, E♯ and F sound the same), make a list containing several examples. How many can you come up with? Include some examples that include double sharps or double flats, such as F𝄪 and G
- The MIDI note numbering scheme allows us to start thinking about notes as numerical data. Middle C can provide a useful reference here. Looking at the kslider in patch 3.2, if the leftmost C is 60 and the C♯ next to it is 61, then what are the MIDI numbers for the rest of the notes? (How many numbers separate the low C from the C one octave above it?)

3.3 Make an Interval

In this section, we will learn how to construct two-note intervals. But what exactly is an interval? It is the difference in pitch between two notes, which you can think about as the vertical distance between the bottom note and the top note. The goal of this section is to learn how to quantify and name that vertical distance. This method of counting will help us understand the relationships between notes with a greater degree of resolution and precision.

Interval types are identified by two variables: number and quality. In order to create intervals using these variables, we will first need to expand upon our understanding of the letter notation system for pitch naming that we first encountered above in section 3.1 "Make a Note." The number of an interval describes its size. Interval sizes are determined, as with stairs and ladders, by counting the number of steps that they span. We count steps using a basic unit of pitch measurement called the semitone. Semitones are also known colloquially as half steps; they are the smallest standard interval sizes we use.[5] (See Chapter 5 for information on the tuning systems that define our interval spacings.)

When we count individual semitone steps, we use a method called inclusive counting that incorporates both the lower and upper notes as the outer endpoints that frame the interval distance. However, you can't simply count the number of semitones and stop there. Intervals exist within a quirky system of weird boundary conditions and established norms. Because we use letter names for notes instead of numbers, "counting" intervals requires more than just simple arithmetic. We have evolved a method for counting and naming intervals that is both precise but also a bit peculiar. The following section digs into the details with as much clarity as possible.

As basic units of pitch measurement, semitone intervals span adjacent pitches but not necessarily two letter names. For example, the interval from C to C♯ is a semitone, and so also are the intervals from E to F and B to C. Although you can perform two notes one semitone apart on most musical instruments, the arrangement of keys on a piano keyboard provides helpful clarity by displaying adjacent notes as discrete keys that are clearly distinguished from each other (see patch 3.2 "Name a Note").

We compute the number of an interval by counting up the total number of letter names contained within its span, including both the upper and lower notes. We count upward from low to high (left to right on the piano keyboard), using the "ordinal" numbers such as second, third, and fourth. For example, the interval between any note with the letter name A (A♭, A♮, A♯) and any adjacent form of the note B immediately above it (B♭, B♮, B♯) is called a "second" because it spans two letter names. But the interval from B up to the next A above is called a seventh, because when you count up from B to A, you include all the letter names in between: B, C, D, E, F, G, and A. We will practice interval counting in detail below, focused primarily on simple intervals of an octave or less. Compound intervals greater than an octave will be addressed briefly later in this section.

The other important variable to consider when identifying an interval is its quality. Quality can be thought of as a modifier for an interval's number that indicates the exact number of semitones. Here are some ways to think about the five qualities of intervals:

- **perfect**—these intervals are considered to be perfect consonances due to their simple frequency ratios and high degree of overtone overlap. The "perfect" label is only assigned to exact unisons, octaves, fifths of exactly seven semitones, and fourths where the upper note is exactly five semitones above the bottom note.
- **minor**—for all non-perfect intervals, the "minor" label (lowercase when abbreviated, as in m3 for minor 3rd) refers to the smaller of the two standard forms—seconds of exactly 1 semitone, thirds of exactly 3 semitones, sixths of exactly 8 semitones, and sevenths of exactly 10 semitones.
- **major**—for all non-perfect intervals, the "major" label (capitalized when abbreviated, as in M2 for major 2nd) refers to the larger of their two forms—seconds of exactly two semitones, thirds of exactly four semitones, sixths of exactly nine semitones, and sevenths of exactly eleven semitones.
- **diminished**—extra-small; all perfect and minor intervals where the upper note is lowered by one semitone.
- **augmented**—extra-large; all perfect and major intervals where the upper note is raised by one semitone.

We will now start applying a two-part method of first counting letter names to determine the number of an interval, and then counting semitones to determine the quality. As you read through this section, follow along using sample patch 3.3 "Make an Interval." Its visual and auditory simulations are designed to accompany the text descriptions: click on each color block to listen to an interval and compare it with the others. Each interval will be played *melodically*, one note at a time, in ascending form where the direction of the interval goes up from the starting note. (In harmonic intervals, both notes play simultaneously.)

In patch 3.3, color indicates interval number and height indicates interval quality. The patch displays intervals in ascending height order, and there are two sets of enharmonically equivalent intervals that share the same height. (These are not the only possible enharmonic equivalents; as an added challenge, see if you can modify this patch by adding a few more intervals that share the same height but have a different color.) You can also compare interval sizes using the piano key note names on the kslider object in patch 3.2. And those who enjoy customizing their patches are most welcome to adjust the color scheme!

We will begin with the simplest example: the perfect unison, sometimes abbreviated P1 or PU. (Instead of "first," we use the special term unison.) Unisons are fairly self-explanatory: a perfect unison is an interval where there is 0 difference between two pitches. Both notes sound the same and are named identically. Unisons are perfectly consonant because there is perfect overlap between the two sounds. They can be modified to have a diminished or augmented quality, where both notes share the same letter names but where the interval size has been adjusted by one semitone using an accidental. For example, G and G♯ form an augmented unison interval, and G♭ and G♭♭ ("G double flat") comprise a diminished unison. These sonorities are considered highly dissonant.

A related but opposite concept to that of the unison is called enharmonic equivalency. This is where two notes share the same frequency and sound the same but use different spellings for their pitch names, such as F♯ and G♭.[6] Notes that are enharmonically equivalent to each other are not considered to be unisons because, as we will encounter later, their differentiated spellings indicate that they have different functions within the tonal structure. The way they are named indicates the role that they inhabit within the society of notes around them.

After unisons, the next most basic type of interval is called the perfect octave. Octaves span eight letter names and are sometimes abbreviated as P8. (Instead of "eighth," we use the special term octave.) Octaves are special cases of intervals: they resemble unisons because their notes share the same letter name and accidental. Like unisons, they are also considered perfectly consonant, because of the high degree of overlap between the overtones for both notes. However, the notes that comprise a perfect octave do not share the same pitch. Instead, they span an interval of twelve semitones. Like unisons, octaves can be modified by raising or lowering one of the notes, thereby modifying their quality to an augmented or diminished octave. A lower E and an upper E♯ (13 semitones higher) comprise an augmented octave, while a lower E and an upper E♭ (11 semitones higher) comprise a diminished octave. Because octaves have a special importance in the way that we organize our tonal system, we will devote some additional attention to them at the end of this section.

The remaining intervals represent subdivisions of the octave and will be addressed in size order. The smallest of these is called the second, which spans two adjacent letter names. Seconds are considered to be dissonant intervals and come in two standard forms: minor and major. The minor second, abbreviated m2, comprises one semitone or a half step, the smallest standard unit of distance between two notes. The interval from E up to F is one such example. The major second, abbreviated M2, comprises two semitones or a whole step. The interval from F up to G or B up to C♯ are examples. The major second can be expanded by one semitone using an accidental to create an augmented second, as in B♭ up to C♯. In rare situations, the minor second can be reduced by a semitone to create a diminished second, as in B to C♭, although the result of that adjustment is enharmonically equivalent to a unison—both B and C♭ share the same frequency and sound the same.

The next largest interval number is the third, which spans three adjacent letter names. (We skip one letter name in between the two notes, as in A up to C.) Thirds are considered to be "imperfectly" consonant intervals and come in two standard forms: minor and major. The minor third, abbreviated m3, comprises three semitones or a whole step plus a half step; the interval from D up to F is an example. Major thirds comprise four semitones or two whole steps; the interval from E up to G♯ is an example. The major third can be expanded by a semitone using an accidental to create an augmented third, as in E up to G𝄪. Minor thirds can be reduced by one semitone to create diminished thirds, as in B up to D♭, which is enharmonically equivalent to a major second. Major and minor thirds are commonly used as building blocks for creating chords, which we will cover in section 3.6 "Make a Chord."

The next interval is the perfect fourth, which spans four adjacent letter names. Fourths are included among the perfect intervals due to the low-numbered frequency ratio between their two notes (4:3); however, in other contexts they are considered dissonant or unresolved.[7] A perfect fourth, abbreviated P4, comprises five semitones or two whole steps plus a half step. The interval from G up to C is an example. A perfect fourth can be expanded by a semitone to create an augmented fourth, as in G up to C♯. This is a special interval known as the tritone, which contains three whole steps. Tritones represent perfect bisections of the octave and are considered to be highly dissonant. Tritones were historically thought to be offensive and generally avoided; for at least three hundred years, they have been called the "devil's interval." It is possible to create a diminished fourth by lowering the top note of a perfect fourth, as in G up to C♭; however, such intervals are highly rare due to their enharmonic equivalence with the major third, one of the most commonly used intervals for making chords.

Next in our progression of intervals is the perfect fifth, which spans five adjacent letter names. Fifths are included among the perfect intervals due to their low frequency ratio (3:2) and high degree of consonance. A perfect fifth, abbreviated P5, comprises seven semitones or three whole steps plus a half step. The interval from G up to D is an example. A perfect fifth can be expanded by a semitone to create an augmented fifth, as in G to D♯. It can also be reduced in size by a semitone to create a diminished fifth, as in G up to D♭, which is the other standard way to create the tritone sonority described above. (Tritones can be spelled either as diminished fifths or augmented fourths; they are enharmonically equivalent and equally dissonant.) Like thirds, fifths are important intervals for building chords and harmonic relationships. This is because when you stack two thirds on top of each other, the outer interval of the resulting combination is a fifth. This idea will be covered in section 3.6 "Make a Chord."

The next largest interval number is the sixth, which spans six adjacent letter names. In addition to thirds, sixths are the only other examples of imperfect consonances. They come in two standard forms: minor and major. The minor sixth, abbreviated m6, comprises eight semitones or three whole steps plus two half steps. The interval from D up to B♭ is an example. The major sixth, abbreviated M6, comprises nine semitones or four whole steps plus a half step. The interval from E up to C♯ is an example. Major sixths can be expanded by one semitone using an accidental to create augmented sixths, as in E♭ up to C♯. (Augmented sixths are enharmonically equivalent to minor sevenths.) Minor sixths can be reduced by one semitone to create diminished sixths, as in E up to C♭. Diminished sixths are enharmonically equivalent to perfect fifths, and therefore are essentially not used (although theoretically possible) because there is no normal scenario in which one would "respell" or repurpose such a basic consonance.

The last of our simple intervals is called a seventh, which spans seven adjacent letter names. Sevenths are considered to be dissonant intervals that often resolve to less dissonant forms. (You can think about them as having a high gravitational pull toward other intervals; intervals with this quality are called tendency tones. Sevenths tend either to resolve downward to sixths or serve as leading tones that resolve strongly upward to octaves.) Sevenths come in two standard forms: minor and major. The minor seventh, abbreviated m7, comprises ten semitones or four whole steps plus two half steps. The interval from D up to C is one example. The major seventh, abbreviated M7, comprises eleven semitones or five whole steps plus a half step. The intervals from F up to E or B up to A♯ are examples. Although technically you could expand a major seventh by a semitone using an accidental to create an augmented seventh, as in B♭ up to A♯, the resulting interval is enharmonically equivalent to an octave and is highly unusual in much the same way as the diminished second and diminished sixth. Minor sevenths can be reduced by one semitone to create diminished sevenths, as in C to B♭♭, although the result of that adjustment is enharmonically equivalent to major sixth and similarly unusual.

3.3.1 A Note about Adjusting Interval Qualities

A careful reader might have noticed that adjustments to interval qualities can be made in two directions. That is, you can expand the size of an interval either by raising the top note or by lowering the bottom note. Similarly, you can reduce the size of an interval either by lowering the top note or by raising the bottom note. Either way is acceptable.

Also, you might occasionally come across intervals that are doubly diminished or doubly augmented. As with other interval qualities, you can reduce the size of a diminished interval by one semitone to make it doubly diminished. For example, a diminished fifth from D up to A♭ can be adjusted to the doubly diminished fifth of D up to A♭♭. Similarly, you can expand the size of an augmented interval by one semitone to make it doubly augmented. An example could be taking an augmented sixth of E♭ up to C♯ and further expanding it by a semitone from E♭ up to C𝄪. Of course, these types of intervals are highly unusual and probably should be avoided unless absolutely necessary.

3.3.2 Interval Inversion

An important concept related to counting and building intervals is interval inversion, which you can think about as matching up mirror-image intervals within an octave. Intervals are inverses of each other if combining them together creates an octave; they are complementary within the octave.[8] For example, if you add a second on top of a seventh, the result is an octave. Similarly, thirds and sixths are inverses of each other, as are fourths and fifths. In addition, the raised version of one inverse pairs with the reduced version of the other, as in major third plus minor sixth, or minor second plus major seventh. The augmented fourth is the inverse of the diminished fifth; both are enharmonically equivalent bisections of an octave. (It is a frequent point of confusion that 2+7, 3+6, and 4+5 all equal eight instead of nine; this situation occurs because we use a system of inclusive counting to determine interval sizes. In the case of a seventh plus a second, the top note of the seventh is the same as the bottom note of the second, so you remove one number from the total because of this overlap.)

Interval inverses share a special relationship that resembles symmetry, and they mirror each other in interesting patterns. For example, a minor third is three semitones from the bottom note of an octave, whereas a major sixth is three semitones from the top note of an octave. Interval inverses also have similar qualities—seconds and sevenths are highly dissonant, thirds and sixths are imperfectly consonant, and fourths and fifths are perfect consonances. Unisons and octaves are also inverses of each other and both are perfectly consonant. To explore the properties of interval inverses, please open up and experiment with sample patch 3.3a "Interval Inversion."

3.3.3 Compound Intervals

Compound intervals are those that exceed an octave. They are named slightly differently: for example, an octave-plus-a-third is called a tenth. Typically, we don't count interval numbers beyond a twelfth—to specify interval numbers larger than that, we often use the word "compound" plus the interval's number and quality, disregarding any extra octaves. For example, an octave-plus-a-fifth is called a twelfth or a compound fifth. An octave-plus-a-sixth could instead be called a compound sixth.

3.3.4 More about Octaves

Octaves are special cases of intervals. We will open up the proverbial hood a little bit here and discuss them in further detail. As was described above in section 3.2 "Name a Note," octaves provide a looping structure that helps us organize our notes, the same way that weeks help us organize how we use our days. Like the seven-day week in our calendar system, octaves define a pitch space that includes seven letter names, and octaves can be used to skip up and down the frequency space from low to high.

Octaves represent a doubling of the frequency; the notes in an octave have a frequency ratio of 2:1, where the higher note oscillates exactly twice as fast as the lower note. This simple ratio provides an important frame within which notes are defined in relationship to each other. For example, if you play a low A on the piano (A2 110 Hz), the A one octave higher is 2× the frequency (A3 220 Hz), the A two octaves higher is 4× the frequency (A4 440 Hz), the next A above will be 8× (A5 880 Hz), and so on.

Most people perceive a quality of "sameness" between notes an octave or multiple octaves apart, and they recognize that this relationship is similar to that of the unison. This perceptual phenomenon is known as the principle of octave equivalence. Although the physiological basis for our perception of octave equivalence is not fully understood, most scholars agree that it arises from the fact that notes share all of their even-numbered overtones with the note one octave higher. While it is believed that all humans can perceive this relationship, not all musical cultures apply octaves in similar ways.

Some scholars have indicated that octave equivalence is one of the rare forms of qualia in music.[9] Qualia are defined as intrinsic qualities of subjective experience associated with specific sensory events, such as the blueness of blue. As with colors, the perceptual qualities of unisons and octaves are experiences that most people can agree upon.[10] And although sound frequencies do not naturally disperse into fixed steps the way light disperses through a prism into the seven constituent colors of the rainbow, we hear the relative relationships between frequencies in a fixed way. This ability allows those of us who don't have perfect pitch to nonetheless recognize intervals through ratios of frequencies.

Octave equivalent notes can be said to share the same pitch class (defined above in section 3.2); because they share the same name, they also share the same bindings and associations within a tonal structure and context. These are sometimes alternatively called chroma, or harmonic pitch class profiles, and they can be used to estimate keys and harmonic features in audio recordings.

3.3.5 Connecting Back to Consonance and Dissonance

One topic that we have deferred for the time being is how to characterize intervals in terms of their frequency ratios and resulting overtone alignments. Although we used frequency ratios and degrees of overtone overlap to describe intervals as consonant or dissonant in section 2.6 "Valence," we had not yet engaged deeply with the complexities of interval counting and naming. Eventually, as you become more comfortable with constructing intervals, you will be ready to loop back around and connect your understanding of intervals back to fundamental concepts of consonance and dissonance. Generally, perfect intervals are consonant, augmented and diminished intervals are dissonant, and major and minor intervals can be either consonant or dissonant. But there is much more remaining detail in this topic that will have to remain "under the hood" while we focus on other areas. (We will return to interval frequency ratios in Chapter 5, where you can explore and compare consonances and dissonances in sample patches 5.1 and 5.2a.)

3.3.6 A Theory about Interval Size

A note about the size of interval leaps and their connection to emotional intensity, as first mentioned in section 2.4 "Intensity": music is an art form that teaches us about movement—how our bodies move physically, and also the ways in which our thoughts and feelings move internally and help us react to the world. In this sense, intervals are sometimes used in music to indicate the variable of emotional intensity. Small intervals like seconds and thirds represent normal, ordinary ways to move. They capture qualities of daily, unsurprising tasks that we do—waking up, brushing teeth, getting dressed, eating breakfast, etc. Stable, routine, expected things involve a low intensity level. However, large leaps represent the surprising, energizing, activating things that we do—falling in love, seeing the Grand Canyon, completing a level in a video game, achieving a new personal best in a sport. In this interpretation, the size of an interval can be compared with the intensity component of Russell's Circumplex model of affect (first mentioned in the endnotes for sections 2.4 and 2.6): it expresses the amount of intensity or activation of a feeling. Interval size is a specific compositional choice that should be used judiciously; larger intervals are often reserved for special moments of emphasis. (As described in section 2.4, volume can also affect emotional intensity.)

Above all, notes get along with other notes in complex ways that resemble aspects of human relationships, and their sonic associations are governed by similar kinds of rules. Some scholars believe that this replication of aspects of human behavior and thought processes is one of the reasons that we have music—to simulate, and therefore view from a safe distance, complex issues and interactions.

3.3.7 These Topics, Skills, and Objects Were Introduced in Section 3.3 "Make an Interval"

- The fpic object is used in these interval patches to display image files in formats such as JPG or PNG. It loads images of rectangles with specific colors tied to the interval number, and sizes tied to the exact number of semitones. Ubutton objects overlaid over each fpic object allow you to click on a colored rectangle and listen to how the interval sounds.
- A warning about fpic: it does not automatically embed or save the image files. When using it, make sure to select "Embed Image in Patcher" in the fpic object's Inspector to store the image with the patch and ensure that it doesn't get lost. (A second-best option is to keep the image files in the same folder with the patch. You can also keep them in a separate folder, but you will need to correctly set the "file path" in the Inspector for them to load properly.)
- In patch 3.3 (hidden using the hide on lock feature), a new object called thispatcher is used to resize the Max window. A message of "zoomfactor 0.75" is sent to thispatcher using a loadbang object, to ensure that the patch opens with a zoom of 75 percent. This allows a large number of objects to be viewable right at the beginning, so that all the interval types are on the screen. (A pipe object ensures that the zoom adjustment happens 50 milliseconds after the screen is drawn, which should give the computer enough time to process the command.)

3.4 Name an Interval

Now that you have learned what intervals are and how to construct them, it could be helpful to reinforce this new knowledge by challenging yourself to identify intervals correctly. You can determine the number and quality of an interval a few different ways, such as starting with note names or even directly from the sound itself. Interval identification is an important skill that enables musicians to assess whether their contributions sound right. It allows them to self-correct without the need for external oversight or feedback. By knowing exactly in what way a performance needs to be adjusted, a musician can more efficiently fix any problems that come up. Legendary stories get passed around about great musicians who can discern subtle note errors: Pierre Boulez, onetime conductor of the New York Philharmonic and founder of IRCAM (where the predecessor language to *Max* was invented), was deeply respected for his ability to hear a tiny out-of-place note in the middle of a dense orchestral texture. Many great popular artists also develop a keen sensitivity to pitch and intervals that helps them quickly create and refine their musical work.

3.4.1 Interval "Spelling"

Sample patch 3.4 demonstrates how you can "spell" or identify intervals by number and quality. Open it up and select different note combinations, pairing lower notes with upper notes to form an interval. The text box displays the number and quality of the interval distance spanned by the note names you choose. Test your knowledge when picking your notes to see if you can predict the correct interval name in advance.

Patch 3.4, shown in figure 3.2, allows for quite a few unusual pairings such as F♭ to G♯, and also reveals some of the weird boundary conditions of our interval naming method. The particular quirkiness of the system comes into full effect when using notes that have accidentals. For example, the interval from A up to B♭ is called a minor second, although the same pitches, if renamed A and A♯, would comprise an augmented unison. The interval from B up to D♭ is a diminished third, but by respelling D♭ to its enharmonic equivalent C♯, the same pitches would comprise a major second. This situation is problematic, but at this point, we are somewhat stuck with it due to its widespread adoption. (In some ways, it is similar to the non-optimal arrangement of keys on the computer keyboard layout design, which originated due to an earlier limitation of the mechanical typewriter—the need to avoid crossing and

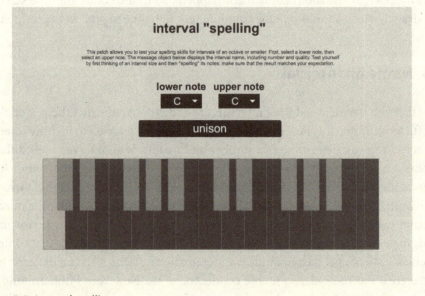

Figure 3.2 Interval spelling

jamming keys.) The worst of the issues with interval spellings can be mostly avoided by minimizing the use of accidentals when possible.[11]

If interval spellings are new to you, it could be helpful to work with patch 3.4 on your own for a few minutes per day. Assign it to yourself for homework. Intervals take a long time to learn and absorb; just reading about them isn't sufficient to internalize and use them fluidly. Just like practicing on an instrument, it helps to do a bit of iterative daily practice in short, intense bursts of time.

In addition to testing your ability to spell intervals, you can also learn to recognize an interval by listening to the way it sounds. This activity can be a bit challenging to start because sound is ephemeral—it fades away quickly, requiring you to develop ways to quickly retain it in your memory. It takes time to learn how to confidently "lock on" to sonic features and connect them to your analytical capabilities. So how do you start to develop facility with auditory interval identification? There are several established techniques that help learners gain a more reliable sense of auditory discernment. In music theory courses, the development of auditory capacities for pitch and interval recognition and production is called aural skills training. Different types of exercises are drilled and practiced including auditory interval identification (ear training), sight-singing on neutral or solfège (do, re, mi, etc.) syllables, writing notes down on blank staff paper (dictation), and sometimes repeating notes back on a keyboard. The ultimate goal of these different activities is to be able to identify and perform intervals without advance preparation, on the spot. It may seem like a daunting prospect if you are at the early stages of aural skills development, but these are critical capacities that are worth building if you want to increase your personal musicianship.

Let's try a few initial experiments in ear training! Go ahead and open up sample patch 3.4a "Interval Ear Training Practice," shown in figure 3.3. This patch is based on a course project originally created by Emily Obenauer, music education major and 2022 graduate from The College of New Jersey; it is used with her permission. Emily designed this code for music students to use for ear training practice—the patch invites users to sing the second note of an indicated interval and determines whether the note is correct or not. The patch starts out in "ascending" mode; this means that all intervals will be counted up from a given starting note. (You can click to select "descending" instead, but beware! Descending intervals tend to be harder to produce. It's probably best to try descending mode after you have gotten comfortable with ascending intervals.)

Click on the yellow circle to hear a starting note; each click here will play a new random note and display a new randomized interval type. If you want to repeat the starting note to practice the interval, you can click on the blue button as many times as you wish. Sing a note matching the intended interval into your laptop microphone input. Your pitch will be measured and compared against the correct note, and the result displayed using highlight colors set in the Inspector settings of the ubutton objects below. Both the starting note and the note you produce are displayed on the kslider object.

112 Constructing Music

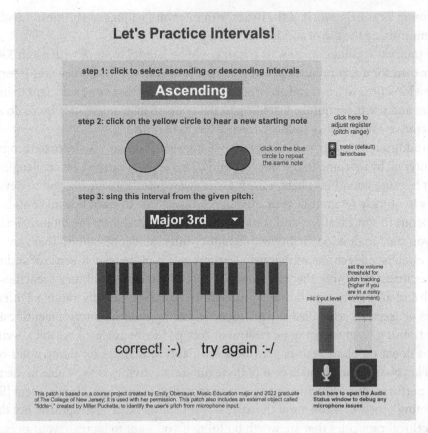

Figure 3.3 Interval ear training practice

Please don't be discouraged if you find this activity challenging![12] Just as with interval spelling, most learners need consistent, repetitive drill and practice to build and retain these foundational ear training skills. It can be helpful to work with this patch on a daily basis; even five minutes per day can go a long way. This will help you develop the capacity called inner hearing: the ability to audiate or perceive intervals silently before producing them. Inner hearing was a core concept in Zoltán Kodály's method of music education, and he defined it this way: "we should read music in the same way that an educated adult will read a book: in silence, but imagining the sound."[13] It is an important skill that enables musicians to determine whether a note is correct or not.

As you work on your sense of inner hearing, you might find it helpful to identify tunes that contain specific intervals; you can use these as mnemonic devices to help you reliably retain and anticipate interval height. (This idea is incorporated into a recommended activity at the end of section 3.4, below.) Another trick is to step through all the intermediate whole and half steps along the way to find your interval; once you get the hang of this skill and begin developing confidence in your perception of intervals, you can then start to group the steps together into successively larger independent leaps. One thing you should try to avoid is to play the second note of the interval on another instrument such as a piano; this may feel good temporarily, but it provides a "crutch" that you might come to rely on that bypasses your inner hearing.

A note about fiddle~, a widely used pitch tracking object that helps to power patch 3.4a: fiddle~ is an example of a *Max* external object. External objects are objects that are not distributed by Cycling '74 with *Max* but are instead created by outside ("third party") individuals and linked into the environment in ways that resemble built-in objects. Because they are defined outside of the official distributed version of the program, they come along with a necessary set of associated helper objects that have extensions such as .mxo, .mxe64, and .maxhelp. A folder has been created to keep all these files together because the patch needs them in order to run. Miller Puckette, the inventor of the software that preceded *Max*, created the fiddle~ external object originally in 1999 for pitch tracking violin sounds in real time. Although fiddle~ is optimized for string instrument timbres, it also works quite well on a range of instruments and voices. Programmers including Isabel Kaspriskie, Ted Apel, David Zicarelli, and Volker Böhm have continued to update fiddle~ and port it to modern computing platforms; it is because of their efforts that we are able to use it here.

3.4.2 These Topics, Skills, and Objects Were Introduced in Section 3.4 "Name an Interval"

- The random object generates a random number between 0 and 1 less than the value of its argument; it is used twice in patch 3.4a, once to generate a random starting note, and once to generate a random interval.
- The fpic object is used in a new way in patch 3.4a to switch the display between indications of ascending or descending mode; it appears as if the same image changes text, but instead different images are swapped out.
- The panel object is used in a new way in patch 3.4a to create a circle image, over which the ubutton creates a clickable area.
- The gswitch object is used in three different places in patch 3.4a: to switch between the two modes of ascending and descending, to ensure that the fiddle~ object only outputs a pitch value when the volume level indicates that the user is purposefully generating sound, and at the bottom to output a correct/incorrect result.
- Activity: As you work on refining your ear training skills, it may help to compile a reference list of familiar tunes that feature specific intervals. Popular examples might include the minor second opening interval in the *Jaws* theme, the major second opening interval in the "Happy Birthday" song, the rising perfect fourth in the *Star Wars* main theme, or the rising perfect fifth interval in "Twinkle Twinkle Little Star." These can serve as mnemonic devices to help you reliably predict interval height, increasing your ability to recognize and generate intervals. Go ahead and create a patch that embeds your favorite tunes with a

series of links to online recordings; you can repurpose the segment of code from tutorial #1 that uses a ubutton object connected to a message object containing the "launchbrowser" command to open a YouTube link. Include as many links as you wish, and customize your patch to make it more inviting. Do what you can to make practicing more fun and engaging, motivating yourself to continue building your skills.[14]

3.5 Make a Scale

In music, a scale is a structured set of intervals that spans an octave, bounded on either end by a lower and upper note called the tonic that serves as the foundational starting pitch. Scales can be thought of as ladders of notes that contain several incremental steps. These steps can have various sizes—usually minor and major seconds, occasionally augmented seconds, and sometimes larger intervals. Unlike the ladders you might use around your home, you have to pay careful attention when running up and down these ladders, so as to not trip on the uneven steps!

The number of steps in a scale is a variable, although the standard number is seven. Five notes are common in the ancient pentatonic scales, covered below. Twelve notes are used in post-tonal music built on the chromatic scale, which comprises only adjacent minor second intervals without any larger steps. There are many different historical and cultural scale patterns; some are in common use and others are quite rare. In this section of the book, we will define several of the most commonly used scale types and simulate them directly using *Max* code to cement our understanding of how they are constructed.

When performing a scale, we usually include the tonic notes at both the top and bottom, one octave apart. This practice helps to frame and define the outer limits of the ladder structure. As a result, we frequently return to the tonic when running up and down the scale steps, in both the ascending and descending directions. The resulting sensation of alternating arrivals and departures feels a little bit like returning home after a trip away and then heading out again. The inclusion of upper and lower tonic notes also expands the seven-note scale pattern to eight notes, which provides a more symmetrical, even-numbered output. This works well for simple metrical patterns, which we will encounter in section 4.2 "Meter," below.

The steps of a scale pattern can be started on any tonic note. Moving a scale pattern from one tonic note to another is called transposition. Transposing a scale shifts the whole pattern up or down; each note is raised or lowered by the same interval as the tonic. Two examples of the same scale pattern are shown in figure 3.4, visualized using piano roll notation in Soundtrap, an online DAW that runs in a web browser. The scale on the left starts on a tonic of C3; the example on the right features the same scale pattern that has been transposed to begin on a tonic of G3.

Additional ladders of eight-note scales can be connected together to extend scalar patterns into higher and lower registers. Most scales contain the same intervals

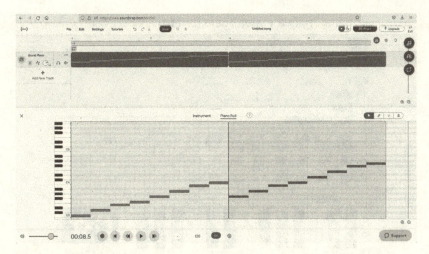

Figure 3.4 Scale pattern transposition in Soundtrap

in ascending and descending forms, although a few include built-in variations featuring changes of direction. (These include the melodic minor scale as well as some Indian ragas, covered below.)

3.5.1 Major Scale Pattern

We will begin by exploring the properties of the major scale. The major scale is a pattern of seven stacked intervals above a tonic that follows this exact sequence: M2 M2 m2 M2 M2 M2 m2. Or, using the whole step (W) and half step (H) convention, W W H W W W H. In MIDI, this pattern is strictly numerical: 2 2 1 2 2 2 1. Proceeding from left to right through the interval steps produces an ascending scale; proceeding backwards from right to left produces a descending scale. Major scales contain seven distinct pitch classes, or eight notes if you include the upper octave.

The way the major scale pattern is often taught to early learners is to play only the lower keys on the piano, starting from C. The upper keys automatically provide spacings of one or two semitones in the right places; by using only the lower keys (and later, remembering those interval spacings), many students gradually start to absorb the basic configuration of the pattern and utilize it with different fingerings and placements on their own instruments, without the physical cues provided by the upper keys.

Now, let's encode the major scale pattern and listen to the result. Open up patch 3.5 "Play a Major Scale" as shown in figure 3.5. This patch extends the code from patch 1.6 in a few specific ways. Play the notes of the major scale by pressing the keys on your computer keyboard or touching the contact points on a Makey Makey. As described in tutorial #6, incoming keystrokes are received by the key object and sorted into separate outputs by the select object. The button objects indicate when a

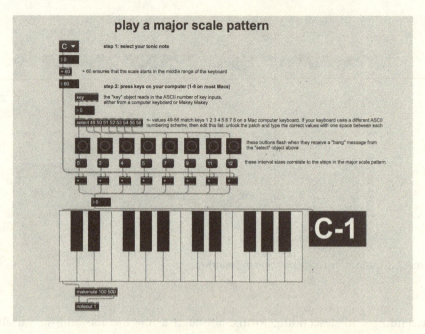

Figure 3.5 Play a major scale pattern

note is triggered. (As was the case in tutorial #6, some computer keyboards use a different numbering scheme. You may need to adjust the arguments in the select object; instructions can be found in the tutorial.)

The starting tonic note in patch 3.5 is middle C, or MIDI note number 60. Step 1 at the top of the patch allows you to change your tonic note and transpose the scale pattern by a fixed interval. Go ahead and try out different tonic notes, noticing how the pattern remains the same while all the notes shift by the same interval.

Numbers 0–12 in the message objects in the center of the patch correspond to the intervals in the major scale pattern. Notice that as you move from left to right across the message objects, the interval numbers increase by amounts that correspond to the major scale pattern: +2 +2 +1 +2 +2 +2 +1. The kslider object displays the pitches of the scale. The number object next to the kslider only displays the sharp symbol (♯) for accidentals, so scales that use flat (♭) accidentals are misspelled with enharmonic equivalents.

For fun, experiment with and modify some of the variables in this patch. Create interesting variations and listen to the result. To transpose the scale one or two octaves higher, add 12 or 24 to the value of 60 in the + object near the top of the patch. Tinker around with the interval numbers 0–12: where two adjacent notes have a difference of two semitones, try changing the interval to one or three semitones. Listen to the sounds and reflect on the different effects that the variable interval qualities cause. (After you learn about other scale types later in this section you can return to this patch, change the pattern to a different type, or invent your own.) Challenge yourself to perform a piece or improvise with your scale for a minute or so. Enjoy a moment of freedom and whimsy! If you like your version of this patch, use File → Save As and give it a new filename to help you locate it later on.

3.5.2 Tetrachords

After playing around with patch 3.5, attentive readers might notice that the major scale pattern contains an inner symmetry in its structure: two smaller groupings of four notes are stacked one on top of the other, separated by a major second in the middle. The intervals in both sets are the same: M2 M2 m2 (+2 +2 +1). These four-note units are called tetrachords: groups of four notes that span the interval of a perfect fourth. Two of these can be stacked together to form eight-note scales. Many different eight-note scale types can be constructed from combinations of two tetrachords, with a spacing of a second interval in between them.

There are four different basic types of tetrachords. They include the major, minor (Dorian), Phrygian (upper minor), and harmonic. Each comprises three intervals of a second that add up to five semitones, with a perfect fourth as the outer interval. These are the four standard tetrachord patterns:

- major tetrachord: M2 M2 m2 (W W H)
- minor (Dorian) tetrachord: M2 m2 M2 (W H W)
- Phrygian (upper minor) tetrachord: m2 M2 M2 (H W W)
- harmonic tetrachord: m2 A2 m2 (H A2 H) (A2 indicates an augmented second)

We can use tetrachords to help us better understand how scales are constructed from smaller groups of notes. As with Legos, first you connect together four individual notes to make a tetrachord pattern, and then you connect together two tetrachords to make an eight-note scale. To experiment with this idea, go ahead and open up patch 3.5a. Here, you can construct scales from tetrachords. First, listen to the different tetrachords in the four panel objects at the bottom of the patch. Use the toggle objects to start and stop playback, and use the umenu objects to select a starting note. Notice that the interval spacings light up as the notes play; this effect is achieved by setting a highlight color for each ubutton object, overlaying a ubutton on each red fpic object, and ensuring that the select object sends a bang message to each ubutton at the correct time. The number objects display the spellings of the notes in each tetrachord.[15] After exploring the four different types of tetrachords ("step 1"), construct a scale by selecting a lower and upper tetrachord ("step 2"), followed by a tonic note ("step 3"). Finally, click on the button to play the resulting scale.

If you are feeling brave, go ahead and take patch 3.5a out of presentation mode to inspect how it is put together! The main structural item to notice is that two gswitch2 objects handle switching between the upper and lower tetrachords for each scale. The gswitch2 object, which you are seeing here for the first time, is similar to the gswitch object—but whereas gswitch has multiple inlets and one outlet, gswitch2 has one inlet and multiple outlets. The radiogroup objects at the top of the patch tell the gswitch2 objects which tetrachord to select.

To create a major scale, pick a major tetrachord for both the lower and upper options. Experiment with other types! (Some common scale types are listed on the right side of the patch with their tetrachord combinations.) As you learn about new scale types below, return back to this patch to construct their tetrachords and listen to the resulting sounds.

3.5.3 Scale Degree Names and Relationships

Until now, we have focused on interval relationships between adjacent notes and tonic endpoints when defining scales. Now that we are hopefully a bit more comfortable with the basic framework of a major scale, it is time to introduce a new level of complexity. The new aspect to observe is that the relationships between notes in a scale don't only occur in a linear progression. That is, in addition to the intervals between adjacent notes, there are other internal scalar relationships to consider. These relationships allow us to more easily hop around the scale steps, perceive their functions within the pattern, and see more clearly the complex web of implied meanings.

To start to make sense of an expanded set of relationships between notes, it can help to assign special names for the pitch class roles that notes inhabit. (It's a bit like saying "Mom" instead of your mother's first name—using a specialized noun for a person denotes the particular role that they occupy in your life.) These names create a layer of abstraction in the form of a generalizable framework that applies to all cases. The naming convention that we will now explore refers to each note in a scale by its scale degree, binding it to a set of intervallic relationships within the scale. As with the use of letter names for notes (A, B, C, D, etc.), using scale degree names can help us more effectively remember their roles.

The first of these scale degree names is the tonic, the starting note of the scale. (We have already encountered this term several times in section 3.5; now it is time to expand that understanding.) The tonic is also called the 1st scale degree, and is often notated with a "caret" symbol above the number (or just to the right), as in: $\hat{1}$. As mentioned above, returning to the tonic reinforces a sense of home, baseline stasis, or resolution. Departing from the tonic creates a sense of tension or heightened emotional intensity, and returning back to it creates a sense of resolution and completion. In this way, scales provide a framework of intervals within which one can experience a sense of internal coherence and balance between sensations of stasis and forward momentum.

In addition to the tonic note, the other scale degrees are named and defined largely by their positions and functions within the scale structure. The supertonic, or 2nd scale degree (notated $\hat{2}$), is so called because it is located directly above the tonic and often leads back down to $\hat{1}$. The mediant, or 3rd scale degree (notated $\hat{3}$), is named to indicate its location midway between the tonic and the 5th scale degree, the two most important scale elements. The subdominant, or 4th scale degree (notated $\hat{4}$), is so called because it sits below the dominant; it often functions as a tendency tone that leads to $\hat{3}$. The dominant, or 5th scale degree (notated $\hat{5}$), is second only to the tonic in its importance within the scalar framework. The submediant, or 6th scale degree (notated $\hat{6}$), is so called because it is the mediant (3rd scale degree) of the scale built upon the subdominant; in its lowered form, it leads strongly to the dominant. The subtonic, or the note that sits a whole step below the tonic, represents the lowered form of the 7th scale degree (notated $\flat\hat{7}$) and leads strongly to the submediant. Finally, the leading tone, the higher form of the 7th scale degree (notated $\hat{7}$), often functions as a strong tendency tone to the tonic.

It can be challenging to memorize the scale degree names described above, and their associations might not be obvious at first glance. Here is one way to think about why the scale degrees are named the way they are, to make better intuitive sense: try visualizing the tonic note as sitting in the center of a scale, with notes above and below the tonic fanning off to either side. Using this visualization of the structure of a major scale, the supertonic and subtonic share the interval of a major second from the tonic, one in either direction—like mirror opposites. Similarly, the mediant and submediant share the interval of a third from the tonic; one above and one below. Finally, the dominant and subdominant share the interval of a fifth above and below the tonic.[16] These interval inverses of each other have similar scale degree names because they share the same distance to the tonic but from opposite directions.

Composers choose to use specific scale degree relationships in their music to reinforce a sense of tension and resolution and enhance the effect of the storytelling. For example, when Dorothy sings "Somewhere Over the Rainbow" in *The Wizard of Oz*, she establishes and reinforces the tonic with the first two notes, defining a sense of home right from the beginning. The two tonic notes are followed by a leading tone, whose tendency toward the tonic provides additional confirmation that those first two notes indeed defined the home from which she was about to depart. Of course, the tendency of the leading tone to progress toward the tonic is thwarted here, as it leaps down to the dominant scale degree. Perhaps this movement enhances the sense of longing and unfulfilled desire to return home, as it delays the return to the tonic. The large size of the opening rising octave interval also indicates that the character of Dorothy feels a high intensity of emotion; in the Hollywood film, Judy Garland enhanced that expression by giving the higher note a bit more volume and lingering on it just a fraction longer than notated, followed by a more extended expansion of time in the notes that followed. We will explore additional ideas related to scale degree relationships in section 3.7 "Make a Key."

3.5.4 Minor Scale Patterns

After the major scale, the next most important scale type is the minor scale. The minor scale comes in a few different varieties including natural, harmonic, melodic, Dorian, and Phrygian. Each type contains a tweak that nudges it toward a particular nuance: natural minor feels somewhat smooth and uninflected, whereas harmonic minor has a distinctive edge, and melodic minor flips between two different patterns based on the context. The harmonic minor scale is also known as the Hijaz, a scale pattern that is ubiquitous in the Middle East and North Africa. The Dorian scale is popular in jazz, funk, and blues styles, whereas Phrygian is commonly used in trap music and flamenco. (Dorian and Phrygian will be covered in detail below, alongside the other modal scales.) Ultimately, the purpose of having different types of scale patterns is to keep your music sounding fresh by enabling lots of variety to attract the attention of the audience. We will start with natural minor, which is the simplest of the three.

The natural minor scale is a pattern of seven intervals stacked above a tonic with this exact sequence: M2 m2 M2 M2 m2 M2 M2. Or, using the whole step (W) and half step (H) convention: W H W W H W W. In MIDI, this pattern is strictly numerical: 2 1 2 2 1 2 2. A careful reader might notice that the tetrachord symmetry of the major scale is missing here. The natural minor scale is constructed out of two different tetrachords: the minor tetrachord (M2 m2 M2) on the bottom, and the Phrygian (upper minor) tetrachord (m2 M2 M2) on the top. If you begin the natural minor scale on a tonic of F♯, you get these notes: F♯ G♯ A B C♯ D E F♯.

There is another way to think about building the natural minor scale: use the major scale pattern, but start on the 6th scale degree (submediant) and reassign it to be your tonic. In other words, the natural minor scale consists of the same elements as the major scale, just starting from the 6th scale degree in the pattern and wrapping around. All the varieties of the minor scale are related to the major scale pattern in this way, with small tweaks as described above. (For this reason, each minor scale can be described as the relative minor of a major scale.)

The harmonic minor scale, or the Hijaz, varies the natural minor scale pattern; building it requires making two modifications from natural minor: the last two intervals, two whole steps in natural minor, are replaced by a larger interval (an augmented second) and a smaller interval (a minor second). Applying MIDI numbers for these intervals, you get: 2 1 2 2 1 3 1. If you begin this form of the minor scale on a tonic of G, you get these notes: G A B♭ C D E♭ F♯ G.

In the harmonic minor scale, the total number of semitones in the scale remains the same as in natural minor, but the top two intervals are resized—one larger and one smaller. A careful reader may notice that the lower tetrachord here is the minor tetrachord (same as in natural minor), but the upper tetrachord is new: the harmonic tetrachord (m2 A2 m2). You can think about this change as raising the 7th scale degree ($\hat{7}$). The resulting effect is an increase in emotional intensity; whereas the two consecutive whole steps of the natural minor pattern feel somewhat ordinary and expected, the expanded size of the augmented second (even though it only changes one semitone) requires extra effort to produce. The change of the 7th scale degree from a subtonic in the natural minor scale to a leading tone in harmonic minor causes an increase in the sensation of a gravitational pull toward the tonic. Although the effect of such a small variation in the placement of a note might seem trivial, it nonetheless significantly influences the way that this scale sounds and feels. The harmonic minor scale tends to convey a greater intensity and heightened sense of emotion when compared with natural minor. The raised 7th scale degree is also the reason why this scale is often called "harmonic" minor: the existence of a leading tone means that this scale includes a built-in dominant chord that creates tension and contrast with the tonic chord. We will address how to construct chords in section 3.6 "Make a Chord" and harmonic relationships in section 4.5 "Make a Harmonic Progression."

Melodic minor provides yet another strategic variation on the minor scale pattern. It combines two different scale patterns—one ascending, and one descending. On the ascending side, the top three intervals are modified from natural minor: M2 m2 M2 M2 M2 M2 m2. This pattern can also be expressed as W H W W W W H or 2 1 2 2 2 2 1. The descending form reverts back to natural minor, following this contour: raise the last two steps (the 6th and 7th scale degrees) on the way up, and lower them on the way back down. If you begin the ascending melodic minor form of the minor scale on a tonic of A, you get these notes: A B C D E F♯ G♯ A; on the descending side, use G♮ and F♮.

A careful reader may notice that the lower tetrachord in the melodic minor scale is the same as that in the natural minor scale (the minor tetrachord), but the upper tetrachord is the same as in the major scale (the major tetrachord). On the descending side, the scale reverts back to the natural minor pattern (Phrygian tetrachord on top, minor tetrachord on the bottom).

These different "flavors" of the minor scale provide musical contrast to keeps things interesting and avoid the stagnation of excessive repetition. Ultimately, music provides our brains with a pleasurable set of signals on which to focus our attention. The human imagination starts to tune out musical signals when they become either too stable and repetitive, or on the opposite side, too noisy or chaotic. Having a range of various scales on hand allows composers to swap out and change up the design of their musical patterns and refresh our senses with new information to absorb and enjoy.

3.5.5 Pentatonic Scale Patterns

A pentatonic scale pattern contains five notes (six if you include both tonics). In comparison to the seven-note scales we have encountered so far, these scales feature empty spots where steps are skipped. For this reason, pentatonic scales belong to a class of scales sometimes described as "gapped" or "incomplete"; they contain at least one adjacent interval larger than a second. In contrast to seven-note scales, pentatonic scales can create a sense of flexibility or openness due to those missing notes. Pentatonic scales are prominently featured among pop and rock and roll melodies, and are thought to have ancient origins. They have been documented in worldwide musical traditions, and it is likely that many historical melodies were pentatonic in nature, containing only steps of major seconds and minor thirds.[17] Sometimes, pentatonic music has been used to evoke a sense of ancientness or otherness; this tendency can edge toward exoticism, at times racist in its reductive depiction of the other as simple.

There are five basic types of the pentatonic scale. We won't cover them all now, although sample patch 3.5b includes all five types. For now, we will review the most commonly used type, often called the major pentatonic scale (or type 1). Its interval pattern is M2 M2 m3 M2 m3 (or, counting semitones in MIDI: 2 2 3 2 3). This corresponds to scale degrees $\hat{1}$ $\hat{2}$ $\hat{3}$ $\hat{5}$ $\hat{6}$ in the major scale. If you begin this form of the pentatonic scale on a tonic of D, you get these notes: D E F♯ A B D. Music theorists have observed that if you stack up a sequence of five consecutive ascending perfect fifth intervals (for example, D → A → E → B → F♯), you will end up with the same notes in the major pentatonic scale, spread across different registers. (If you then reduce those notes to pitch classes fitting within a single octave, you can list them in scale order.)

The singer Bobby McFerrin demonstrated the powerful pull of pentatonic scales in a presentation he gave at the World Science Festival in 2009. The video of his segment is worth watching: https://youtu.be/S0kCUss0g9Q?t=3534. In this example, he hops around the stage to define locations corresponding to notes in the scale. McFerrin seemingly effortlessly elicits a type 1 pentatonic scale from his audience without preparation, using a few movements, some vocal feedback, but no instructions! By moving his body to locations on the stage, sometimes while singing, sometimes not, he sets up a situation in which presenting the notes in a particular order leads the audience to expect and unanimously agree on what note comes next. In particular, here were his steps:

- establishing and alternating $\hat{1}$ and $\hat{2}$ leads to a higher expectation of $\hat{3}$
- noodling around $\hat{1}$, $\hat{2}$, $\hat{3}$ and landing on $\hat{6}$ below leads to a lower expectation of $\hat{5}$.
- from $\hat{5}$, the lower expectation leads to $\hat{3}$ and then $\hat{2}$ below.

McFerrin's presentation was part of a conference in which leading musical scholars were invited to debate whether our responses to music are hard-wired or culturally determined.[18]

3.5.6 Modal Scales and the Diatonic Pattern

Let's return once more to the arrangement of the lower keys on the piano keyboard that helped us define the C major scale pattern above. In between the seven-note sequence C D E F G A B, the five upper keys have been purposefully placed in their own interstitial repeating sequence: C♯ D♯ F♯ G♯ A♯. The upper keys are distributed within the lower ones in two groups: starting from C and ascending upward for an octave, three lower keys surround two upper keys, followed by four lower keys surrounding three upper keys. Looking up and down the piano keyboard, you will see that these groupings repeat across the seven full octaves (plus four additional notes) that comprise the 88-key standard layout.

This arrangement of keys, sometimes called the "seven plus five" layout, was first devised in the fourteenth century to simplify the performance of major scales on the organ.[19] This pattern has another name that we haven't used yet: diatonic. The word diatonic refers to a configuration of seven notes that fit within an octave, including interval spacings of five major seconds and two minor seconds, where the minor seconds are separated as far as possible from one another.

You can think of the upper keys on the piano as representing spacing intervals for the diatonic pattern built on a tonic of C. The diatonic pattern is shared by the major scale, the natural minor scale, and a group of scalar patterns called the modes (sometimes also called the diatonic modes, church modes, or Gregorian modes). As with the major and minor scales, the modes contain seven distinct pitch classes; the inclusion of an upper tonic completes the pattern with eight total notes.

The modes have a long history in European religious music dating back over a thousand years, and they continue to be used in popular music today. We will skip the interesting historical bits here and efficiently get to the point: the modes are constructed by rotating the diatonic pattern. That is, you can start the diatonic scale pattern on different scale degrees, reassigning the tonic to any of the seven notes. The diatonic pattern continues to provide the framework of whole steps and half steps, with the tonic note reassigned as a changeable variable.

If you choose your tonic to be the first scale degree of the diatonic pattern, the result is a major scale. But you can choose your tonic to be any other note in the pattern, resulting in a set of closely related scales. Regardless of which note you choose to serve as the tonic, you get a full octave scale by wrapping the pattern around and extending it into adjoining higher octaves as needed. It can help to think about the diatonic pattern as a loop or a bracelet with seven beads that can be slipped around to the other side so that any of them can be the first element in the pattern.

For example, Dorian mode starts on the second step of the diatonic pattern. Dorian is very popular these days because of its common usage in styles such as rhythm & blues and funk. It features this set of intervals above the tonic: W H W W W H W. A careful reader might notice that this is nearly the same as the major scale pattern, with one exception: the whole step interval that was on the bottom of the major scale has now wrapped around and moved up to the top of the Dorian scale. The whole sequence of intervals has been translated over by one step. This translation happens for each of the modes, as you step through each of the scale degrees in the diatonic pattern. Table 3.1 contains a list of the modes and their interval patterns (with W for whole step and H for half step).

Table 3.1 Modal scales with corresponding interval patterns

Ionian	W	W	H	W	W	W	H
Dorian	W	H	W	W	W	H	W
Phrygian	H	W	W	W	H	W	W
Lydian	W	W	W	H	W	W	H
Mixolydian	W	W	H	W	W	H	W
Aeolian	W	H	W	W	H	W	W
Locrian	H	W	W	H	W	W	W

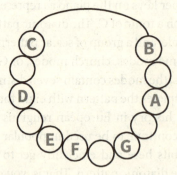

Figure 3.6 Mode bracelet metaphor

Notice how, as you move down through the rows of table 3.1, the whole pattern shifts to the left. At each row, the leftmost step (W or H) from the mode above jumps all the way to the right side of the neighboring mode below it. However, the way that Ws and Hs are listed makes it hard to distinguish visually. Instead, it may be more intuitive to visualize the set of modes using the metaphor of beads on a looped string, as described above. Using the bracelet idea, any of the beads can be slipped around to the other side to become the first element in the pattern.

This idea is sketched out in the drawing shown in figure 3.6. In this arrangement, whole steps are indicated with empty beads in between letter-named notes. Beads can slide across the empty spot on the top of the loop, and the sequence can start on any letter.

Notice also that each of the modes has its own unique set of tetrachords. Dorian mode consists of two stacked minor tetrachords (W H W); Phrygian mode consists of two stacked Phrygian tetrachords (H W W); Lydian mode consists of an unnamed tetrachord on the bottom (W W W) and a major tetrachord on top (W W H) separated by a half step. Mixolydian mode has a major tetrachord on the bottom (W W H) and a minor tetrachord on top (W H W). Locrian mode, the least used of all the modes due to a dissonant tritone in place of the usual tonic-dominant perfect fifth, has a Phrygian tetrachord on the bottom and the same unnamed tetrachord (W W W) shared with Lydian mode, on the top.

You can think about the modes simply as the collection of lower keys on the piano starting from any note. For example, Dorian mode may be thought of as the set of lower keys starting on D. However, this way of understanding the modes enables a common misconception to persist that we should avoid: because modes are often associated with lower-key starting notes, some students think Dorian mode always has a tonic of D, Phrygian mode always has a tonic of E, etc. Instead, you should think about Dorian mode as an interval pattern that can be visualized using the lower keys starting on D, and similarly, Mixolydian mode as an interval pattern that can be visualized using the lower keys starting on G. Meanwhile, it's important to remember that each of the modes can be constructed on any note.

To start any of the modes on any note, just build the interval pattern beginning on your intended tonic. For example, applying the Dorian mode interval pattern (W H W W W H W) to a tonic note of F, you get these notes: F G A♭ B♭ C D E♭ F. Or, if you want to start the Mixolydian mode interval pattern on a tonic note of C, you get these notes: C D E F G A B♭ C. Using the chart of interval patterns shown in Table 3.1 above, try playing a few modes starting from arbitrary tonics. (The kslider object in patch 3.5 can provide a helpful way to explore this idea.) Test yourself and see if you can select the correct notes to match the whole and half steps in each pattern.

As you play around and listen to the different modes, you might notice that they share similarities with the more familiar major and minor scales, with one or a few differences. For example, Dorian mode sounds a lot like natural minor, with one difference: it has a raised 6th scale degree. That one change is subtle but adds just enough variety that it strikes the listener as different. Dorian mode is often used in films and video games to establish a sense of ancientness, reference the Medieval/Renaissance time period, or evoke a land out of time, as in the Legend of Zelda game series.

Similarly, Mixolydian mode resembles the major scale, with the one difference of a lowered 7th scale degree. As a result, Mixolydian sounds like major with a subtonic. This reduces the powerful pull of the leading tone toward the tonic and results in a more relaxed aspect. Mixolydian mode was frequently used in rock music of the 1960s and 1970s, such as "Norwegian Wood" by the Beatles. A more recent example of music written in Mixolydian includes "Clocks" by Coldplay.

One final point to make about modes is that they combine well together; this is known as modal mixture. (Once that diatonic wheel starts to spin, it often likes to keep on going!) As you move up and down a scale, you can mix and match all sorts of patterns into successive ascending and descending phrases, providing ever-renewing variations that keep your audience on their toes.[20]

3.5.7 Other Scale Patterns

There are many different types of scales out there to be explored! It's fun to create your own scales, or to seek out unusual examples. They can add freshness to your music, sources of inspiration, and new ideas. One scale that is worth investigating further is the whole-tone scale; it has six notes, each a M2 apart. This scale gained some popularity in the early twentieth century among European composers who were interested in experimenting with "orientalist" and exotic sounds. (One such example can be found in *Jeux* by Debussy, a musical poem written for dancers in the Russian Ballet.) Another slightly rare example is the octatonic scale, which is constructed using alternating whole steps and half steps. It is often associated with Russian composers of the late nineteenth and early twentieth centuries who were trying to create music that was both emotionally expressive and strikingly modern. (Examples can be found in Stravinsky's *Rite of Spring*, as well as works by Scriabin, Rimsky-Korsakov, Rachmaninoff, and in the haunting trumpet solo for Charles Ives's *The Unanswered Question*.)

Sample patch 3.5b provides a way to easily compare and switch between the many different scale types that have been discussed in this "Make a Scale" section of the book. Go ahead and open the patch, select a tonic note, and choose from among the nineteen scale types listed. Play the notes of each scale exactly as you did in patch 3.5; press the same keys on your computer or Makey Makey and make any necessary adjustments to the arguments in the select object. A radiogroup object allows you to choose your scale type, and the new coll object stores all the scale patterns. A row of number objects displays the pitch names of all the scale degrees. To view or modify the scale patterns, take this patch out of presentation mode but make sure that it remains in patching mode. Then, double-click on the coll object; this will open up a window displaying its contents. Each row lists the numerical scale degrees of each scale type; coll outputs these numbers as a list when it receives a number corresponding to one of its rows. Add new scale types here if you wish; this coll object is set to save its data with this patch (via its Inspector). The coll object provides a way to structure and organize the scale data so that you can apply each scale as a pattern instead of manually typing in each note. (You can implement the pattern once and then compute the notes based on whatever tonic is currently selected.[21])

Using the patches that have been provided in this section (3.5, 3.5a, and 3.5b), give yourself permission to experiment with the standard scale patterns! Cobble together bits of code to explore unusual scale patterns. Invent your own unique scale types, and allow them to inspire you to generate new creative ideas.

3.5.8 Ragas

Many different scale types have been developed in cultures and traditions around the world; some are quite ancient, and some are newer. But the musical cultures of

South Asia are particularly admired for their innovative designs of scale patterns and the abundant melodic variety that results. These scale forms are known as ragas or raags; you can learn about their profuse forms in two distinct classical genres that coevolved on the Indian subcontinent: the Hindustani music of North India and the Carnatic tradition in South India. The content that follows is not a comprehensive survey of these traditions but rather an introduction to the basic concepts.

The Hindustani tradition provides a large body of literature and performance practices on which there is much consensus, although as with many cultural traditions, there are points of disagreement and controversy. Over a thousand ragas have been documented, although the exact number is not known. They exist within a comprehensive system that organizes them according to their features. Ragas share similarities with the scale types described earlier in this section, and they also incorporate unique components that are not included in other scale systems. The Hindustani system essentially shares the same seven diatonic scale steps and twelve semitones that have been described previously, although there are some differences around tuning (including shrutis, or microtones) and various ways to move between adjacent notes. The set of seven basic scale degrees that comprise the major scale (diatonic collection) are called the saptak in the Hindustani system, and the individual notes of the scale are called the shuddh swaras, or pure (correct) notes.

The Hindustani system organizes the types of scale patterns into scale families called thaats. There are ten basic thaats that are categorized by sequences of interval steps (including sharps and flats), similar to the scale types defined above. Ragas are individual variants derived from these thaats; they each incorporate unique modifications that utilize the notes of the thaat in which they belong. Most ragas include 7, 6, or 5 notes, and sometimes they add or skip specific notes or feature characteristic melodic contours. Ragas provide a structure for the melodic material that a Hindustani classical musician can use to perform a composition. The structure often includes a set of syntactical rules that determine the way that certain notes are to be prioritized, the order in which notes can be sequenced (chalan), and conventions about how to arrive at and depart from notes in ascending and/or descending directions. Ragas are defined by a set of allowable ornamental devices, tuning variations, and specific melodic patterns (pakads). They are also associated with specific moods, times of day, and seasons.

This elaborate set of definitions and expectations imparts special identities onto specific ragas, not unlike characters in a play or musical character themes (Leitmotivs), which will be discussed in Chapter 4. It also imparts an aspect of "gamifying" the listening experience in a live performance: one of the joys of listening to a Hindustani music concert is identifying the raga as it unfolds during the early part of the composition. Once all the notes in the thaat have been performed, the presence of certain melodic patterns and other identifying elements provides a breadcrumb trail of clues that the audience can use to arrive at the correct conclusion. (This experience is a bit like reading an Agatha Christie murder mystery;

sometimes the artist will purposefully lead you astray and distract you with spurious clues before arriving at the definitive solution.)

Compositions in the Hindustani tradition are partly improvised and partly based on fragments of traditional fixed compositions (bandishes) with poetic texts that impart additional cultural or emotional meaning. Not unlike jazz and other music traditions that incorporate improvisation, one of the goals of a performing artist is to establish a musical reference and then reinforce it with increasingly complex levels of variation before landing back on a resolution. In the traditional teaching method, also called the guru-shishya parampara, the teacher instructs the student by slowly elucidating the notes of the raga with increasing melodic expansion and variation, eventually ending up at the bandish along with a set of alankaras, or prepared melodic improvisational materials that can be connected and combined in different ways.

Having established some basic information about ragas and how they are constructed, we will now investigate an initial example: Raga Bhairav. It belongs to the thaat that is also called Bhairav, for which it is the defining raga. Bhairav thaat is comprised of two stacked harmonic tetrachords with lowered scale degrees: $\hat{2}$ and $\hat{6}$. (The rest of the notes are shuddh, corresponding to the major scale.) Lowering the second and sixth scale degrees causes an augmented second interval in both the top and bottom half of the scale; this sounds similar to the upper part of the harmonic minor scale. Raga Bhairav contains all seven notes in the scale, and its intervals therefore have this pattern: m2 A2 m2 M2 m2 A2 m2. If you build this raga as if it were a scale with a tonic note of D, here are the notes you will get: D E♭ F♯ G A B♭ C♯ D. Bhairav is characterized by a stepwise progression of notes (a straight chalan); passages typically progress without many changes of direction. Its most important note is $\hat{6}$ and its second-most important note is $\hat{2}$, both of which take the lowered form. Characteristic melodic patterns (pakads) include examples such as $\hat{3}$ $\hat{4}$ $\hat{6}$ $\hat{6}$ $\hat{5}$, $\hat{3}$ $\hat{4}$ $\hat{2}$ $\hat{2}$ $\hat{1}$, and $\hat{5}$ $\hat{6}$ $\hat{4}$ $\hat{5}$ $\hat{4}$ $\hat{3}$ $\hat{4}$ $\hat{2}$ $\hat{1}$. Raga Bhairav is typically performed in the early morning, and it can be sung in any season. Its mood is associated with seriousness but also calm. It is often used for devotional music. You can listen to the basic notes of Raga Bhairav by opening patch 3.5a and selecting the harmonic tetrachord for both the lower and the upper tetrachords.

Scales and ragas represent important ways to organize musical structure. Take some time to explore the many available options and listen to how the subtle ordering of intervals affects nuances in the music that results. Give yourself permission to experiment with the different scale types and explore new musical ideas. You can modify the code from the patches in this section to create new options and try them out.

3.5.9 These Topics, Skills, and Objects Were Introduced in Section 3.5 "Make a Scale"

- The gswitch2 object is used in patch 3.5a "Make a Scale from Tetrachords" to switch between the different tetrachords in the lower and upper positions of

the scale. It functions similarly to the gswitch object, with the difference that the original gswitch selects among multiple inlets to send to one outlet, whereas gswitch2 sends from one inlet to one of multiple outlets.
- The coll object, introduced in patch 3.5b, stores and edits a collection of data as a text file. Individual data elements are indexed by row number. Double-clicking on the coll object while the patch is locked will open the editing window, allowing modifications to be made. Select "Set Data with Patcher" in the coll object's Inspector to ensure that coll data remains with the patch; otherwise, data must be saved as a separate text file.
- Activity: there are additional tetrachord types that are theoretically possible but not represented among the four basic types listed in patch 3.5a. How might you modify patch 3.5a to construct them and listen to the result?

3.6 Make a Chord

Now that we have defined lots of different intervals and scale types, let's turn our attention to the structures that interact with them. The first of these is the chord. What is a chord? Metaphorically, it is a sonic pillar. Like the ancient Greek columns in the Parthenon or the Persian columns of Persepolis, chords are designed to hold up the roof of a piece of music so that the horizontal aspects can proceed unimpeded. Like marble pillars, chords provide helpful stability and context that supports time-based structures and allows them to soar.

Chords serve as the basic building-blocks of harmony: the system we use to organize how simultaneous notes relate to each other along the vertical dimension of music. Harmony usually begins with the structuring of chords, which are the labels we use to describe the simultaneous sounding of two or more notes together. Individual notes interact with each other to create intervals; when multiple intervals stack up to create chords, we ascribe qualitative associations to them. Harmony also has a horizontal aspect called harmonic progression, which we will encounter in section 4.5 "Make a Harmonic Progression."

Typically, in everyday tonality (general tonal practice), chords are constructed by stacking successive third intervals. The most common chords have three pitch classes; the prefix "tri-" means three (from both Greek and Latin), and for that reason these three-note chords are called triads. When triads are tightly stacked in adjoining thirds, the bottom note is called the root and the triad is considered to be in root position. (The note that serves as the root note is often used to name the chord.) The middle note is called the third because it occupies the position a third above the root when the chord is in root position. (The third is the only chord element that belongs to both the bottom third and top third of the triad.) The top note is called the fifth because it is an interval of a fifth above the root in root position. We typically define the quality of a triad by identifying its lower third (from root to third), its upper third (from third to fifth), and outer fifth (from root to fifth).

The adjacent thirds in a chord can be swapped around to different registral placements called inversions, where other chord tones besides the root occupy the lowest note positions. When the third (middle note) of the chord is on the bottom, the triad is said to be in first inversion. When the fifth (top note) of the chord is on the bottom, the triad is said to be in second inversion. Additional thirds can be stacked above the fifth, including sevenths, ninths, elevenths, and thirteenths. Each of these larger chords has its own set of inversions—the number of possible inversions available for a chord is determined by the number of notes it contains. (Any note can be the bottom note.)

Like intervals and scales, chords are characterized by the number of notes they contain and the exact steps that are used to construct them. Chords are usually referred to by root note and *quality*, determined by the interval relationships between the notes in the chord. Next, we will enumerate these variables for the most common chords, starting with the four main types of triads. As you read through this section, open up patch 3.6 "Make a Chord" and explore the different chord types and interval relationships. Click on the colored blocks to hear the ways in which individual notes relate to each other to create a coherent pattern and quality.

The most common triad quality is the major triad. It consists of a major third on the bottom and a minor third on top. For example, if you build a major triad on a root of F♯, you get the three notes F♯, A♯, and C♯.

The next most common triad quality is the minor triad. You construct it by inverting the structure of the major triad—start with a minor third on the bottom and then place a major third on top. The notes in a minor triad built on a root of F♯ are F♯, A, and C♯. While major and minor triads stack their thirds in opposite order, they share the same outer interval of a perfect fifth.

Two more examples complete the set of four basic triads. In these latter two triad types, the outer fifth is not perfect. Perhaps for this reason, they are not quite as commonly used as the ubiquitous major and minor chords. The first of these, which is still fairly commonly used, is the diminished triad. It consists of two stacked minor thirds. As a result of both thirds being minor, the outer interval is a diminished fifth. The notes in a diminished triad built on a root of F♯ are F♯, A, and C. The diminished triad is considered to be dissonant and strongly leads toward a harmonic resolution. Because its outer interval, a tritone, was considered to have diabolical connotations in earlier times, European music in the common practice period almost never featured this triad in root position. Much more commonly, the diminished triad was voiced in first inversion because that is the only position in which it does not contain a tritone interval with its bottom note. (In first inversion, the diminished triad features a minor third and major sixth above the bottom note.)

The augmented triad consists of two stacked major thirds. Because of its larger inner intervals, the outer interval that frames the whole chord is an augmented fifth. The notes in an augmented triad built on a root of F♯ are F♯, A♯, and C♯♯. Although the augmented triad is considered to be dissonant, popular groups such as the Beatles,

Chuck Berry, and the Beach Boys sometimes used augmented chords to achieve specific effects. Augmented chords, because of their dissonance, have a strong tendency to resolve toward other chords.

3.6.1 Seventh Chords

After the basic three-note triads, the next most common chords contain four notes. These are called seventh chords because they feature intervals above the root of a third, fifth, and seventh. Like triads, seventh chords are constructed out of consecutive stacked thirds, where the top note of each third interval becomes the bottom note of the next higher third. The outer interval from lowest to highest note in root position is a seventh. The five different basic seventh chord types are listed below from largest to smallest; notice that as you progress from one type to the next, one of the intervals changes its quality.

The major 7th chord, also known as the major-major 7th chord, consists of a major triad plus a major seventh interval above the root note. You typically see this chord constructed using the tonic note or the subdominant note as the root.

The major-minor 7th chord, also known as the dominant 7th chord because of its association with the dominant scale degree, consists of a major triad plus a minor seventh interval above the root note. It is the most commonly used of the seventh chord types. The most basic construction of this chord uses the 5th scale degree for its root, although a dominant seventh chord can be created on any scale degree by using accidentals. Originating with the African American blues tradition, many twentieth-century popular music styles have routinely featured major-minor 7th chords on the 1st and 4th scale degrees. (This was especially true in early rock and roll songs by artists such as Chuck Berry and Little Richard and later emulated by groups such as the Beatles.[22])

The minor 7th chord, also known as the minor-minor seventh, consists of a minor triad and a minor seventh interval above the root note. In the European classical tradition, this chord is typically constructed on the supertonic, mediant, or submediant scale degrees; in popular music styles, it also commonly appears on the tonic, subdominant, and dominant chords.

The half-diminished 7th chord consists of a diminished triad and a minor seventh interval above the root note. You typically see this chord constructed using the leading tone scale degree as the root note.

The fully diminished 7th chord consists of a diminished triad and a diminished seventh interval above the root note. You typically see this chord constructed on the leading tone as the root, but with the 7th interval reduced by one semitone using an accidental. This chord is also frequently written in first inversion, similar to the diminished triad listed above. (The fully diminished 7th chord is often used to accelerate harmonic motion toward a cadence, or as a pivot to a "secondary dominant"—an altered chord that helps "modulate" to a new key.)

132 Constructing Music

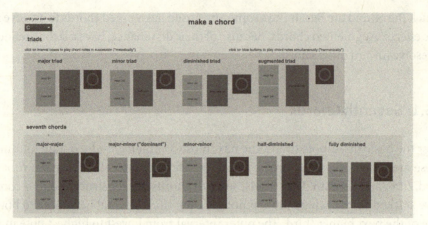

Figure 3.7 Make a chord

Patch 3.6 "Make a Chord," shown in figure 3.7, demonstrates how to construct triads and seventh chords using the same color blocks that were first introduced in patch 3.3 "Make an Interval." Notice that colors here represent interval numbers (third, fifth, etc.), whereas interval sizes are indicated by the height of the rectangle. Using this scheme, smaller intervals are shorter, and larger intervals are taller. Presentation mode hides quite a few of the complexities "under the hood." Observe the use of design elements in this user interface, including color, typeface, and the arrangement of objects together on the screen. Once you have explored the front panel, go ahead and take the patch out of presentation mode to see how it is put together.

3.6.2 These Topics, Skills, and Objects Were Introduced in Section 3.6 "Make a Chord"

- There are, of course, many other varieties of chords that we have not had time to address here; extend the functionality in patch 3.6 by creating your own chords and listening to their qualities.
- Activity: The Stradella Bass System is a series of buttons that are arranged in columns on the left-hand side of an accordion; musicians press these buttons to trigger chord playback. How might you create a *Max* patch that creates a similar arrangement, laying out a range of chords in an organized, easy-to-use structure? (Then, how might you implement inversions for each chord?)
- Activity: Make a *Max* patch to experiment with quartal harmony, making chords out of fourth intervals.

3.7 Make a Key

Now that you have started learning how to construct intervals, scales, and chords, you may be ready to encounter the concept of musical keys. Even if you are not completely confident in all the details yet, please do not worry. We have covered a lot of content in this chapter, and it may take some steady, iterative review for you to feel like you have a solid grasp over it. Feel free to loop back and tinker with any of the previous sections or code examples in this chapter for helpful refreshers as you proceed through this section.

The key of a musical passage is an abstract idea that encompasses a unified set of notes, intervals, scales, and chords. A key is defined as the orientation of all the pitch-based structures around a local tonic that serves as a metaphorical "home." In the shared tonal system called everyday tonality, most chordal and melodic patterns share a tendency to eventually return back to the tonic. Keys provide hierarchical structures that define how notes should function in relationship to each other; they frame the diatonic pattern and establish a tonic note that forms the foundation of that structure. (Using another analogy, the key of a piece of music metaphorically "unlocks" hidden relationships in the underlying framework within which musical meaning and coherence can be found.[23] The key gives a piece its tonal identity.)

Some composers emphasize the ephemeral qualities of keys and associate them with emotions, colors, or personality characteristics. Composers sometimes have a favorite key within which they like to work, or that they associate with features that they can apply to create a particular effect. Musicians who have perfect pitch or synesthesia, a condition in which the senses are fused, might also have fixed associations with keys that are consistent and specific.[24]

A key comprises a diatonic set of notes. The presence of a key allows you to identify the scalar patterns and chords that fit within it. In any key, the most commonly used modes are major (Ionian), minor (Aeolian), and Dorian. The major mode starts on the tonic of the key, the minor mode starts on the 6th scale degree, and Dorian mode starts on the 2nd scale degree. (The modes are "related" to each other because they share the same notes but different tonics; for example, the A minor scale is the relative minor of C major, whereas G major is the relative major of E minor.)

Our system of tonal organization comprises twelve keys, one for each pitch class. Because of strange overlaps in the letter-note naming convention, we usually include three enharmonically equivalent keys for a total of fifteen. There are three keys that can each be named two different ways: D♭/C♯, G♭/F♯, and C♭/B. Each of the twelve keys preserves its diatonic set of half steps and whole steps by using a unique number of accidentals. The key of C contains only natural notes; it has no sharps or flats. The seven sharp keys include the following: G (one sharp; F♯), D (two sharps; F♯ C♯), A (three sharps; F♯ C♯ G♯), E (four sharps; F♯ C♯ G♯ D♯), B (five sharps; F♯ C♯ G♯ D♯ A♯), F♯ (six sharps; F♯ C♯ G♯ D♯ A♯ E♯), and C♯ (seven sharps; F♯ C♯ G♯ D♯ A♯ E♯ B♯). The seven flat keys include: F (one flat; B♭), B♭ (two flats; B♭ E♭), E♭ (three flats; B♭ E♭ A♭), A♭ (four flats; B♭ E♭ A♭ D♭), D♭ (five flats; B♭ E♭ A♭ D♭ G♭), G♭ (six flats; B♭ E♭ A♭ D♭ G♭ C♭), and C♭ (seven flats; B♭ E♭ A♭ D♭ G♭ C♭ F♭).

The list of accidentals associated with a key is called a key signature; in combination with a tonic note, the key signature defines the exact set of notes that are included in the key. In conventional music theory courses, key signatures are often memorized and drilled because they are necessary components of notated sheet music. For our purposes, we won't memorize and drill these lists of sharps and flats—computer code can do that for us! We just need to understand how they function at a higher level of abstraction and then re-derive them as needed. The following section will show us how to do this.

A careful reader may have noticed a pattern in the list of keys above: as you move through the increasing accidentals for the sharp keys, you hop up by the interval of a perfect fifth. It turns out that if you start down at the bottom of the piano keyboard on C and keep hopping consecutively up in perfect fifths, you will hit all twelve chromatic notes, ending up back on C seven octaves higher. Here is how the notes progress upward in fifths from left to right: C–G–D–A–E–B–F#–C#–G#–D#–A#–E#–B# (B# is enharmonically equivalent to C). You can visualize this on the 88 keys of the piano keyboard as a bouncing ball hopping up a perfect fifth interval, twelve times in a row. *Max* patch 3.7 "Circle of fifths" demonstrates how this can happen from low to high (left to right in the piano keyboard) using an 88-key kslider object.

Patch 3.7 works as follows: clicking on the blue button at the top of the patch initiates an ascending sequence of perfect fifths, starting from C0 (MIDI note number 0), all the way up to C6 (MIDI note number 84). The + object adds 7 semitones to each value, which generates each next perfect fifth higher. The pipe object ensures that each note is separated in time by one second. Notice that there is a loop here, going from the pipe object all the way back up to the + object. The loop can be stopped at any time by clicking on the red toggle object on the left-hand side of the patch. The loop is governed by the gswitch object, which we have encountered in earlier code examples. In this patch, the control inlet to gswitch is handled by an object called > ("greater than"), which compares the number arriving in its left inlet with its argument (77). Once the incoming number exceeds 77, > sends a value of 1 to gswitch that tells it to change over to its other inlet track. Because that second inlet track is empty, this effectively shuts off the system, creating an on/off switch that responds to input. Pitch numbers from the outlet of gswitch get sent to the modulo object below.

The function of the modulo object is to divide one number by another and output the remainder, the amount left over after the computation. In this patch, modulo divides all MIDI pitch numbers coming out of the gswitch object by the number twelve. It then outputs a remainder indicating the pitch class of the note, here indexed by number from 0 to 11. (If we had instead used the division arithmetic object in place of modulo, it would have yielded the octave number, or register, of the note.)

Octave equivalent notes can be said to share the same pitch class because they share the same name; they also share the same bindings and associations within the tonal structure and context. For example, the result of dividing middle C (MIDI note number 60) by 12 yields an integer 5, and a remainder of 0. All notes with the pitch class of C happen to be integer multiples of the number 12, and thereby will all have a remainder of 0. Similarly, the result of dividing G4 (MIDI note number 67) by 12 yields 5 with a remainder of 7. All notes with the pitch class of G will output a remainder of 7.

Folding down the octaves using modulo in this way allows us to see that a sequence of twelve consecutive ascending perfect fifths not only lands us back on our starting note, but it also generates all twelve pitch classes. This structuring of pitch relationships is often called the circle of fifths; in recent years, it has also been described as a spiral. The circular arrangement of consecutive fifths, displayed on the right side of patch 3.7, helps reveal how key relationships work. The key of C major, which has no accidentals, is listed at the top. Descending in a clockwise direction from C are the seven "sharp" keys, which slowly increase in their number of sharps: beginning with G (1 sharp) and ending with C♯ (7 sharps). Descending on the other side, in a counterclockwise direction from C, are the seven "flat" keys, beginning with F (1 flat) and ending with C♭ (7 flats). The three overlapping enharmonically equivalent keys are all located at the bottom of the circle.

Hidden under the hood in patch 3.7, all the pitch classes from the left side of the patch are sent over to the right side; bang messages from the select object cause the ubuttons to highlight when their pitch is sounded. The modulo object (with a value of 12 as its argument) provides a compact way to fold down the octave registers so that all twelve notes fit within a one-octave span. This reduces pitch numbers to pitch classes that are independent of octave registration. Instead of spanning seven octaves to hop from C to C by fifths, you can compress all that hopping down to one octave. This is similar to what Music Information Retrieval experts do when identifying pitch by "folding down" the overtone patterns. As mentioned earlier in section 3.3 "Make an Interval," these are sometimes alternatively called chroma, or harmonic pitch class profiles, and can be used to estimate key and harmonic features in audio recordings.

To explore patch 3.7, unlock it and play around with adjusting the variables. To change the pacing of the notes, edit the arguments for both pipe objects by manually replacing 1000 milliseconds with another number. Alternately, you could create a new slider with a range of at least 1000 or 2000 milliseconds, and input that value into the right inlets of the pipe objects. Then, lock up the patch again and control the speed in real time by moving your slider.

Or, you could change the direction of your sequence of perfect fifths. Instead of sweeping up from low to high, you can sweep downward from high to low. If you start from the same top note (84) and hop down in perfect fifths, you will end up at the same bottom note (0) in the same number of steps. Accomplish this by replacing the number 0 in the message object near the top with MIDI note number 84. Then, replace the "+" symbol with "−" and change your "greater than" object (> 77) to a "less than" object (< 7). (In addition, you will also need to delete the patch cord going from the 84 message object to the left inlet of gswitch.) Save and close the patch to reset its state; then open it again. Now, your sequence of fifths should descend from near the top to the bottom of the pitch range. A cool feature of this modification is that the note names around the circle of fifths will highlight in inverse order!

3.7.1 Diatonic Chords

Within any key, there is a standard set of chords that structurally occur on the scale degrees. We can use Roman numerals to identify these chords according to their relationship to the tonic, with uppercase for major and lowercase for minor. (If you prefer instead, you can simply use letter names to indicate the root note of a chord, although its function within the key structure is not indicated that way.) Here is the regular set of diatonic chords within any major key:

- I tonic (major)
- ii supertonic (minor)
- iii mediant (minor)
- IV subdominant (major)
- V dominant (major)
- vi submediant (minor)
- vii° leading tone (diminished)

These Roman numeral labels can be useful when placing chords in relation to each other in a sequence. We will cover this idea in section 4.5 "Make a Harmonic Progression."

3.7.2 The Basis of Tonal Music

In summary, musical keys provide an organizing framework that holds together all the pitch structures we have encountered so far: notes, intervals, scales, and chords. Keys define interdependent systems of relationships between these structures, within which notes are held together by one central pitch class. Similar to the arrangement of planets around a central star in a solar system, the chords and melodies circle around the tonic, are held in fixed orbits in relation to that star, and are affected by its gravity.

This constellation of key relationships defined by the structure of keys forms the basis of the diatonic system or the tonal system. The diatonic system comprises all intervals, scales, and chords that fit within the twelve keys. In the tonal system, each note functions based on its relationship to the tonic. However, quite a bit of flexibility is allowable within those constraints—the use of chromaticism is tolerated and even encouraged, as long as it does not compromise the basic framework within which all tonal music works.

The diatonic system, which is essentially a vertical construct, is stretched out to a horizontal, holistic construct when it is deployed as a key. The diatonic system also, in a way, is greater than the sum of all of its interrelated parts: it includes the relationships of scales to their tonic notes, the melodic possibilities of a scale, and the set of chords that fit within a scale. All of this can get very confusing, so the thing to remember is that the role of the diatonic system is to provide a sense of stability and coherence. Once this pattern is established, it causes a sense of expectation that can then be manipulated and modified for expressive, artistic effect.

3.7.3 These Topics, Skills, and Objects Were Introduced in Section 3.7 "Make a Key"

- The modulo object divides one number by another and outputs the remainder (the amount left over after the computation); it is used in patch 3.7 to create all the pitch classes that define the twelve keys.
- Activity: now that you have started to learn about keys, see if you can apply your knowledge toward a creative goal. Pick any key; C major provides a good, simple starting place. Using a Max patch, keyboard, or other instrument, first play the notes of the C major scale. Then, play the notes of the diatonic chords associated with each of the scale degrees. (The tonic chord contains C, E, and G; the supertonic chord contains D, F, and A; the mediant chord contains E, G, and B, etc.) Create little patterns and play around with these chords to get a sense of how they all fit together within one diatonic system. After noodling around a little bit in the key of C major, try composing a short melody and adding diatonic chords to it. For an extra challenge, repeat the same activity in a different key.

4
Time-based Structures

Next, we will explore how basic musical building blocks and simple pitch-based structures can be grouped together to create intermediate forms that include the element of time. In this chapter, we will engage with aspects such as tempo, meter, melodies, arpeggios, and harmonic progressions. These compound structures require specific sequences of events; sometimes, several consecutive or overlapping steps are involved. (Although the intervals, scales, and chords covered in Chapter 3 also contain "steps," they do not strictly define the order in which those steps must occur over a duration of time.)

The introduction of the time aspect represents a significant shift in emphasis at this point in the book. The vertical (pitch-based) and horizontal (time-based) components of music represent two fundamentally different processes. The vertical element is based on acoustic frequencies, whereas the horizontal is based on patterns that evolve over time. It should be mentioned here that pitch-based structures are strongly emphasized in traditional Western music theory pedagogy. In the classical method of teaching music theory, lessons tend to progress through the pitch-based topics in great detail and cover the rhythmic elements as quickly and compactly as possible. There are good reasons to devote significant attention to the vertical, pitch-based dimension of sound. However, it's also important to understand that the use of time is a critically important element in all forms of music, and therefore it should not be minimized or undervalued.

The topics in this chapter belong to the "time domain" of music. As was first introduced in Chapter 2, you can think of an audio waveform recording as belonging to the time domain, with the progression of time laid out horizontally on the x-axis and the amplitude on the vertical y-axis. Similarly, musical score notation marches horizontally from left to right, reflecting the flow of time in the same direction. Sheet music can be thought of as expressing moments of *discrete* time, or time that is carved up into individually distinct units, whereas an audio waveform is an example of *continuous* time, or the nearly unbroken re-creation of the original vibrations captured from the sound itself. (Although digital audio files are *not* continuous, they simulate continuous audio signals by taking "snapshots" or *samples* of amplitudes at individual moments in time that are so close together as to sound seamless to most listeners.)

Thinking again about the structures of music as combinations of basic Lego building blocks in different configurations, let's now tackle these intermediate topics with continued focus and dedication. Here is where music making starts to actively take shape. It's an exciting moment; we are on the threshold of getting a chance to activate and engage with our creative capacities. We will begin with the important concept of *tempo*.

4.1 Tempo

The word "tempo" simply means "time" in Italian. In a musical context, tempo describes the speed or pacing of sound events. It is a variable that defines the rate at which consecutive beats arrive. In some contexts, the terms "tempo" and "beat" are used interchangeably to mean the same thing. However, we will make a clear distinction between the two: a beat is a single pulse, whereas tempo describes the speed of playback of multiple consecutive beats.

The rate at which beats occur is calculated as the number of beats per unit of time. It can be steady and unchanging, as in settings on digital metronomes and DAW transport controls, or it can be flexible, as in certain styles of acoustic music where the tempo ebbs and flows in synchrony with the emotional energy of the performers. In some cases, time-based tempo variation is intentional and planned, as in *rubato*, where the tempo is purposefully fluctuated to emphasize important musical elements for expressive effect. Rubato means "stolen" in Italian, and refers to the "stealing" of time internally by speeding up and slowing down locally in a way that balances out and eventually returns to the original tempo of the piece. Playing with time and shaping phrases with rubato is a valued part of the performance practice in classical music. In that context, tempo doesn't usually ramp up and down in straight lines, but instead uses curves comprising logarithmic and exponential functions. The effect is intended to feel a little bit like riding a roller coaster: slowing down as you climb up a hill helps you anticipate the upcoming descent, and accelerating through a downward curve enhances the overall thrill of the experience. These techniques provide additional ways to create variety in musical performances.

Historically, before precise mechanisms for measuring time became widely available, it was common to use poetic adjectives to describe musical tempo. These words were used to convey the spirit or experience of the pacing, not strictly its velocity. In English-speaking regions, it was fashionable to adopt terms from Continental European languages such as Italian or German to evoke a special effect. For example, *allegro*, meaning "cheerful" in Italian, is often used to convey a brisk or fast tempo. Alternately, *kräftig* means "powerful" in German, and is used to encourage a performance that is not too fast but vigorous or forceful in character.

4.1.1 Playback Speed

The most rudimentary way to think about tempo is as a form of *playback speed*, which we first encountered in tutorial #4 when playing MIDI files with the seq object. Playback speed can be calculated as a simple *ratio*: a relationship between two values expressed as one value divided by the other. The result of the division of the two values can be simplified to a simple floating-point number. A playback speed ratio can be computed by taking the intended playback speed of an audio file and dividing it by the original speed of the source file (typically 1, if recorded normally). A ratio of 1 (obtained by dividing 1 by 1) will give you the original tempo of the recording. A value higher than 1 will increase the speed; for example, a ratio of 1.5 (obtained by dividing 1.5/1) results in a playback speed 50 percent faster than the original. Conversely, a value lower than 1 will decrease the speed; 0.5/1 yields a ratio of 0.5, with a resulting playback speed that is half as fast as the original. A value of 2 will double the speed, and a value of 0 will stop playback entirely. (All the other values lie on a continuum in between.) Values higher than 2 or lower than 0.25 tend to cause noticeable distortion on an audio signal, and for that reason tend to be avoided. There is an inverse relationship between speed and duration: the faster a piece plays, the shorter it takes to reach the end. Doubling the speed will take half the time for the audio to play; halving the speed will take double the time for the piece to play.

Playback speed can be explored in software using incremental steps or a slider with continuous values. The idea of controlling playback speed has become somewhat commonplace since YouTube (https://www.youtube.com) first implemented playback speed controls in 2010. Even prior to the rollout of this feature, people used third-party applications to speed up or slow down YouTube videos. In order to enable this functionality, special implementations of the *phase vocoder* algorithm were developed that were capable of changing playback speed in real time without affecting pitch or audio quality.[1] Playback speed controls have also been popular on podcast distribution platforms.[2] On some web browsers, the YouTube playback speed feature is located under the "Settings" menu in the bottom right corner of the video window. (On other web browsers, you must first install an extension in order to enable this feature.) Users are able to select from among the following ratios: 0.25, 0.5, 0.75, "normal," 1.25, 1.5, 1.75, and 2. A "Custom" control feature allows users to adjust a slider using floating-point increments of 0.05. Selecting "normal" is equivalent to a value of 1 and will give you the original tempo of the recording. A value higher than 1 will increase the speed, and a value lower than 1 will decrease the speed. Although a playback speed value of 0 is not available on YouTube's playback speed menu, you can just press the regular "stop" button to achieve the same effect of stopping the video.

Patch 4.1 "Playback Speed Ratio" allows you to experiment with playback speed controls for digital audio files. Audio playback functions are handled by the groove~ object that we first encountered back in tutorial #5. An audio file has been pre-loaded for you in the buffer~ object, containing a short excerpt from "Hide and Seek" by Imogen Heap. Click on the green button to start the file playing normally. Then, grab the slider and play around with the playback speed ratio. Have fun with this! I love slowing down this recording to really fine levels of granularity; it's compelling to hear the artist slowly grab a breath or hang on a note with extra expressive emphasis. This patch allows you to explore speed ratios at a much finer level of detail than YouTube does; the slider is set to output 2000 individual values between 0 and 2. You can explore even smaller levels of granularity by using the Inspector to edit the Range and Output Multiplier settings for the slider object. (In order for new values to work well, make sure that when you multiply them together, they equal 2. The default values of 2000 and .001 accomplish that for you.) Take the patch out of presentation mode to see how it works. Note that the "timestretch" box has been checked; this decouples pitch from playback speed, avoiding having the pitch rise when you go faster or fall when you go slower.

4.1.2 Beats per Minute

Whereas adjusting playback speed is a little bit like pressing the accelerator pedal on a car, a more nuanced method for controlling tempo is available using the variable of "beats per minute," abbreviated as BPMs. BPM values were historically associated with *metronomes*—mechanical devices that were first invented around 1815[3] to generate steady reference tempos. Initially, metronomes were used by composers to help them select precise tempo values for their pieces. Later, metronomes came into common usage to help practicing musicians learn musical passages by gradually bringing them "up to speed," one increment at a time. Swinging pendulum mechanisms were used in early metronomes to generate steady clicks; they were occasionally and sometimes notoriously unreliable. Today's musicians often use mobile phone apps and software click tracks instead of physical metronomes to reproduce tempo values; thankfully, these digital options are accurate to a very high degree of precision. Some offer additional benefits: *DrumGenius* is a metronome app that enhances the quality of the practice experience by providing recorded clips of real drummers performing at specific BPMs, instead of electronic tones. Many drummers appreciate listening to the "feel" or *groove* of a rhythmic pattern performed by a human musician, rather than a quantized, metronomic pulse train.

During the past century, various uses for BPM measurements have emerged. Film and media composers use BPMs to help fit their music precisely into predetermined scene durations. Video editors align the beats in a musical track to character movements on the screen. DJs perform complex feats of *beat matching* to enhance and sustain energy levels on the dance floor. Content creators adjust the BPMs of a song so they can seamlessly combine it with another track to create a *mashup*. And music streaming services such as Spotify and Pandora seek to accurately detect the tempo (and other features) of popular music tracks so they can effectively recommend similar tracks to new audiences. In recent years, many academic and industry research efforts have sought to enable computers to automatically and accurately extract beats and tempo from audio sources.[4]

The BPM value provides a way to quantify tempo as a variable. It is a numerical representation of the rate of speed, or the number of beats that occur within a fixed period of time. In order to calculate BPMs, you need a steady sequence of beats called a *pulse train*, where the spacing between beats is somewhat consistent or fixed. When you tap your foot along to a song, you are creating your own version of the pulse train provided by the song. If, however, you are the drummer in a band or the conductor of a group of musicians, you are actively generating a pulse train for others to follow. Depending on the style of music in which you are working, the distances between beats in a pulse train might be similar but not necessarily equal. Subtle differences in spacing between successive beats can have a significant impact on the emotional power of a song. On the other hand, tracks in highly electronic music styles such as EDM usually establish an unwavering BPM value, which creates a different kind of impact in that context.

A simple way to determine the BPMs in a piece of music is to use an interactive *tap tempo* tool; examples can be found on popular websites and smartphone apps. Tap tempo calculators receive inputs from keyboard or mouse clicks and continuously recalculate BPMs with updated tempo estimates. In the following section, we will learn how to build our own "tap tempo" functions in *Max* and use them to determine the tempo of a piece. As you read through this section, follow along with the instructions to construct the different steps along the way. Afterward, open up patch 4.1a "Tap Tempo Machine" and compare it with the version you made yourself.

To determine a BPM value, you first need to measure the time distances in between consecutive beats. These time intervals, known as *interonset interval* values, define the spacing distance between two adjacent onset times. (The use of the term "interval" here means something different from our earlier usage in Chapters 2 and 3; here it describes an interval of time, not pitch.) We usually measure time intervals using milliseconds—increments of one-thousandth of a second.

To begin measuring interonset intervals in *Max*, go ahead and create a blank new patcher. Near the top of the window, add a button object and a new object called "timer." Much like a stopwatch, the timer object receives bang messages from the button object and reports back the time difference between them. Go ahead and draw two patch cords from the button object—one to the left inlet of timer, and the other one to its right inlet. Add a number object (press "i" for integer) and draw a patch cord from timer to the number object to display the interonset interval number. Now, click on the button repeatedly, creating a pulse train of somewhat regular beats. Notice that the number object displays the number of milliseconds that have elapsed in between the two most recent beats. (The very first click will generate a spurious large value, because the distance between the first beat and a nonexistent prior beat is undefined.)

Once you are able to see and update this "instantaneous" interonset interval value, we can then apply a simple mathematical formula to convert it to tempo in BPMs. Here is the formula: BPMs = 60,000 / interonset interval. This equation defines the relationship between two variables: tempo (in beats per minute) and the millisecond distance between beats (interonset interval). Here, the number 60,000 represents the standard unit of time of one minute: 60,000 milliseconds fit within a minute—there are 60 seconds per minute and each second contains 1000 milliseconds. Perhaps the best way to make sense of this formula is to allow it to convey the insight that tempo and interonset intervals share an inverse relationship within a fixed duration of time. As the number of beats (BPMs) increases, the distances between consecutive beats get smaller. Conversely, as you expand the interonset spacings between beats, BPMs decrease and the tempo slows down.

To implement this formula in *Max*, we will make use of a new object called "expr" that computes simple mathematical expressions including arithmetic, Boolean operators, and other common functions. To continue where we left off, create a new object below the previous number object, and type into it this exact string of characters: "expr 60000./$i1". Draw a patch cord from the previous number object to the new expr object. Add a flonum object beneath and draw a patch cord to it from the expr object. Click on the button a few times; the flonum object should display the current tempo value, as measured between the two most recent beats.

Some explanation is probably needed to understand what is going on here with these new objects. The string of characters called "$i1" tells the expr object that any variable ("$") arriving into its first and only inlet ("1") will be accepted if it is an integer ("i"). The value 60000 represents the number of milliseconds per minute, and its decimal point "separator" (".") indicates that it is formatted as a floating-point data type. The expr object receives an integer representing the interonset interval in its inlet, divides the fixed value of 60000 by that integer, and outputs a floating-point number representing the current tempo value in BPMs.

This method of computing the beats per minute value does not require waiting for an entire minute worth of beats to elapse. Here, we have calculated the BPM value instantaneously, updating it on a beat-to-beat basis. However, there is a classic problem with this beat-to-beat method. To test it out, go ahead and click repeatedly on the button at the top of your patch; observe the output value in BPMs below. After a series of steady, consistent clicks, you may notice that the resulting tempo tends to jump around a bit. It is likely that tiny inconsistencies in your untrained mouse-clicking efforts are causing fluctuations in the instantaneous BPM measurement. This common problem in the processing of signals is called *jitter*: variations in the timing of regularly occurring events. Here, small deviations in the human-generated input data are causing jaggedness or irregularities in the output data.

Small perturbations due to jitter can be improved upon by taking a slightly longer view. To achieve a less jumpy tempo value, we can apply a simple *moving average*. Moving averages are helpful for smoothing out the rough edges of different types of patterns. They are a good first step to try that doesn't require an intensive intervention. It could help to use a short time window of a few seconds or a longer time segment of up to perhaps 10–15 seconds. There are trade-offs with either option: averaging over too few values could yield a tempo that still jumps around; averaging over too many values could cause an output that updates too slowly. Figure 4.1 displays a *Max* implementation of a simple moving average.

In this code snippet, incoming new values are averaged with the seven preceding values using the "bucket" object. Bucket is named that way because it passes values

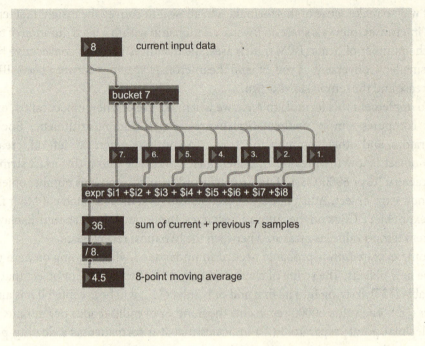

Figure 4.1 8-point moving average

one at a time to the next output location on the right, just as firefighters in earlier ages might have passed a water bucket in a "bucket brigade." It functions like a *shift register*, a venerable method for storing and moving data that has been used in computers for many decades. The bucket object can move its contents between outlets in either direction.

To use an 8-point moving average to compute BPMs, please open up patch 4.1a "Tap Tempo Machine." On the left side of the patch is the code that we built earlier for the instantaneous tempo calculation. Branching out on the right side is another segment of *Max* code that includes the eight-point moving average from figure 4.1. Compare it with your earlier version by clicking repeatedly on the button at the top. The timer object measures and outputs the time interval between successive taps. The bucket object outputs the most recent 7 values prior to the current value; the 7 values plus the current value represent the 8 beats over which you will compute the running average. The eight most recent interonset values are added together and the result is divided by 8; this gives us a moving average value. We then apply the BPM formula in the expr object, and it outputs a current tempo estimate. (Since we are averaging over 8 values, you will need to click 8 times before you get a valid answer.)

Explore the features of the tap tempo code in patch 4.1a, shown in figure 4.2. It can be fun to tap alongside a favorite audio recording while watching the BPMs displayed below. To determine the tempo of a particular song, just open up any audio file or web clip on your computer, or use the code that has been provided for this purpose on the right side of the patch. Click on the message object labeled "replace"

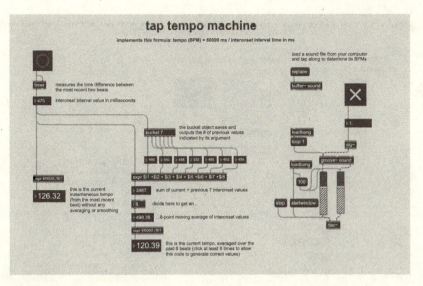

Figure 4.2 Tap tempo machine

to select and load a sound file from your hard drive. Clicking on the toggle object will cause the sound file to play and stop.

Feel free to modify the objects in this patch as you sort out how it works. One thing you can try is to change the argument for the bucket object (currently, 7). (You should also adjust the amount of number objects and "$i" input values in the expr object accordingly.) Test the resulting changes by clicking on the button quite a few times to create many successive interonset intervals; listen carefully and compare how the same data sounds when smoothed across smaller or larger numbers of values, called "window sizes." This will help you determine a reasonable window size to use in your moving average calculation.

You can also invert the tempo calculation and proceed in the opposite direction, converting from BPMs to interonset intervals. (This can be useful if you are given music with the tempo indicated in BPMs and need to know how long your quarter notes should last. For example, to run patch 1.1 Loops with a new song, you will need to calculate and update the pipe arguments to match the new tempo.) To do this, flip around the terms of the BPM formula: interonset intervals = 60,000 / BPMs. Use patch 4.1b "Inverse BPM to Interonset," shown in figure 4.3, to compute this inverse form of the equation. Select your BPMs with the slider, and observe the exact interonset intervals in the green number object below. (A software note: if you recently used patch 4.1a, you may need to first quit and restart *Max* to use patch 4.1b. Sometimes after the digital audio functions have been activated, the MIDI driver needs to be relaunched.)

Now that you have learned how to work with playback speed and BPMs, you can combine the two variables to solve interesting musical problems! Return back to patch 4.1 and add a few objects that will allow a BPM ratio to control a playback

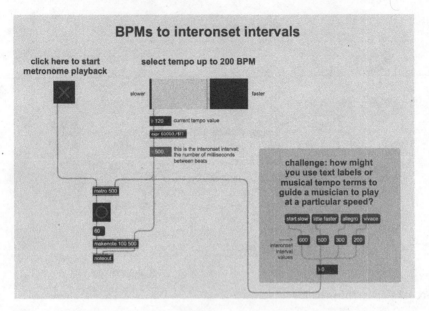

Figure 4.3 Inverse BPMs to interonset intervals

speed ratio. For example, if you have an audio track that was recorded at 120 beats per minute that you want to play a little faster or slower, copy the tempo slider code from patch 4.1b and send its output to an object that contains "/ 120". This will create a BPM ratio, which you can then connect to the playback speed slider in patch 4.1.

Another thing you could try might be to display text labels or musical tempo terms on the top-level interface to guide a musician to play at a particular speed. A starting place for this idea has been drafted in patch 4.1b and left there for you in the bottom right corner to experiment with if you like.

4.1.3 Some Additional Considerations about Tempo

Similar to the phenomenon of absolute or "perfect" pitch mentioned in section 2.3 "Frequency," some expert percussionists and drummers are able to reliably demonstrate *absolute tempo*. It's not clear exactly how they are able to recreate exact timings, but it is thought to be a skill that can be exercised through consistent repetition and careful self-assessment.[5] Related to the issue of perfect precision in tempo is the notion that a particular tempo "feels" a certain way—how a passage of music might have a speed that it naturally "works" in. Often, there is a general consensus about the range of speeds in which certain musical structures seem more correct, more exciting, flowing, etc. Drummers sometimes talk about finding the right "pocket" in which a set of rhythmic patterns sits comfortably, although there can be a range of opinions about what feels appropriate. The "rightness" of a tempo, it seems, has more to do with the individual decisions of an artist about how to make it work within their vision. When developing a new interpretation of an existing work, recording artists often consider the selection of a specific tempo to be an important element that makes their version unique and interesting.

While there haven't been many research studies about this,[6] there is a general idea that has been around for some time that the "rightness" of a tempo has to do with the internal rhythms of our physical bodies and the ways in which our bodies move. Tempos align with embodied sensations that we recognize as authentic to our experiences (or not). Oscar-winning Hollywood film composer Hans Zimmer has asserted that tempos can be used to establish particular moods. He likes to use a "heart rate tempo" of 120–130 BPMs to convey a sense of activity and excitement. (Zimmer has observed that a high number of hit singles have been written in this tempo range.)[7]

As mentioned before in section 2.5 "Rhythm," terms such as "pulse" and "beat" are associated both with music as well as with the functioning of our hearts. It is not much of a leap to connect the dots and notice that the same words are used for both music and the individual heartbeats that pump blood around our bodies. It is likely that music's ability to simulate the signals in our bodies may explain its great power to engage both our attention and our emotions; just as with our physical heart rates, musical beats also speed up and slow down, indicating changes of energy or excitement. As early as 1482, musicians began to ascribe physiological and physical bases for tempo decisions, including heartbeat rate,[8] breathing rate,[9] and walking period.[10]

Heart rate signals are complex measures that reflect interactions between physical, emotional, and cognitive experiences. Heart rates can directly indicate our levels of emotional excitement, intensity, and stress (physiological "arousal" or activation) because the sympathetic nervous system directly stimulates heart activity through nerve impulses. Heart rates are also influenced by physical activity, as well as inputs from the parasympathetic branch of the autonomic nervous system, which decreases our heart rates when we are resting or relaxed. In much the same way that our pulse quickens when we watch a scary movie or the speed of our footsteps increases while exercising, an increase in tempo can simulate similar effects in music and stimulate our bodies to respond. Musical tempo speeds up in places to increase excitement (tension) or motivate suspense (anticipation), and it slows down when preparing to resolve or providing a respite in which to recharge before getting ready to build up to another peak.[11] It has been observed that common tempos align well with the average human heartbeat rate, which generally lies between 60 and 100 BPMs. However, during workouts and other moments of intensity, heart rate can increase well beyond 120 BPMs. Given the modern digital tools available today, some of these associations can be studied and measured.

4.1.4 These Topics, Skills, and Objects Were Introduced in Section 4.1 "Tempo"

- The *metro* object outputs a bang at regular intervals indicated in milliseconds; it acts like a metronome.
- The *timer* object reports the elapsed time between two events in milliseconds.
- The *expr* object is used in patches 4.1a and 4.1b; it computes simple mathematical expressions including arithmetic, Boolean operators, and other common functions.
- Activity: take some time to listen to a few of your favorite musical tracks, paying attention to how tempo values are used to enhance the excitement level or emotions in the music. Think about the speed of the music as a purposeful decision that the artists made; how does the overall tempo (and any tempo changes in the middle) affect the way that you react to the sounds you are hearing?

4.2 Meter

It can be challenging to try to understand the time component of music using abstract concepts like pulse trains and beats per minute. Meter provides a helpful way to organize time that is easier to follow and more practical to use. Just as your caregivers may have cut up your food into small pieces when you were a child, meter helps us carve up long sequences of pulses into manageable chunks so that we can more easily take in, digest, and engage with the structures of rhythm.

Way back in section 2.5 "Rhythm," we explored the basic rhythmic pattern generated by our hearts. The human heartbeat features a shorter and softer first sound followed by a longer and louder sound, resulting in the characteristic "lub-dub" pattern that is so familiar and fundamental to our lives. It is a simple two-note grouping; there isn't anything particularly complicated about the musical aspect of the sound itself. However, a special feature of this biological pattern is that it repeats seemingly without end in a pulse train that extends out over our entire lifespans—hopefully, with a duration of many years! Individual pieces of music generally aren't intended to last as long as a human lifetime. However, they must contend with a challenge that our hearts don't have to deal with: music should ideally remain interesting to listen to, even over many repetitions. While an uninflected sequence of heartbeats keeps us alive, it eventually becomes tedious as a soundtrack. Simply placing equal beat after equal beat in a long line creates monotony and an uncomfortable, unresolved sense of infinite marching toward nowhere. Although we rely on our hearts as important engines that power our lives, we usually don't think of them as sources of musical inspiration. (Some medical professionals and scientists would disagree.[12])

The need to keep beats and rhythms interesting is a design challenge for musical creators. For sounds to remain compelling over extended repetitions, they must initially capture the attention of listeners and then sustain that engagement by varying their elements. Meter provides a framework for this purpose: it establishes a looping structure of regular time units within which rhythmic patterns can be created, developed, and then nimbly respun to keep things fresh.

Meter is the system of organizing short groups of beats into regular, repeating units that function much like frames. Instead of counting beats in a single unbroken line upward all the way from 1 to infinity, we use a simple mechanism of recurring units within which we count a small number of beats, and then loop back to start counting from 1 again at the first beat of the next one. We call these units *measures* (or bars). Measures provide a sense of regular structure by delimiting time into manageable chunks. They establish a looping framework within which rhythmic patterns are perceived to "fit" and in relationship to which they derive their expressive power. Measures establish reliable guideposts within which the push and pull of rhythmic activity takes place; they provide opportunities for both coherence and variety. In metered music, measures themselves can be grouped together into ever larger patterns, providing yet another mechanism for variety: like walls made up of bricks, music is composed of numerous small individual measure units, some of which are identical, and others of which provide necessary contrast or irregularity that imbue the whole construction with a sense of uniqueness and character.

As was first mentioned in section 2.5 "Rhythm," we typically establish the beginnings and endings of measures by alternating heavy and light beats in recognizable patterns, where volume levels are used to indicate the amount of emphasis. Heavy beats are sometimes called "accented" or strong; light beats are sometimes called "unaccented" or weak. In some styles of music, the first beat is the heaviest beat in the measure; in other styles, such as rock and roll, soul, and funk, the snare drum *backbeat* is the loudest beat in the measure and the one that clearly delineates the metrical grouping boundaries. (Backbeats usually occur on the second or fourth beats of a measure, less commonly on subdivisions of those beats.)

As was also mentioned in section 2.5 "Rhythm," the standard unit of beat duration is called the *quarter note*; it can be subdivided into smaller durations such as *eighth notes* and *sixteenth notes*, as well as combined into larger durations, such as *half notes* and *whole notes*. Any of these durational levels can be picked to serve as the beat unit, although the quarter note is most commonly used. Usually, measures contain 2, 3, or 4 beats, with 4 being the most common grouping. Metrical groupings with 4 quarter-note beats per measure are often called *common time*, which indeed is statistically the most commonly used meter. Figure 4.4 uses Hyperscore software to display a measure of common time containing quarter notes, eighth notes, and sixteenth notes. It also features a strong backbeat on the fourth beat in the cymbal part.[13]

In *duple* measures containing 2 beats, alternating patterns of emphasis can occur either with a heavy first beat (as in | heavy light | heavy light |), or with the light beat followed by a heavy backbeat, as in | light heavy | light heavy |. Regardless of which type you use, these 2-beat groupings help to define the measure boundaries. For *triple* measures containing 3 beats, there are a few different options. You often see

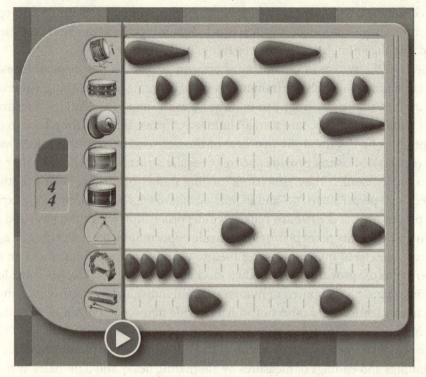

Figure 4.4 Common time in Hyperscore

triple measures framed as patterns of | heavy light light | heavy light light |. In other cases, you might find that the third beat leads back toward the stronger first beat by increasing its strength, as in | heavy light medium | heavy light medium |. And there are more elaborate triple patterns that embed a duple emphasis across alternating measures, as in | heavy light heavy | light heavy light |. These grouping patterns can be compared to familiar patterns of movement that make use of our 2 feet, such as marching (| left right | left right |) or 3-step dances like the waltz or the *Fandango*, a folk dance from Spain (| right left right | left right left |).

As soon as you start to use multiples of 2 beats, implied sub-groupings emerge. In a *quadruple* measure containing 4 quarter notes, the repeating 4-beat measure pattern can be interpreted as 2 duple measure patterns smushed together. In some cases, as in a standard funk groove, both duples could have heavy backbeats: | light heavy light heavy |. On a drum set, this effect can be realized by alternating between kick and snare drums. In other cases, one of the 2 duple pairs could have slightly less emphasis, as in: | heavy light medium light |. Essentially, the "heavy light" pair of beats forms a "heavy" group, and the "medium light" pair of beats forms a "light" group, echoing the smaller structure of the duple metrical pattern over the larger duration of 4 beats.

Meters where each measure contains 5 or more beats are considered to be *compound*. Their measures are often "subdivided" into multiple smaller units of 2, 3, or 4 beats. For example, a measure containing 5 beats typically is reinterpreted as a duple meter containing one implied grouping of 2 and one grouping of 3. One of those groups may be weaker than the other, as in: | heavy light medium light light | (2 + 3) or | heavy light light medium light | (3 + 2). And if a measure contains 6 quarter notes, we typically "hear" or interpret it as a duple pattern where each beat contains a triplet grouping. We call these higher-numbered measures of 5 or more beats "compound" because of their nested sub-groupings. Figure 4.5 uses Hyperscore software to display a measure in the compound meter of 6/8. This measure contains 6 eighth notes; see if you can discern its 2-part structure, where each section contains 3 beats.

To explore a simulation of how meter works, please open up patch 4.2 in the sample code. Just to the right of the start and stop buttons is a set of radiogroup controls from which you can select different numbers of beats per measure. Listen and compare the standard patterns of heavy, medium, and light emphasis that accompany the options. First compare the *simple meters* of duple, triple, and quadruple (2, 3, and 4 beats per measure), and then listen to the compound meters of 5, 6, 9, and 12 beats per measure. MIDI velocity values of 120, 90, and 60 map to heavy, medium, and light emphasis; text labels flash when each corresponding loudness value is triggered. Once you have a sense for how metrical patterns sound at the default

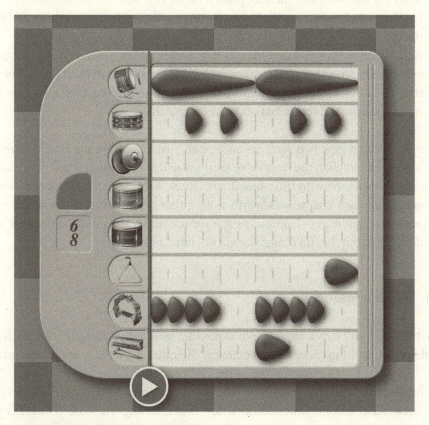

Figure 4.5 Compound 6/8 meter in Hyperscore

speed of 120 BPMs (displayed in the patch using the interonset interval value of 500 milliseconds), crank the speed higher by moving the slider to the right. Listen to how the emphases in the patterns seem to come into greater focus as the speed increases. This may be more evident with the compound meters; at faster speeds, you may be better able to perceive their higher-level groupings of 2, 3, and 4.

There are many more details about meter that would be great to get to! For those who are interested in going deeper into topics of meter and rhythm, it can help to have a good reference on this subject.[14] Musical cultures around the world use metrical systems with slightly different feature-sets; one example is the Indian system of *tala*, which uses many more types of metrical cycles than are typically used in the West. Beat-making and software-based drum loop creation are major components of modern music production activities. How do you apply concepts of rhythm, tempo, and meter in your own creative musical work?

4.2.1 These Topics, Skills, and Objects Were Introduced in Section 4.2 "Meter"

- The *counter* object is used in patch 4.2 to count upward for a fixed number of beats per measure and then loop back to the first beat at the next measure. Its two arguments represent the lowest number followed by the highest number in the loop.
- Activity: now that you understand how meter works and how you can group beat patterns together, return back to the beat-making activity at the end of section 2.5 "Rhythm" and challenge yourself to continue to develop it further. Feel free to borrow and remix bits of code from patch 4.2.

Whereas the previous two sections addressed structures that used only time and emphasis (heavy/light), the next three sections will feature pitch structures that are uniquely intertwined with time-based structures. While the following sections do not need their own chapter, it's worth noting that the reintroduction of the pitch component is significant—combining the vertical and horizontal components back together, filling out the full dimensionality of what music can be.

4.3 Make a Melody

What is a melody? It is a sequence of notes that lasts approximately the length of a single breath and functions like a sentence. Melodies are usually complete musical utterances that have a beginning, middle, and end—much like a narrative arc. They can function independently with or without accompaniment, and sometimes they contain words that contribute additional layers of meaning. The *Oxford Music Online* dictionary defines the contents of a melody as "pitched sounds arranged in musical time in accordance with given cultural conventions and constraints."[15] As we first learned in section 2.6 "Valence," those conventions and constraints also determine how we perceive consonance and dissonance. They affect the decisions composers make when writing music to please their intended audiences, and they also enable melodies to convey a coherent sense of narrative by structuring elements into patterns of tension and resolution. Here is one of the foundational ways to structure such a pattern: start resolved, build up tension, and resolve back to stasis at the end.

Melodies occupy a prominent place among the most beloved horizontal structures in the time-domain component of music. Great melodies are thought of as valued cultural artifacts that can easily be shared with others through singing, without the need for any additional tools or technologies beyond our built-in physical equipment. Great vocalists are celebrated for their abilities to connect the melodies they perform to our most deeply held inner feelings; they model safe ways for us to express and acknowledge our thoughts and emotions through the medium of sound.

More specifically, a melody is set of related notes that fit within a scale and follow a particular order, featuring intervals of various sizes and directions. Melodies often start on a tonic note and proceed through alternating moments of ascending and descending motion, usually returning back to end on that same tonic note. Intervals between adjacent notes tend to emphasize *conjunct* (stepwise) motion of major or minor seconds. The decision when to use leaps, or *disjunct* melodic intervals greater than a second, requires a little more nuance. In general, leaps are less common than stepwise motion. Smaller leaps tend to be preferred; third leaps are commonplace, while fourth and fifth leaps are less prevalent but nonetheless present. Larger intervals are reserved for moments of special emphasis.

Within a melodic context, the size of an interval can be associated with emotional intensity; this is the magnitude of feeling being expressed, represented as the vertical component in Russell's Circumplex model of affect (mentioned above in sections 2.4 "Intensity," 2.6 "Valence," and 3.3.6 'A Theory about Interval Size). Interval size is an important variable to consider when composing a melody. Larger intervals are often reserved for special moments of emphasis, perhaps because they imply a greater investment of energy and a greater risk of error. Large leaps could indicate higher emotional intensities because, just as with physical movement, traversing a greater frequency distance requires more effort and speed. (You have to move much faster to hop up an octave, compared with stepwise movement of a major second, in the same duration of time.)

Another important concept in melody creation is *contour*, which can be described as the shape or outline that the notes make, including the kind of movement in between them—whether more gentle or more angular. Melodic contour governs not just note-to-note movement, but the overall shape of a set of notes and the relationships or patterns that determine those steps and leaps. You can think about melodic contour as the difference between walking over a small hill or hiking a steep mountain range; both excursions involve going up and down, but the shape of the second experience is much more extreme, acute, and varied (and perhaps more exciting as a result).

Now that we know something about melodies, we can construct one of our own and listen to it in *Max*. One straightforward way to accomplish this is to reuse the sample code from section 2.5 "Rhythm," repurposing its "daisy chain" structure for pitched notes instead of rhythmic patterns. To try out this approach, please open up patch 4.3 "Simple Melody Maker." Here, you will see a modified version of patch 2.5 that uses the same interconnected daisy chain sequence, where each note triggers the one that follows it. Notes are assigned MIDI pitch numbers using message objects, and their durations are controlled by the arguments in the pipe objects that follow them. The purpose of the pipe objects is to control durations in between notes, in a similar way to the interonset intervals we learned about in section 4.1 "Tempo." The slider in the top right corner controls the playback speed of the melody; the trick here is that these melody notes don't all have the same durations, so a ratio has to be implemented three different ways to accommodate the different (but proportionally related) durations of quarter notes, eighth notes, and sixteenth notes. This patch also retains the loop control mechanism from patch 2.5; melodies don't necessarily loop, so you might want to disable this feature by clicking once on the yellow toggle object.

As you explore the code in sample patch 4.3, shown in figure 4.6, I encourage you to "make it your own" by editing the notes and durations. Instead of the classic Hollywood film song currently in there, pick out one of your own favorite melodies or, better yet, go ahead and compose a new one! As you carefully edit the MIDI pitch numbers and pipe durations, you may also want to increase the number of notes. Just insert as many new message and pipe objects as you need, cutting and pasting them into the daisy chain. If you don't need this new melody to loop, then just delete the patch cord that connects from the last note back into the gswitch object. Take care to

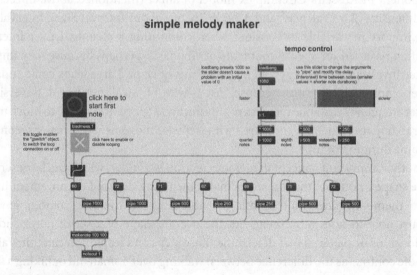

Figure 4.6 Simple melody maker

ensure that your patch cords attach objects together in exactly the same way as in the sample code.

OK, that was fun, but it leads us to an important question: how do you construct a high-quality melody? Before we had modern statistics and software to help us analyze music, we had a general set of rules that were passed down for hundreds of years in the European classical tradition. The rules were refined over many generations based on a consensus about what sounded good. Of course, musical tastes evolve a great deal over time! But for now, let's take a look at a widely used historical example.

One of the earliest manuals for melodic creation was penned by Johann Fux in 1725.[16] Fux's text proposed a few desirable melodic characteristics that composers should observe; they comprise a preliminary list of "conventions and constraints" that make a decent melody (although probably not a great one). Many music theory textbooks have refined Fux's list over the intervening 300 years. Below is a compilation of melodic rules, synthesized from a variety of scholarly sources and textbooks on classical music. They are admittedly somewhat old-fashioned and problematic, but they nonetheless provide a practical starting set of heuristics:[17]

1. Use a simple rhythm, allowing for some variety.
2. Notes should fit within a diatonic framework (key and scale).
3. Mostly start and end on the tonic note and return to the tonic occasionally in-between.
4. Limit the total pitch range to approximately 1½ octaves so it is comfortable to sing for most people.
5. Maximize stepwise (seconds) motion between notes; this establishes a sense of orderly progression.
6. Add occasional leaps to increase variety or to create tension. Leaps should generally be smaller (thirds and fourths); use larger leaps (fifths, sixths, sevenths, octaves) sparingly and for special effect or emphasis.
7. Create a pleasing contour, incorporating a mix of ascending and descending motion.
8. Create a sense of melodic direction (progression) by not repeating the same notes too many times ("noodling") or leaping around too much.
9. After large leaps, typically change direction.
10. Mostly avoid dissonant melodic intervals, especially sevenths, augmented intervals, and tritones.
11. Minimize chromatic motion; maximize diatonic intervals.
12. Observe tendency tones: $\hat{7}$ is usually followed by $\hat{1}$, and $\hat{4}$ often is followed by $\hat{3}$.

This list of features may seem like a lot to manage! In past generations, music students would dutifully write out their melodies on staff paper note by note, observing the rules one at a time and iteratively reviewing them for correctness. Nowadays, that technique is considered somewhat antiquated, although aspects of it remain relevant and useful. One thing to keep in mind about this list or any other list of melodic rules is that although it may be a useful pedagogical tool for teaching students (some regard it as a cruel torture mechanism), it should not be used as a source of absolute truth. It is more of a general set of guidelines or principles than a rule book. Great works of music tend to align with the rules in most places, but also artfully break them in ways that transcend standard techniques, confound educators, and delight audiences!

Having reviewed the guidelines above, we can now apply them to create our own melodies using *Max* code. At this stage, we are not aiming for elegance; merely a passable sonic result will suffice for now. This initial experiments will use techniques from *algorithmic composition*, a method for encoding rules and heuristics into algorithms that create music. It is a field of study that is worth delving into, with popularity growing around the use of Artificial Intelligence (AI) and Machine Learning as tools for musical creativity.[18]

In the descriptions that follow, we will learn how to use algorithms to encode our melodic writing rules. The outputs of these algorithms can provide interesting starting places from which to create new melodies. Rather than construct and evaluate our melodies on paper, we will instead enact a set of step-by-step procedures in *Max*. Sample patch 4.3a, shown in figure 4.7, acts as a "melody machine" that implements several of the melodic writing rules. The resulting melodies represent statistical simulations of the possibilities available within the constraints established by the rules. Generally, these algorithms will create passable melodic structures, although they might benefit from a little light editing to be truly worth keeping; while it is statistically possible for the algorithms in this patch to compose melodies that compare with beloved gems by Timbaland or Taylor Swift, it's probably not likely. Open up patch 4.3a to get started; the following section provides instructions on how to use it and make sense of the results.

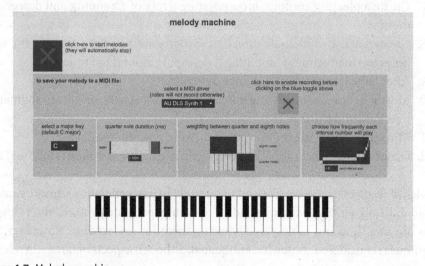

Figure 4.7 Melody machine

To use patch 4.3a, click on the blue toggle object in the upper left-hand corner and listen to the melody that it generates. It will automatically stop on its own; after 10 beats elapse, the next arrival of a tonic note will trigger it to conclude. Click on the blue toggle repeatedly to create additional melodies. Pay attention to qualities such as interval size, rhythm, ascending/descending motion, contour, a sense of melodic "direction," etc. You may find some similarities between melodies, but statistically each one should be unique. If you want to save your melodies as MIDI files, take two steps before clicking on the blue toggle: select a MIDI driver from the blue umenu object, and then click on the yellow toggle object to enable recording. When the melody stops, the system will prompt you to provide a filename (Make sure to include a ".mid" extension at the end of the filename.). The next few paragraphs explain how the code works, step by step. Take the patch out of presentation mode and follow along with the descriptions of the code blocks "under the hood."

Clicking on the blue toggle object sends a value of "1" to the *metro* object directly below it. We first encountered metro above in section 4.1 "Tempo"; it operates like a metronome, outputting bang messages at regular intervals when it receives a "1" or a bang message in its left inlet. This metro object starts sending beats with an interonset interval of 1000 milliseconds, generating a tempo of 60 BPM. These quarter-note beats provide the basic pulse mechanism that powers each melody. Use the slider located to the right if you wish to adjust the underlying tempo.

Below the metro object is a small group of objects framed by a pink panel labeled "simple rhythm." As we saw earlier, the panel object is a visual interface element that organizes and delineates areas of the patch. Its appearance can be customized via the Inspector to change variables such as color and transparency. Access the panel object's Help file by right-clicking on it to view more information. The code inside the pink panel implements melodic guideline # 1: "use a simple rhythm, allowing for some variety." At the top of the panel is a random object connected to an *itable* object. Random, which we used in patch 3.4a "Interval Ear Training Practice," receives a bang from metro on every beat. It has an argument of 10 that causes it to function like a 10-sided die, outputting random numbers between 0 and 9. The itable object receives the number sent by random and uses it to locate an index number along its horizontal axis; it outputs the value (either 0 or 1) at that location. Using itable in this way creates a *distribution* of values; a set of statistical probabilities of each outcome. This affects the rhythm by specifying the percentage of time the two types of note durations will occur: quarter notes (1 beat) and eighth notes (½-beat). In the current itable setting, 60 percent of the beats contain one quarter note and 40 percent output two eighth notes. This distribution results in simple rhythms, where quite a few notes last for one beat but where there is also a good chance of helpful rhythmic variety. You can change the proportional weighting of quarter and eighth notes by clicking on itable when the patch is locked. (Click on the top half of the itable object to increase the percentage of eighth notes.) Try rebalancing the percentage of quarter notes and eighth notes and listen to the resulting rhythmic combinations.

Located at the bottom of the pink "simple rhythm" panel, the *int* object is responsible for sending each new note. It functions a bit like a storage locker: it stores one value at a time, sending that value out when it receives a bang message in its left inlet. Values arriving in its right inlet are held until the next bang message. Eighth notes are triggered to play by an "if" object above "int" that contains an "if/then" *conditional statement*. This "if statement" functions like a traditional text-based programming command; it evaluates any value it receives in its inlet ("$i1"). If the input equals 1, then it sends a bang message ("b") out of its outlet ("$o1"). This enables it to switch between quarter notes and eighth note durations: if it receives a quarter note indication (0) from itable then it does nothing, but if it receives an eighth note indication (1), then it triggers a new ½-beat note by sending a bang to the pipe object. The pipe object receives that bang message, holds it for 500 milliseconds, and then sends it to the int object to create a new eighth note. (The pipe object's argument of 500 is overwritten by any updated tempo indications from the slider object above.)

Melodic guideline #2 (notes must fit within a specific key and scale) is implemented in the green panel object at the bottom of the patch, constraining notes within the diatonic key of C major. Here, the note numbers have been "hard-coded" for a major scale (similar to patch 1.6), which means that they are written out in number boxes instead of derived dynamically from a scale pattern. This aspect can be updated at a later time by swapping in new code that treats scale types as user-selectable variables, such as in patch 3.5b "Scale Switching." It could be really interesting to hear this same melody generator work with different scale types!

The first part of melodic guideline #3 (start on the tonic note) is handled by the code in the orange panel object. Here, the "loadbang" object establishes a tonic note of 60. (It also establishes a vibraphone timbre, using voice #12 in the General MIDI sound set.) The *togedge* object, used here for the first time, receives values from the blue toggle object above and reports when they change. At the "rising edge," when going from 0 to 1, togedge sends a bang out its left outlet; at the "falling edge," when 1 changes to 0, it sends a bang out its right outlet. Togedge is used here to handle switching from the end of one melody to the beginning of the next one—it sends pitch 60 as a starting note at the beginning (toggle "on") of every new melody.

Melodic guideline #4 ("limit the total pitch range") is observed by the code in the red panel on the right side of the patch. This section defines the outer limits of the melody to two octaves (a little bit larger than the 1½ octaves recommended by the rule). The < operator ("less than") sets a lower boundary; if the melody descends below its value, the < object outputs a 1, causing the gswitch object to reset the minimum pitch value. Conversely, the > operator ("greater than") sets the upper boundary, outputting a 1 if pitch values exceed the upper limit, causing the other gswitch object to reset the maximum pitch value.

Melodic guidelines #5 and #6 (maximize stepwise motion between notes and emphasize smaller leaps; use larger leaps sparingly) are both addressed by the code in the yellow panel on the right. In this section, the random object receives a bang from metro on every beat; an argument of 100 causes it to output a random number between 0 and 99. This value is received by the itable object, which displays interval sizes on its vertical axis and the probability that the interval will be selected on its horizontal axis. The very lowest interval is a unison, the next one a diatonic second, then third, fourth, etc. As you go progressively higher, you can see that the percentage chance of getting a sixth, seventh, or octave gets quite low. The itable object sends its output to the two blue panels on the left, which both jointly govern the mix of interval sizes and directions.

Melodic guideline #7 ("create a pleasing contour, incorporating a mix of ascending and descending motion") is implemented in the small blue panel in the middle. Here, when any new note is triggered, the "random 2" object randomly outputs a 0 or 1, like a coin toss. This causes the *gswitch2* object, which we used earlier in patch 3.5a, to switch between ascending (0) or descending (1) motion. The size of the ascending or descending intervals is controlled in the "+ 1" and "– 1" objects, which are updated with new values coming from the large blue panel to the left.

Finally, the code for melodic guideline #8 ("create a sense of melodic direction") is included in the large blue panel on the left side. Its purpose is to foster a sense of progression by not repeating the same notes too many times ("noodling") or leaping around too much. It accomplishes this task in two parts—one for intervals of a second, and one for thirds. The section on the right ensures that there aren't too many seconds in a row (i.e., too much stepwise motion). It accomplishes this by keeping track of the previous four notes, repurposing the bucket object that we used in section 4.1.2 'Beats per Minute' for this task. It then measures the differences between those four notes and computes the absolute values of the differences (to obtain just the interval sizes without ascending/descending information). It uses the "==" object to compare two numbers; it outputs a 1 if they are equal and a 0 if they are not. If the previous four notes were all a second interval apart, then it forces the next interval to be a third. The code block on the left side does the opposite: if the past three intervals were all a third, it forces the next interval to be a second. This diminishes the chance of repetitive "noodling" and helps increase a sense of "direction" in the resulting melody.

Melodic guidelines #9–12 have not yet been implemented in patch 4.3a. However, this patch represents a solid starting place with which to build a sophisticated understanding of algorithmic composition. How might you improve upon it? Perhaps you might implement more advanced features such as tendency tones (e.g., leading tones must usually be followed by tonics), non-scale notes, or non-chord tones (passing tones, appoggiaturas, escape tones, suspensions). It would make a fascinating project to progressively enable features and evaluate whether the melody gets more pleasing over time. See if you can turn on and off individual melodic rules one at a time and perceive the resulting effects. I invite you to adjust the parameters of the melody machine patch and push the results in different directions. If you are dissatisfied with its sometimes awkward, flawed, or problematic results, then I encourage you to tweak and revise the "cultural conventions and constraints" so they result in melodies that are pleasing to you!

4.3.1 Themes and Characters

As we have been discussing melodies, it would be a shame to leave out the concepts of *character* and *theme*, with which melodies are closely associated. A theme is a sentence-length bit of musical material that has a clear sense of identity, "usually having a recognizable melody and perceivable as a complete musical expression in itself."[19] Not entirely distinct from melodies, themes usually last for the duration an average singer can sustain without having to take a breath.

Once a thematic identity is established, it can also be varied. Variations in musical features such as melodic contour, interval relationships, tempo, rhythm, orchestration, texture, and instrumentation are used to modify the original theme and convey new qualities of emotion or energy for audiences to enjoy. Themes are often constructed from *motives*, brief musical ideas with distinctive rhythms and contours. They are the shortest components of a theme that are still identifiable as independent ideas, and they provide bits of melodic material that can be combined together with other fragments to create full melodies.

Character is a related concept that is used to explain the ways that music conveys, implies, or transmits subtle qualities and nuances of musical emotions. These precise shades of mood are often associated with human personality traits and can be thought of as expressions of personal temperament or identity. Jeffrey Chappell defines *character* as "the quality of a feeling" that one can express musically with purposeful choices in variables such as timbre, dynamics, articulation, tempo, beat division, and rubato.[20]

When attached to characters in stories, themes can contain musical qualities that identify and relate them to those characters. One of the most important methods for associating specific qualities with characters in storytelling media is the *Leitmotiv* technique. Leitmotivs are musical identities or themes that are assigned to major characters in a narrative, containing embedded structures and variables that reflect aspects of the characters' personalities or actions. The purpose of Leitmotivs is to help audiences subconsciously recognize characters and bind emotional attachments and empathies to them in order to evoke specific feelings when they are played. Leitmotivs have been used in many genres including opera, film, and video games. German composer Richard Wagner developed entire systems of Leitmotivs for his operas; later, John Williams applied similar ideas in his film scores, most famously in *Star Wars*.

Leitmotivs establish thematic identities when characters are introduced in a narrative. They are then transformed to reflect new situations; Leitmotivs change and adapt along with the characters they portray, conveying the range of emotion, energy, and action that the character experiences. They can also help contextualize the time period or culture with which the character is associated. Orchestration helps reveal personality by associating it with individual instruments or groupings. Additional musical features such as interval patterns, scale types, dissonance, and melodic contour are attached to characters to distinguish them from each other. For example, the Siegfried character in Wagner's Ring Cycle operas is portrayed using French horns and brass instruments, denoting his heroism. Siegfried's Leitmotiv melody is written in the key of C minor, indicating that he has a tragic fate. During moments when he displays heroism and accepts his destiny, his theme modulates to the key of G minor and is assigned a lower register, indicating greater maturity. During Siegfried's funeral, his theme is returned back to his original key of C minor and orchestrated with a huge array of brass instruments, signifying the weightiness of his passing. Williams made similar choices for the Jedi theme in *Star Wars*, attaching it also to the French horn and the key of C minor; the characteristic rising fourth interval at the beginning of the Jedi theme is also a distinguishing characteristic.[21]

Character themes help music to enhance visual media by providing subtle backchannels that subconsciously influence our mechanisms of perception and emotion. Composers use thematic techniques to exploit audience emotions and enhance their experience of stories by emphasizing plot structure, supporting story elements, using tension and resolution to manipulate emotions, and cueing anticipation, suspense, and memory. These techniques enable music to remind us of past action and also serve as a harbinger of future events, providing foreshadowing and suspense. The best character themes powerfully support the story and transform a good script into a great piece of art!

4.3.2 These Topics, Skills, and Objects Were Introduced in Section 4.3 "Make a Melody"

- The *panel* object is an interface object that visually delineates an area of the patch.
- The *random* object generates a random number when it receives a bang, outputting a value between 0 and 1 less than the value of its argument.
- The *itable* object is an editor that stores a set of data to be used either for graphing purposes or to output values.
- The *int* object stores and outputs one integer value at a time. Updating a value in its right inlet sets the value without outputting it; updating a value in the left inlet sets and outputs the value. A bang message received in its left inlet outputs the current value without changing it.
- The *togedge* object reports zero/non-zero transitions, at the "rising edge" when 0 jumps to 1 or at the "falling edge" when 1 jumps to 0. Togedge sends out bang messages from the left outlet for 0-to-1 transitions and from the right outlet for 1-to-0 transitions. If it receives bang messages, it alternates which of its outlets output a bang.
- The == object (double equal signs) compares two numbers, outputting a 1 if they are equal or a 0 if they are not.

- Activity: How might you refine the algorithms that generate melodies in patch 4.3a? For example, how might you use code from patch 3.5b "Scale Switching" to create melodies in minor keys or Dorian mode? Or, rather than randomizing the variable that controls the mix of ascending and descending motion, what would happen if you started each melody with a bias toward ascending motion, and then gradually adjusted it to emphasize descending motion near the end?
- Activity: how might you use *Max* code to create a Leitmotiv and vary it to accompany a character's experiences in a video game?

4.4 Make an Arpeggio

Now that you have a working knowledge of how to create chords and melodies in *Max*, we can start to explore a new structure that combines both elements together: *arpeggios*. What is an arpeggio? It is a series of notes, similar to a melody, where the set of pitches is limited to the elements of a chord (root, third, fifth, seventh, etc.) rather than utilizing all available notes in a scale. Arpeggios are sequential lines of notes that combine the horizontal aspects of melodies (including pitch range, contour, ascending/descending intervals) with the vertical structures of chords.

Another way to think about arpeggios is as chords in which the individual notes are played non-synchronously, using "melodic" (sequential) instead of "harmonic" (simultaneous) intervals. For this reason, arpeggios are sometimes called "broken" chords—where the individual note onsets arrive in a staggered fashion, rather than all at once. The concept of the arpeggio originated, perhaps unsurprisingly, with an Italian term: "arpeggiare," meaning "to play on a harp." This linguistic connection to the harp implies that the individual notes in an arpeggio are on different strings that are strummed by the fingers in a sweeping progression, either upward or downward. Arpeggios can be played on a range of monophonic and polyphonic instruments, using different techniques that allow them to play chords in a melodic manner, one note at a time. Arpeggios provide interesting opportunities to incorporate rhythmic variety and other effects into harmonic progressions.

Synthesizers can also perform arpeggios with the help of *arpeggiators*—hardware or software systems that encode the rules, variables, and procedures that create arpeggio patterns with electronic sounds. Arpeggiators started appearing in analog electronic synthesizers in the late 1960s; early examples included the "Electronic Organ Arpeggio Effect" patented by the Hammond Organ company and the Triadex Muse synthesizer. Arpeggiators remain popular tools for enhancing electronic sounds by creating patterns of notes and rhythms that fill up the frequency and time domains. The resulting effect can be compared with the pointillist paintings of Georges Seurat: you can zoom in to perceive the individual dots as separate elements, but when you zoom out, all the different points merge together into a unified texture. In a similar way, arpeggiators create a sense of density in sound by generating clouds of notes that enchant listeners with their bouncy energy and fuller, richer sonic textures. (It may be an auditory version of the pointillist illusion, but that sense of fullness can be helpful in smoothing over some of the harshness and artificiality in electronic sounds.) Analog synthesizers by Moog, Oberheim, Kurzweil, and other manufacturers included arpeggiation features that allowed users to select variables and listen to the result; their sounds can be heard in popular music tracks such as Kraftwerk's "Pocket Calculator" and the Eurythmics' New Wave classic "Sweet Dreams (Are Made of This)." Today's Digital Audio Workstations (Logic Pro X, Ableton, Pro Tools, and others) offer arpeggiation effects using plugins and editing tools.

The variables for creating an arpeggiator pattern include root note, chord quality, lowest note (not always the root), upper limit (# of octaves), direction of movement (sometimes called pattern variations: up, down, up and down, down and up, intermittent hopping, octave displacements, etc.), rhythm, and rate (tempo). These aspects can be shaped and modified in real time. Arpeggiators also usually apply a looping structure whereby they reach the end of their predetermined sequence, return to the top, and repeat as often as indicated.

How do you build an arpeggiator in software? You could just reuse the code from patch 4.3 "Simple Melody Maker" to preset ("hard code") the individual pitch values. However, that approach, while quick and simple, would not allow you to use all of the variables that make arpeggiators interesting! It could produce a quick result but ultimately would not be flexible enough to handle all the necessary variety. Instead, we are going to start using higher levels of abstraction as we program the patterns in *Max*. We will use a new technique called *data structures* to keep track of and manage our data.

The components of an arpeggiator can be implemented in *Max* by combining together existing bits of code from previous patches. Once you know how to build intervals, chords, and melodies, you have all the raw materials. Let's start by opening up patch 4.4 "Simple Arpeggio Maker," shown in figure 4.8. It provides a good starting place for our arpeggiator system; go ahead and click on the blue toggle object to start it up, and click around on its interface objects to explore the controls. The root note is selectable from the umenu on the left. Right now, the chord qualities are limited to just major triads; this aspect should probably be expanded. The lowest note is currently set at MIDI note number 60; this can be changed as needed with a slider or other interface object. The upper pitch limit right now is only a fifth, but that could also be adjusted by adding more int objects and chord notes. Pattern variations are handled by the radiogroup object on the right side; three options are currently available for changing the direction of movement. Tempo (rate) is adjustable using the slider on the top right.

How might you take this idea to the next level? Well, one way to begin might be to not just think about constraints, but also aim for efficiencies and elegant design elements. There are many options with arpeggiators: different chord qualities, root notes, inversions, rhythmic patterns, numbers of octaves, pattern variations, etc. And these variables sometimes interact with each other; as we saw with the melody

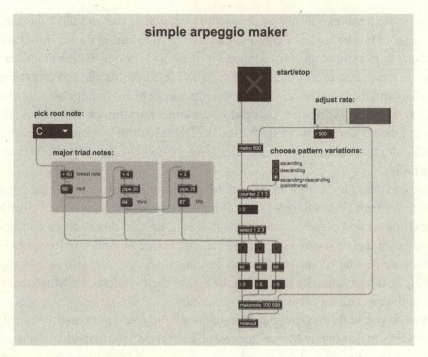

Figure 4.8 Simple arpeggio maker

machine patch (4.3a), changes to one component can affect others. I encourage you to think about patch 4.4 as the starting place for an exploration where you can apply your own creative ideas!

In addition to the purely musical features of arpeggiators, there are also interesting opportunities to use visual design elements that make the user experience more intuitive and engaging. Sample patch 4.4a "Arpeggiator Machine," shown in figure 4.9, presents a model for the expert interface design of arpeggiation variables. This patch is based on a course project created by Everett Huynh, interactive multimedia major and 2022 graduate of The College of New Jersey; it is used with their permission. Click on "activate" to start and stop the arpeggiator. Try the different options, observing how Everett arranged the visual display to highlight categories of variables: root note choices are located around a seven-pointed star, each with their own color, whereas chord quality options are outlined using white text on shaded message objects arranged around an eight-pointed star. Pattern variations (labeled "direction" here) each have their own icon to distinguish them, and speed and volume are on sliders. A "randomness" button activates two itable objects (one for root note, and one for chord quality) that cause the arpeggiator to launch into a mode of revolving changes, such that random returns to C major are striking and notable when they arrive.

The arpeggios tool in Google's Chrome Music Lab[22] provides a different way to arrange and visualize the variables in an arpeggio. Click on the colored segments of the circle to select among different major and minor chords; notice that the outer

Time-based Structures   165

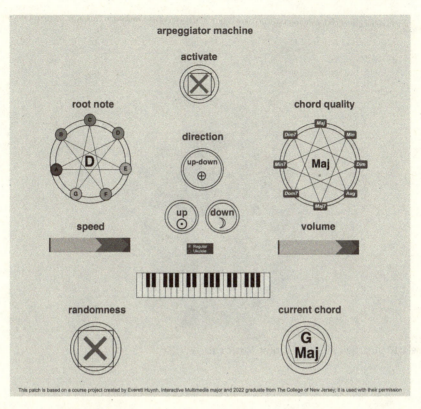

Figure 4.9 Arpeggiator machine

ring of this circle resembles the circle of fifths concept that we explored in section 3.7. Clicking on the arrows switches to different pattern types; you can also change the harp to a piano sound and adjust the tempo. Compare these features to Everett's design in patch 4.4a and consider the many ways to display the complex variables in an arpeggio. Figure 4.10 displays the visual interface of Chrome Music Lab's arpeggios tool.

4.4.1 These Topics, Skills, and Objects Were Introduced in Section 4.4 "Make an Arpeggio"

- Sample patch 4.4a "Arpeggiator Machine" uses the panel object in new ways. As in patches 3.4a and 3.7, panel objects are being used to create circles.
- The fpic object here is also used in a new way by loading and displaying images containing geometric shapes, contributing to the interface design.
- The message object is also being used in a new way here by displaying symbol characters in a specialized font ("Segoe UI Symbol").
- The coll object, last used in sample patch 3.5b, is being used here to store interval patterns for the eight different chord types.

166   Constructing Music

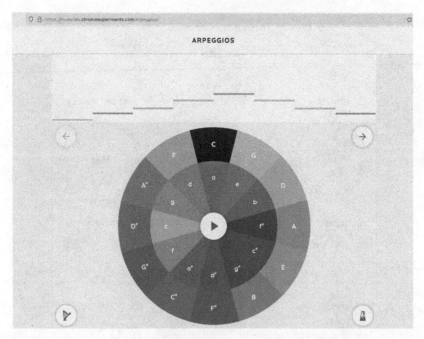

Figure 4.10 Arpeggios tool in Chrome Music Lab

4.5 Make a Harmonic Progression

A harmonic progression is a set of chords played in a specific sequence. Harmonic progressions create a sense of momentum that propels the musical energy forward by modulating the amounts of tension (dissonance) and resolution (consonance) at different moments in time. Composers purposefully place individual chords in relation to each other to create a sense of a varying, contoured harmonic landscape and provide an emotionally satisfying journey for listeners.

Certain chord sequences sometimes function like "formulas" because they appear in similar configurations within music of the same style. For example, in Western classical music, the dominant (V) chord is often followed by a tonic (I) chord, although sometimes it might instead progress to the leading tone (vii°) or submediant (vi) chord for a little change of pace. Other chords are less predictable—for example, the subdominant (IV) chord can be followed by the supertonic (ii), the dominant (V), the leading tone (vii°), or the tonic (I), depending on context and artistic license. Each diatonic chord has a set of chords that it typically proceeds from and leads to.

In other styles of music, chord "formulas" are constructed differently. For example, in many genres of popular music, chord sequences aren't designed to progress to a conclusive harmonic endpoint, but rather to loop. The most famous of these is the "four-chord" sequence: I V vi IV. Other commonly used looping sequences include sequences of three or four chords:

I vi IV V
I IV vi V
vi IV I V
I V IV
I IV V

In Western classical music, sequences of chords conventionally progress toward an eventual goal or arrival point called a *cadence*. Cadences conclude passages and serve as forms of musical punctuation. There are many types of cadences, each of which offers unique ways to resolve harmonic tension or extend it a little bit longer. "Authentic" cadences provide convincing endings by resolving on the tonic chord (I); they function like periods at the ends of sentences. The most common example is the *perfect authentic cadence*; it features the dominant chord (V) moving to the tonic chord (I), with both chords in root position and the top note in the I chord landing on the tonic. Another example is the leading tone *imperfect authentic cadence*, where a first-inversion leading tone (vii°) chord substitutes in place of the dominant chord and progresses directly to the tonic chord (I). Other types of cadences are "progressive" in the sense that they sustain (or don't fully stop) the musical momentum. Examples of those somewhat unresolved cadences include half cadences that end on the dominant chord (V) and deceptive cadences that move from the dominant (V) to the submediant (vi) chord. Many chord progressions follow patterns that incorporate aspects of the circle of fifths that we encountered in section 3.7 "Make a Key."

Sample patch 4.5, shown in figure 4.11, simulates chordal movement in harmonic progressions, with each progression terminating in a cadence. This patch extends upon a course project originally created by Thomas Ploskonka, music education major and 2015 graduate from The College of New Jersey; it is used with his permission.[23] Click on the blue button in the upper left corner of the patch to hear a randomly generated progression. Each diatonic chord is visually identified by a Roman numeral representing its position within the key of C major; its button flashes when it plays. Along the bottom, comment objects display information about the chord and cadence types. As with the earlier "melody machine" patch, this "harmonic progression machine" implements algorithms that enact the general guidelines for chordal movement, reducing the set of possible options to those that fit the "cultural conventions and constraints." A statistical model is used to determine what chord should arrive next in the progression. This results in well-behaved but conventional harmonic movement. (Sadly Although, this patch is not likely to generate great art, hopefully it will reveal important information about the ways in which chords follow each other.) Listen to the results a few times, and then take the patch out of presentation mode to see how it has been implemented.

168   Constructing Music

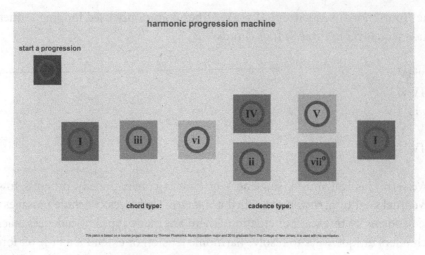

Figure 4.11 Harmonic progression machine

When you take patch 4.5 out of presentation mode, the underlying code reveals that clicking on the "start a progression" button automatically sends a I (tonic) chord. After the tonic chord is triggered to play, it initiates a random number generator in combination with an itable object. As we have seen before, the itable stores a set of statistical probabilities for each outcome. Here, the itable is configured for a specific distribution of chords that can follow the I chord: 20 percent of the time I will progress to ii, 5 percent to iii, 30 percent to IV, 25 percent to V, 15 percent to vi, and 5 percent to vii°. Each consecutive chord has its own random object and itable configuration that creates a unique distribution of chords to which it can progress. In this way, each chord selects and triggers the one that follows it. The "final" tonic chord on the right side is the only one that does not trigger any other chord, therefore terminating the progression with a cadence. Any chord that triggers the "final" tonic will also trigger a "set" message along with the name of the cadence to display in the comment object on the front panel.

While this way of creating chord progressions may seem abstract and disconnected from music making, composers really do purposefully place sequences of chords in a particular order to evoke specific reactions in listeners. In this way, composing is a little bit like being a chef; the goal is to delight or inspire audiences by engaging their attention with lots of complex sensations and textures that trigger emotions and bind them to experiences. To refine the harmonic progression machine to function in exactly the way a human composer would, you may want to first undertake a thorough statistical analysis of the chord progressions created by a specific artist. (It may be instructive to look at unusual examples, such as in Stevie Wonder's "Golden Lady," 1973.)

Another way to learn more about this topic is to create your own harmonic progressions to accompany melodic lines and study how composers you admire have approached this activity. Songsmith, a project by Sumit Basu at Microsoft Research, implemented this idea by automatically generating musical accompaniments to real-time vocal inputs; it worked by training a Hidden Markov Model on a database of prior examples.[24] Harmony is a fascinating component of music and worth digging in to understand better, whether through a *Max* patch or more conventional means!

4.5.1 These Topics, Skills, and Objects Were Introduced in Section 4.5 "Make a Harmonic Progression"

- Activity: How might you expand upon patch 4.5 to feature different cadence patterns such as half cadences, deceptive cadences, or common harmonic formulae such as the cadential 6-4 progression?
- Activity: Now that you can make both an arpeggio and a chord progression, try to create a patch that combines both aspects. For those who have been trained in classical music, you might implement any instrumental etudes that arpeggiate a fixed chord progression. (Here is a standard example: i–I–iv^{64}–IV^{64}–i°–V^7/IV.)
- Activity: Certain beloved musical traditions are especially known for using specific chord progressions. One of the most important of these is the blues, a musical style that originated in the African American diaspora in the nineteenth century. Blues music is cherished for its poignancy of expression and is strongly associated with particular rhythms and grooves, as well as the frequent use of microtonal intervals called "blue notes." The style features a repeating 12-measure structure with one chord per measure: I I I I | IV IV I I | V V I I. (Each group of four measures is grouped into a phrase grouping, and the use of a tonic seventh chord adds a unique characteristic to the way that tension and resolution work within the form.) Within this looping structure, there are many possible variations for both harmonic and rhythmic choices. Given the limitations of coding, it could be problematic to try to capture the blues in software. How would you respond to the challenge of representing the blues progression in a *Max* patch? How might you structure the experience to maximize the expressive power of the style? (What are the limits of code in trying to simulate a deeply human, heartfelt musical art form?)

5
Finer Granularities

Many of the topics in this book contain their own built-in rabbit holes that invite further exploration as soon as you start to dig around a bit and ask a few questions. One of the rabbit holes we left behind in Chapter 2 (section 2.3 "Frequency") deserves returning back for deeper inspection: how exactly do we convert frequency to pitch? The techniques we use have implications for the ways in which we perceive consonance and dissonance.

There are many different methods for carving up the continuous frequency domain into fixed-pitch stair steps, and many ways to organize how we *tune* or align note frequencies so they sound good together. Tuning is a mechanism of production and performance, and it is absolutely necessary if you are playing more than one note at a time, for example, in music created by ensembles of musicians. When music features frequent vertical interactions between multiple instruments or voices, advance coordination is required to align those intervals. Tuning systems set the exact frequencies for notes and provide a consistent, shared framework that allows instruments and voices to play harmoniously together without needing to negotiate the terms on a case-by-case basis.

Tuning systems have been defined, discussed, and debated for thousands of years! There are many complexities involved, and for that reason, tuning usually requires some basic knowledge of mathematics and physics to understand properly. Luckily, *Max* can simulate some of the math equations, allowing us to listen to the sounds, compare them, and develop a better understanding of the differences between the various systems. In addition to the *Max* patches presented in this chapter, interested readers might also want to explore other software-based methods for controlling tuning parameters including the MIDI *pitch bend* function, plug-ins such as Auto-Tune, and applications like MTS-ESP that share information across DAW plug-ins. In this chapter, we will dig in a little more to understand the complexities at a finer degree of resolution.

5.1 Just Intonation

> "When you play the 12-string guitar, you spend half your life tuning the instrument and the other half playing it out of tune."
>
> —Pete Seeger

Many historical tuning systems have used some form of *just intonation*, in which intervals are tuned using whole number frequency ratios derived from the overtone system. Those ratios result in pitch relationships that have been described as "pure" because the overtones of the two notes align well and cause minimal *acoustic beats* (volume fluctuations that are perceived as rough or dissonant). This way of using frequency ratios was introduced and discussed in section 2.6 "Valence," where *perfect consonances* were defined as interval ratios with numbers of 4 or lower, and *dissonances* were defined as interval ratios containing numbers higher than 4. The methods of just intonation have been implemented in many different ways across various cultural contexts, and continue to be actively used in music traditions around the world, including in China and India.

Patch 5.1, pictured in figure 5.1, presents the exact interval tunings specified by the system of just intonation. The patch plays a full octave of standard twelve semitone intervals[1] tuned according to their commonly used whole number ratios. To use patch 5.1, click on the row of purple message objects at the top of the patch; they contain values correlated with the ratios listed above them. Each purple message object also triggers a green message object to send its value of 220 as the frequency of a lower reference note, A3 (220 Hz). The patch works by multiplying the interval ratios with the reference note to yield final frequencies that are synthesized using sine waves by the cycle~ object. Click on the purple 0 message object to stop the sound. It can help to play the A3 tonic note simultaneously with the upper note to perceive the complete interval relationship; the simultaneous combination of both notes together is called a *harmonic interval*. Click on the blue toggle object to play the tonic A3 in the right channel and compare it against the upper note in the left channel.

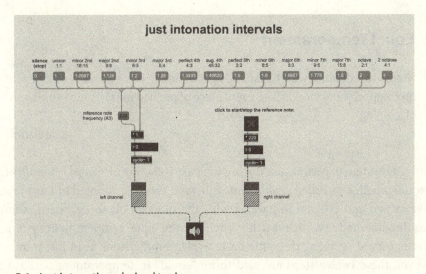

Figure 5.1 Just intonation–derived tunings

5.1.1 These Topics, Skills, and Objects Were Introduced in Section 5.1 "Just Intonation"

- Patch 5.1 further explores the concept of multiplying a sound frequency by a fixed ratio, which we first encountered in Chapter 2 (section 2.6.2). When you click on any of the purple message objects in patch 5.1, you are sending both an interval ratio value (e.g., 1.3333) and a reference frequency of 220 Hz. When both numbers arrive at the "*" arithmetic object, they are multiplied together and the product is sent to the flonum object below. In this case, 1.3333 * 220 = 293.326 Hz, which is then synthesized with a sine wave. The new note, D4, is a perfect 4th above A3 in the just intonation tuning system. Multiplying a frequency by 4/3 or 1.3333 will automatically transpose its pitch up by the interval of a perfect 4th. Similarly, multiplying a frequency by 5/3 or 1.6667 will automatically transpose its pitch up by a major 6th. Multiplying a frequency by 2 will transpose it up an octave.
- Activity: Looping back to the concepts of consonance and dissonance that were first introduced back in section 2.6 "Valence," remember that any two notes are considered to be perfectly consonant if the ratio between them contains numbers of 4 or lower. Conversely, dissonance is defined as any two notes whose ratio contains numbers higher than 4, especially above 7 (e.g., 8:7, 9:8, 10:9, etc.). This definition is somewhat antiquated and perhaps could use some new attention. Now that you have a framework in patch 5.1 that allows you to compare frequency ratios, how might you use it to test the standard definitions of consonance and dissonance? Listen carefully to the different interval ratios and decide for yourself which intervals are consonant and which intervals are dissonant.

5.2 Equal Temperament

> "Because it determines what sounds good, tuning has a pervasive influence on compositional tendencies. Every piece of pitched music is the expression of a tuning."
>
> —Kyle Gann[2]

The tuning system in general use during the past 100 years of *everyday tonality* (general tonal practice) is called *equal temperament*; it was first adopted in Europe about 400 years ago and evolved in parallel with the modern piano keyboard, although it was documented in China much earlier.[3] In the equal temperament system, the octave is carved up using the same basic twelve subdivisions as in just intonation. However, these twelve steps are said to be "equal" in temperament because they share the same frequency ratio. Note that "equal" here doesn't mean that adjacent semitones are separated by equal numbers of frequencies; instead, the use of a ratio means that the actual frequency distances between notes actually increase as the pitch gets higher. But our pitch perception system hears them as equally spaced, so the system works reasonably well. Like Lego bricks, each note fits with all other notes—the system is governed by universal design criteria that ensure interconnectability.

In order to apply the mathematically identical semitone ratio to all notes in equal temperament, the whole number ratios in the just intonation system had to be adjusted slightly. Altering those pure intervals is called "tempering": shifting interval ratios by a small amount in order for the whole system to work well. For example, the perfect fifth interval between A4 and E5 is exactly 3:2 in just intonation (660 Hz for E5 and 440 Hz for A4), but in equal temperament the frequency of E5 is 659.255 Hertz.

One of the benefits of making these tempering adjustments is that they allow music to be fully transposable in all twelve keys, regulating every interval size by the same ratio. You can think of this like using a grid layout, where all structures can shift up or down by the same number of cells. (In just intonation, the cells are of different sizes, which makes those shifts awkward and problematic, causing significant dissonances called *wolf intervals*.[4]) Equal temperament also helps keep large instrumental ensembles in tune. Its adoption may have enabled the expansion of ensemble sizes and structural complexity of European music during the sixteenth–nineteenth centuries; it also allowed composers like J. S. Bach to write keyboard pieces that purposefully include all keys, such as *The Well-Tempered Clavier* (1722). Although just intonation does not transpose well between keys, its primary advantage is that it allows for perfectly ringing resonant overtones on a chord-by-chord basis, and for that reason it is frequently preferred by string ensembles and *a cappella* (unaccompanied) vocal groups, where slight tuning adjustments can be more easily made. It was not practical to implement exact equal temperament tuning until the twentieth century, when modern devices became widely available that could ensure the necessary precision. During the eighteenth and nineteenth centuries, *meantone tuning* provided a middle ground between the mathematically accurate intervals of equal temperament and the sweeter, purer intervals of just intonation.[5]

The semitone ratio used in equal temperament is often called the *twelfth root of two* ($2^{1/12}$, or 2 to the 1/12th power) and is used to convert frequencies to pitch numbers. It is an irrational number, which means that it is a floating-point number with an infinite number of non-repeating decimal places. For practical purposes, we will truncate its value to 1.059463. We can apply the twelfth root of two to find the frequency of one semitone above a given note through simple multiplication: starting from A4, you can calculate the frequency of the adjacent note above (A#4) by multiplying 440 Hz (the frequency of A4) by 1.059463, resulting in a frequency of 466.164 Hz. To compute the frequency of any interval above a given note, multiply its frequency by 1.059463 to the power of the number of semitones in the interval—a process you can explore using the patch described below.

To see how equal temperament can be implemented, please open up patch 5.2 "Equal Temperament Semitone Intervals," pictured in figure 5.2. Click on the

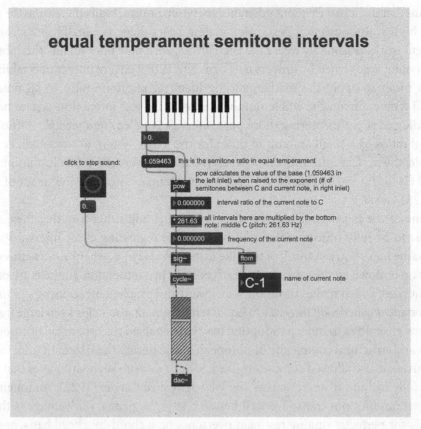

Figure 5.2 Equal temperament semitone intervals

notes of the kslider beginning with C on the left-hand side; each key should produce an equally tempered note separated exactly one semitone away from its neighbor. The kslider outputs 25 notes across two octaves (including an additional C at the top); each note number indicates its distance in semitones from the lowest note. These note numbers are sent from the kslider to the right inlet of the *pow* object. Pow calculates the value of its left input (the base) when it is raised to the exponent provided in its right input. Here, the left input to pow is the twelfth root of two (1.059463); the right input to pow represents the number of semitones between the current note and middle C. Essentially, the pow object here multiplies the ratio by itself as many times as there are semitones in the interval. This calculation results in a new ratio representing the difference between C and the current note. This value is then multiplied by the frequency for middle C, yielding a new note frequency that is synthesized as a sine wave by cycle~. The ftom object converts the frequency number to a MIDI note number, shown here in a number object displaying the letter name and octave register.

This is not the first time we are using the ftom object; we used it once before in patch 2.3 "Frequency." Now may be a good time to review how it works in more detail. The ftom object converts frequency to MIDI pitch numbers using this formula derived from the twelfth root of two: m = 69 + 12 * $\log_2$(f/440). Here, f represents the frequency that you want to convert, and m represents the MIDI pitch number of the resulting note. The components of the formula relate the doubling of the frequency at the octave ($\log_2$) to the 12 semitone subdivisions, pegging the frequency of A 440 Hz to MIDI note number 69.

The relationship of frequency to pitch is an exponential function, evidenced by the fact that frequencies double in value over each octave. You can therefore use powers of 2 to calculate octave frequencies. For example, to find the frequency (f) for a note x octaves higher than a note with frequency y, you compute $f = y*2^x$. For example, if you play the lowest C on the piano (C1, frequency 32.7032 Hz), the note one octave higher (C2) is 2 times higher (32.7032*2^1 = 65.4064 Hz). One octave higher than that (C3) has a frequency that is 4 times higher than C1 (32.7032*2^2 = 130.8128 Hz). One octave higher again (C4, or middle C) is 8 times higher than C1 (32.7032*2^3 = 261.6256 Hz).

Exponential and logarithmic functions are inverses of each other. When you multiply two inverse functions together, you get a straight line. That, therefore, is the role of the formula used in the ftom object (m = 69 + 12 * $\log_2$(f/440)): to apply a logarithmic function ($\log_2$) to an exponential function (2^x), and thereby linearize the relationship between frequency and pitch. The result is a linear sequence of semitones with MIDI numbers 0–127, or, in musical terms, one long chromatic scale encompassing 10½ octaves.

The best way to comprehend the differences between tuning systems is to experience them viscerally. Patch 5.2a "Just vs. Equal Intervals" provides an opportunity to listen and compare just intonation with equal temperament. Listen carefully to the results and decide for yourself! Open up the patch, start up the tonic note by clicking on the blue toggle object, and then alternate between the corresponding just and equal tempered intervals. Minor and major seconds may not have very noticeable differences, but you will probably find the thirds to be quite distinct from each other (most people prefer the just intonation version). Although the fifths are numerically close together, the tiny difference may be noticeable. And the major sevenths are very different from each other. Enjoy spending time attending to the finer details of sound here! Careful listeners may hear some acoustic beating effects. Feel free to modify the code to play both versions of each interval simultaneously; be forewarned that the acoustic beats can occasionally get ferocious, however.

Listening to tunings is a little bit like going to a wine tasting; there can be real aesthetic pleasure and appreciation in noticing slight differences of emphasis. Sometimes, after exploring a range of options, you may return back to an earlier favorite only to discover that it isn't quite as great as you remembered it. Enjoy the journey! There is no objective right or wrong answer to be found here. Having reviewed the technical explanations of tuning systems in this chapter, it may seem ironic that so much math doesn't yield a conclusion about which is the "best" tuning system. After all, it really just comes down to taste and what you find pleasing.

176 Constructing Music

Ultimately, whatever tuning system you decide to use in your performance practice is a matter of personal taste and style—what sounds good to you, and the choices you make while navigating the framework of norms and constraints in which you find yourself.

5.2.1 These Topics, Skills, and Objects Were Introduced in Section 5.2 "Equal Temperament":

- The *pow* object computes a numerical base to an exponential power.
- The *sig~* (last seen in Chapter 1) object converts a number into an audio-rate signal (44,100 kHz sampling rate).
- Microtonal tunings are often characterized in *cents*, or 1/100 of a semitone. Our examples have been worked out in terms of ratios and frequencies; how might you convert them to alternate units such as cents?
- Cycling '74 provides "external objects" and packages in the Max Package Manager that offer "libraries" and pre-computed tables for the just intonation system; try the Just Intonation Toolkit for this purpose.

5.3 Playing in Tune

This final section of the chapter will address how musicians approach tuning during practice sessions. Many monophonic instruments require diligent work and continuous adjustments to perform in tune, especially string instruments and voices. String players and vocalists, as well as other musicians, undertake regular practice regimens in which they slowly and carefully attend to the pitch center of notes and make subtle changes as needed. To get good at this important skill requires a secure sense of inner hearing, as described earlier in section 3.4 "Name an Interval." Inner hearing is the ability to "hear" or audiate notes internally without making any audible sound.

Confidence in one's own inner hearing requires development and reinforcement through regular practice and feedback. Some students find this process difficult because they have to first overcome self-doubt about their ability to identify and lock on to correct frequencies without an external reference. (Of course, for the lucky few who possess perfect pitch, this is not so much of an issue.) In order to develop confidence with this skill, it can help initially to practice in relation to a source note provided by a *drone* or a sustained tone called a *pedal point*. After working in that way for a while, a next step might be to practice with a digital tuner—Korg made a popular series of DT models in the 1990s, and these functions are now widely available in smartphone apps. Tuners provide precise feedback by displaying a meter with a needle moving around a center line. Markers on either side indicate how close or far

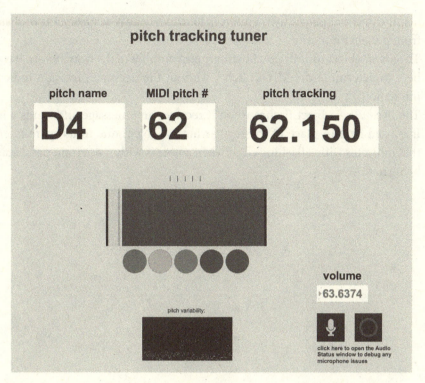

Figure 5.3 Pitch tracking tuner

your pitch is from the desired frequency. Perhaps by now it will not be surprising to discover that this idea can be conveniently adapted to a *Max* patch!

Patch 5.3 "Pitch Tracking Tuner," depicted in figure 5.3, provides a software simulation of the digital tuner idea. It uses Miller Puckette's fiddle~ external object, previously used in patch 3.4a, to accurately track pitch down to 1/1000th of a semitone, in order to assess intonation at a high degree of resolution. A few displays provide the closest pitch letter name and register, MIDI pitch number, and pitch value with three decimal places indicating how much above or below the pitch center you are. A slider object provides a rudimentary display, enhanced by "live.button" objects below it. If the pitch is within 20 percent of the closest semitone, the green button will flash; if between 20 and 40 percent, the yellow buttons will flash, and if greater than 40 percent, then the note is out of tune and the red buttons will flash. Adjust the settings to fit your particular needs.

5.3.1 These Topics, Skills, and Objects Were Introduced in Section 5.3 "Playing in Tune"

- The "!-" object reverses the subtraction process, by subtracting its left input from its right input. In patch 5.3, this means that the nearest whole number semitone is subtracted from the full floating-point number value, outputting

just the decimal places by themselves to evaluate as measurements of distance from perfect intonation.
- The *round* object rounds up a floating-point number to the next integer. It is used here to determine the MIDI pitch ♯, without the decimal precision indicating intonation.
- The *live.button* object flashes when it receives any message and sends a bang. It is used here in place of the regular button object due to its spare interface that indicates with a flashing color when a note is within a certain percentage of being in tune.

6
Reflections

We have covered quite a bit of content in this book! But there are many more aspects to this story—in some ways, it feels as if we have just scratched the surface. I sometimes like to tell my students, after they have completed a substantial task, that the learning process is a little bit like the old "bear went over the mountain" song. That is, you climb and strive and challenge yourself almost to the breaking point, and then one day you find yourself at the top of that proverbial mountain—and suddenly, now you are able to see all the other mountains, as far as the eye can see! Acquiring knowledge and experience expands one's awareness of the remaining knowledge and experience yet to be gained. This insight can be humbling and frustrating, but it also presents new opportunities. With your hard-won skills in music and coding, what new possibilities can you now explore? How might you take this content and make it your own? What exciting live performances and new sounds will you invent? How might you integrate technology into your creative work?

6.1 On the Role of Technology and Invention in Music

Music is an ancient art form that can be traced back at least 40,000 years in human history, and likely much further. From the earliest beginnings of our musical endeavors, we have used tools to help us make music. Music has always been inextricably influenced by the technologies of the time; as technologies have evolved and become more complex, so has music itself. The record player was the music technology that was accessible for my family when I was a child in the 1970s; later, we got a piano that expanded our options, and then a computer in the 1980s that didn't initially inspire sonic possibilities. By now, most of us have computers that are well suited for music production, and our creative possibilities have expanded with the available tools.

Tools facilitate progress and creativity in two ways: they extend our bodies to accomplish actions that we cannot physically manage alone, and they expand our minds by facilitating ideas that might otherwise be inconceivable. In music, our tools are instruments. Although we don't generally think about them this way, instruments are also inventions—not handed down from on high, but painstakingly designed and engineered over many years. Even simple, ancient instruments provide evidence of imagination and design thinking. There is a 40,000-year-old vulture bone flute from Hohle Fels cave in Germany that contains fragments of mammoth ivory; it lends evidence that music may have given the early modern humans a strategic advantage over Neanderthals. Stradivarius and Guarnerius were the acknowledged experts of classical European violin-making, whose instruments enabled new playing styles and musical possibilities. Their instruments provide great examples of iterative design; it took 1,000 years to get from the primitive medieval viol to the sixteenth-century Baroque era form of the violin. During those many years, the materials used to make violins also changed—varnishes improved, methods adjusted. Strings, originally made from animal innards, were replaced by metal.

During the current era of space exploration and wireless digital communications, it is probably not surprising that our music production processes have increasingly moved away from mechanical methods to digital computers, software, and sensors. Modern electronic and digital technologies support musical activities such as performing, recording, editing, producing, broadcasting, and distributing. Arguably, the new instruments of the twenty-first century are interactive music systems that combine hardware together with software intelligence. But they are still tools that extend our human hands and minds.

Musical cultures and practices are deeply influenced by the newly available technical affordances of their time. Historical accounts reveal that great composers and musicians often embraced the technologies of their age. A well-documented example of this phenomenon is provided by W. A. Mozart (1756–1791): although he had grown up playing the harpsichord and composed on it for most of his life, he enthusiastically adopted the newly invented pianoforte when he encountered it in Vienna in 1782. The pianoforte, a precursor to the modern piano, improved upon the harpsichord's intonation, volume control, articulation, and hammer speeds.[1] Mozart quickly incorporated its properties into his music and liked it so much that he wrote fifty works for this new keyboard instrument during the nine years prior to his passing in 1791. He also collaborated with clarinetist Anton Stadler, whose new basset clarinet influenced Mozart's decisions in writing his Clarinet Concerto, completed during the last two months of Mozart's life. He innovated all the way up to the end—not only in structure, form, and melodic invention, but also in the mechanisms of production.

The study of musical history yields many similar examples of prominent composers who leveraged the technical advancements of their day. Other memorable examples include Giovanni Pierluigi da Palestrina, whose ornate polyphony and counterpoint were influenced by the striking acoustical properties of Renaissance cathedral architecture; Palestrina used special techniques such as hocketing and echoing to emphasize the natural panning and reverb that those spaces provided. In the early twentieth century, Olivier Messiaen incorporated new electronic instruments including the Theremin and Ondes Martenot into his instrumental compositions, and George Antheil experimented with diverse arrays of horns, whistles, cranks, sirens, and player pianos to express the frenetic energy of American industrialization. These composers are just a few of the many who enthusiastically adopted innovative approaches to create the sounds of their time.

Creativity is important! It invites a sense of possibility, and it can enhance learning by authentically connecting us to our interests and passions. But creativity isn't easy. It requires time, effort, and iteration. It causes change, which sometimes challenges the status quo and threatens entrenched interests. It can bump up against systemic resistance and long-standing culture issues that are tricky to address. True innovation requires a long time horizon, a methodical process, a high degree of commitment, and an understanding of the implicit risks. It can also help to not be fearful of being embarrassed, as new ideas can be really weird. (Sometimes, the weirder the better!)

New technologies can profoundly impact and cultivate creativity. In New Jersey, where I live, we have gradually forgotten about how this manifested historically in our state. Before the hub of American technical innovation shifted to Silicon Valley during the latter half of the twentieth century, New Jersey was a major powerhouse for the development of technologies that powered massive achievements in science, electronics, and media technology. These inventions propelled New Jersey from a primarily agricultural economy (thus its nickname, the "Garden State") into an internationally significant center for technical innovation. Industrial leaders such as the Edison Manufacturing Company, Bell Telephone Laboratories, Radio Corporation of America (RCA), and other companies created an ecosystem of corporate innovation that drove massive industrialization during the period between approximately 1900 and 1980. Cities like Trenton, Camden, and Newark were engines of industrial production. And interestingly, when you take a look at the totality of inventions created by those companies, a surprisingly high percentage directly involved sound and music. Music played an outsized role in their development and financial success. These companies invented products that enabled, for the first time at scale, the general public to afford access to the production and consumption of sound. (Up until this time, recreational music listening was an expensive luxury often reserved for the wealthy.)

For example, Thomas Edison invested considerable corporate resources into the phonographs and wax cylinder recordings that helped popularize music listening in the home. RCA's early radios, produced at a rate of 9,000 per day in 1932, distributed free music wirelessly to a population primed by the Jazz Age and Roaring '20s. The RCA Theremin, produced between 1929 and 1931 and powered by RCA vacuum tubes, was one of the very earliest sound synthesizers and featured realtime interactive gesture control, nearly eighty years ahead of its time. The NBC Symphony (1937–1954), the world's first corporate-sponsored orchestra, promoted classical music to an empowered postwar American public that was eager to see itself as culturally equal to the great powers of Europe.[2] Early programming for the televisions produced by RCA featured musical performances and variety shows, which may have helped to popularize new music forms like rock and roll, doo-wop, swing, and rhythm & blues. Max Mathews at Bell Labs was credited with inventing the foundational digital audio technologies that allowed not only telephone communications to function, but afterward, enabled an entire landscape of computer-based music production and distribution. Later, RCA permitted Milton Babbitt of nearby Princeton University to access the Mark II synthesizer at night in their headquarters to compose music beginning in the 1950s, widely acknowledged to be some of the first great musical compositions ever made on computers.

Music is deeply intertwined with the history of human invention itself. Many of the engineers and scientists who developed the technologies that powered twentieth-century innovations were also personally invested in making music during their spare time. Perhaps music is the special ingredient without which these important landmark technologies might never have been invented. And it is perhaps also worth noting that American influence and power abroad during the twentieth century was also tightly correlated with its musical innovations that were exported and enthusiastically embraced worldwide. Perhaps music and innovation share one necessary creative element: belief in the power of an idea to transform the world.

6.2 Creative Technology Enables Access and Inclusion

There is also an important social justice component embedded in our technical tools for music production. At times, technological developments have enabled new opportunities for diversity, equity, and inclusion in music production. When the tools of musical recording became commercially available in the 1950s and 1960s, the means of production were finally obtainable by African American artists. This empowered a generation in which authentic cultural voices began to emerge. Studio systems were established that invented whole new genres of music, including Motown (Hitsville U.S.A. studio in Detroit), the Philadelphia Sound (associated with Gamble & Huff, Philadelphia International Records, and Sigma Sound Studios), and Afrofuturism (Labelle and Sun Ra's Arkestra). Audio recording and editing hardware bypassed the written requirements of earlier musical styles and the postgraduate gatekeepers in music theory, notation, and scoring. Now, musicians could jump directly to the creative process through direct, embodied interaction in the recording studio. This broke open the canon of acceptable modes of engagement in music with activities including composing, arranging, and producing being taken on by African American artists.

Today, digital instruments and software are again opening up the canon by allowing new styles of music to be included in higher education curricula. Pop, rock, rap, electronic dance music, etc. are being taught, as well as new modes of musical production and performance. A wider range of repertoire attracts students whose identities are not foregrounded in the cultural, racial, and stylistic norms of the Western Classical tradition. This approach embraces "a plurality of style to decenter whiteness,"[3] thereby fostering inclusion.

These changes have led to rethinking the "primary instrument" requirement for college-level music study; musical identity formation now goes beyond just one's instrument, viewed through new lenses and intersectional perspectives that do not disadvantage students based on their socioeconomic backgrounds and educational preparation. In some institutions of higher education, students are allowed and even encouraged to learn music on laptops as their primary instrument, using software as the mechanism of musical production. To accommodate these changes, instructors are enacting project-based learning activities instead of traditional notation-based drills and graded exercises. Students from many different socioeconomic backgrounds are doing these activities on their own time outside of school, so it makes sense to find ways to include computer-based music production in our classrooms as well.

6.3 Defining Music Broadly

Having engaged with the broad sweep of historical, technical, and musical ideas in this book, you may find that your working definition of music is starting to expand. Funny enough, it's difficult to pin down exactly what music is, and to define it with precision. Most likely, music is a suitcase word for an integrated set of complex experiences that comprise thinking, feeling, emoting, performing, creating, and listening. But here is a starting place: music is the human activity of creative expression through sound. It is an ancient art form that encodes and reflects important aspects of human experience. It teaches us about how things interact, move, and change, including bodies, thoughts, and emotions. It involves physical embodiment and cognitive perception, revealing in its patterns essential aspects of both. Ultimately, music is one of the most characteristic of human activities, and one of the best ways to learn about the special features and limitations of being human.[4]

Perhaps music might also be described as a proto-form of Artificial Intelligence. Even before computers existed, we simulated, imitated, and evaluated our thoughts and emotions through the means available to us at the time. A striking example is provided through the experience of music. Before the development of modern computer languages, algorithms, and computational processes, music provided a useful procedural simulation platform on which to work out and enact abstract ideas. (This is probably true for other forms of art as well, although music most closely mirrors AI because of its abstract symbolic qualities.) Composition and music production enable us to express our thoughts, memories, and feelings by encoding them as shapes and contours in patterns of sound. In the aesthetic reception and reflection processes of musical listening, we re-form and re-enact those shapes and contours in our own imaginations and learn about the ways other minds work across the range of human experience.

In suggesting that music has proto-AI qualities, I am not suggesting that music produces the outcomes of thinking, such as the decisions, language models, images, code, and other results of modern generative AI systems. Rather, music simulates the *experience* of thinking; what it feels like to think in someone else's head. Music serves as a way to inhabit another person's cognitive processes in our own mind. Musical sounds flow by at the speed and scale of human thought, mimicking thought-like processes through patterns of pitch, intensity, rhythm, valence, timbre, texture, etc. Listening to music helps us perceive the features and structures of another person's thoughts—to hear how they think. Repeated listenings yield new insights, new explorations, and reinforce prior discoveries. For example, listening carefully to all the voices in a multilayered contrapuntal texture gives you the experience of seeing things from multiple perspectives, exploring a range of sonic collaborations. By exploring the musical ideas and feelings of others through our own auditory imaginations, we can interpret them from a safe distance, build empathy, and derive therapeutic value for ourselves. This helps us feel better emotionally and think new thoughts.

6.4 Music, Coding, and Constructionism

Finally, in using code to better understand how music is put together, we have not completely forged a new unique path. Instead, we have been standing on the shoulders of giants by applying a learning theory called *Constructionism*. *Constructionist* learning theory extends the *Constructivist* philosophy of Jean Piaget (1896–1980), who asserted that learners actively create their own knowledge by interacting with the world and integrating new information with what they already know. Constructionism takes that idea one step further by integrating it with creative technology and describing how students actively construct knowledge by making things in the world. Both philosophies place the individual at the center of the knowledge creation process, eschewing the traditional "sage on the stage" model of knowledge transmission from teacher to student. Constructionism instead focuses on the process of "learning to learn," emphasizing the conversation-like steps that learners undertake when making things, and how these experiences facilitate the construction of new knowledge.

Seymour Papert developed the Constructionist learning philosophy at MIT in the 1980s, based on earlier collaborations with Marvin Minsky that produced the LOGO programming language and "turtle" interface for elementary school children in the 1960s and 1970s. Decades before the STEM movement, Papert theorized that the creation of new technological artifacts enabled students to engage in a turn-taking process of iterative revision with evocative objects that Papert called "things to think with." He observed that it was helpful to give students projects to work on to encourage those internal conversations to take place. Constructionist projects emphasized playfulness and placed a high value on diverse materials and simple kits that did not include too many specific tasks or predefined plans to execute.

There have been many powerful outcomes of the Constructionist framework. Constructionism has directly led to modern programming platforms such as Scratch and Processing, as well as popular digital environments such as Minecraft and Roblox. We can also draw strong connections between Constructionism and the Maker/DIY movement, popularized by Make Magazine, Instructables.com, the growth of Makerspaces, and hardware prototyping platforms such as Arduino, Raspberry Pi, Makey Makey, and LittleBits. Powerful pedagogical results of the Constructionist method include teaching practices that are project-centered and oriented toward demos and public presentations as both extrinsic and intrinsic motivators. Constructionist teaching environments have an immersive quality—students get absorbed in the act of solving problems with a tangible goal. Ideally, the instructor cultivates an environment that is safe and supportive of creativity, openness, invention, and risk-taking, providing necessary conditions for progress. Constructionist teaching practices focus on collaborative problem solving, teamwork with individualized deliverables, and careful mentorship. They also emphasize the synthesis of interdisciplinary skills and concepts, and encourage synergies between design, coding, hardware, musical/artistic content, and user experience assessment. Constructionist methods require flexibility and nimbleness to change directions when things get stuck, which they sometimes do. And the best projects are usually motivated from big ideas first: first develop a "pie-in-the-sky" vision, and then implement.

Constructionism can also be applied to help us make music. There are strong similarities between Papert's process-oriented learning theory and the ways that we learn music. Musical creativity is good not only for making sound, but also for developing our minds. From this perspective, music itself becomes an evocative object, a teaching machine, or a *thing to think with*. And human musical perception becomes a learning system that can be modeled and studied. So, in engaging with the activities of this book, you have been learning music fundamentals through a Constructionist framework. This approach is well grounded in theory and research literature, and hopefully it worked for you.

6.5 Looping Back; Final Thoughts on Creative Coding and Music

Well, what exactly did we learn in the process of constructing music through code? In addition to the core music theory concepts, we also engaged with important music technology content such as MIDI, digital audio, signal flow, algorithmic composition, and interactive music systems. We undertook procedural and quantitative approaches to creating music, applying elements of computational thinking. We also introduced foundational concepts in the design of new media including user interface design, human-centered design methods, and the iterative design loop. And we gained introductory familiarity with fundamentals of object-oriented computer programming, including variables, functions, data types, Boolean logic, loops, pointers, arrays, data structures, the concept of "state," sequential processing of instructions, algorithm design, modularization, and encapsulation. We learned a little bit about external objects and the knowledge base of the worldwide *Max* user community, and observed the ethical citation of outside sources for our code projects. Finally, we explored the value of interdisciplinarity and observed how combining different perspectives can enhance the overall learning experience. As you move on to next steps in your own development process, I hope you will continue to explore new possibilities in music and coding, build upon your skill set, and make awesome creative work! There is so much more to discover, learn, and enjoy.

Notes

Introduction

1. Marvin Minsky, "Keynote Address at the Music, Mind, and Invention Workshop," March 30, 2012, at The College of New Jersey, Ewing, NJ, video, 23:38, https://youtu.be/gmeiJlbcVDo?t=1418. A longer quotation segment provides additional context: "So, what are the meanings of musical phrases? We don't have an agreed-on language of discourse for talking about such things. It's curious. Such a popular activity, and most uneducated people actually unconsciously—or inarticulately—know a great deal about music and know when something's wrong, and know when a piece is coming to the end, and so forth. But it's not part of popular discourse to talk about it. And in technical music discussions there's precious little agreed on things to say about it. So I think that's annoyed me because I spent a lot of time trying to get better at music and improvising and trying to understand how did Bach or Beethoven pull such a thing off, and no-one could actually tell you. It's a fascinating field that. . . . It's like chemistry before the Periodic Table, and there's lots to do."
2. Kort, Reilly, and Picard proposed that as people move through the learning process, they experience a variety of positive and negative emotions. For example, learners might start out curious or fascinated by a topic; then they can become confused or puzzled as they seek a better understanding. In later stages, they may engage with negative emotions such as frustration when they actively grapple with the issues and solve problems. Finally, as they consolidate their knowledge and become aware that they are making progress, they may start to feel hopeful and optimistic about next steps. Additional research by D'Mello et al. found that when measuring facial expressions of learners, faces that displayed confusion preceded learning gains. See Barry Kort, Rob Reilly, and Rosalind W. Picard, "An Affective Model of Interplay between Emotions and Learning: Reengineering Educational Pedagogy—building a Learning Companion," *Proceedings IEEE International Conference on Advanced Learning Technologies* (2001): 43–46; and Sidney K. D'Mello et al., "Integrating Affect Sensors in an Intelligent Tutoring System," in *Affective Interactions: The Computer in the Affective Loop Workshop at the International Conference on Intelligent User Interfaces* (2005): 7–13.
3. One example of a widely used music theory textbook: Stefan Kostka and Dorothy Payne, *Tonal Harmony*, 8th ed. (New York: McGraw-Hill Higher Education, 2017).
4. Figures I.1 and I.2 display an excerpt from the iconic Kool & the Gang hit song, "Celebration." Ronald N. Bell et al., "Celebration," Kool & the Gang, De-Lite/The Island Def Jam Music Group, 1980, https://youtu.be/3GwjfUFyY6M.
5. The College Music Society released a report by its Task Force on the Undergraduate Music Major in 2014. Among other recommendations, the report advocated for greater emphasis on creativity, improvisation, technology, and contemporary musical styles in music curricula. While controversial, the report has generated robust discussions within the academic music community about the need to update teaching materials and methods. Edward W. Sarath, David E. Myers, and Patricia Shehan Campbell, "Transforming Music Study from Its Foundations: A Manifesto for Progressive Change in the Undergraduate Preparation of Music Majors," in *Redefining Music Studies in an Age of Change* (New York: Routledge, 2016), 59–99.
6. John Harbison, "Symmetries and the 'New Tonality,'" *Contemporary Music Review* 6, no. 2 (1992): 71–79.
7. Philip Tagg, *Everyday Tonality II: Towards a Tonal Theory of What Most People Hear* (New York: Mass Media Music Scholars' Press, 2014).

8. The concept of layers of abstraction relates to the "spiral curriculum," a learning design model in which topics are presented repeatedly at deepening levels of detail. As learners develop knowledge about topics, they progress through the abstraction levels, moving from short summaries at the highest level to detailed explanations at the lowest level. Jerome S. Bruner, *The Process of Education*, rev. ed. (Cambridge, MA: Harvard University Press, 1976).
9. We can also use suitcase words "to conceal the complexity of very large ranges of different things whose relationships we don't yet comprehend." Marvin Minsky, *The Emotion Machine: Commonsense Thinking, Artificial Intelligence, and the Future of the Human Mind* (New York: Simon & Schuster, 2007), 17. (See 109–12 for a description of how suitcase words are used in psychology.)
10. It is worth noting that there is no intrinsic reason why piano keys were given a black and white color scheme; this was a design decision. During the early days of keyboards this arrangement was not standardized, and Mozart himself owned a keyboard with black lower keys and white upper keys. In light of our current understanding of structural racism, we cannot ignore the use of color in this context: in the standard configuration, white was chosen for pleasing diatonicism and black was chosen for chromaticism and "accidentals." For this reason, this book refers to keys as "upper" and "lower" instead of black and white. In addition, all code examples featuring a keyboard layout use an alternate color scheme, and readers will be encouraged to creatively reinvent the colors for the keyboard layouts in their work.
11. MUSIC (versions I–V) was developed by Max Mathews at Bell Telephone Laboratories, 1957–1966. GROOVE (Real-time Generated Operations On Voltage-controlled Equipment) was developed by Max Mathews and Richard Moore at Bell Telephone Laboratories, 1968–1978. Csound was first developed by Barry Vercoe at the Massachusetts Institute of Technology in 1985. SuperCollider was released by James McCartney in 1996. Miller Puckette began developing Pd (Pure Data) at The University of California, San Diego in 1996. ChucK was released by Ge Wang and Perry Cook at Princeton University in 2004. Sonic Pi was invented by Sam Aaron in 2012.
12. "Max (software)," Wikimedia Foundation, last modified December 11, 2022, https://en.wikipedia.org/wiki/Max_(software)). Francois, "A brief history of MAX," Free Software @ IRCAM, archived 2009, https://web.archive.org/web/20090603230029/http://freesoftware.ircam.fr/article.php3?id_article=5.
13. Dan Derks, "Algorithms in Motion: Elementary Cellular Automata in Max and Max for Live," Cycling '74 tutorial, last modified April 28, 2020, https://cycling74.com/tutorials/algorithms-less-concepts-max-for-live-device-cellular-automata.

Chapter 1

1. V. J. Manzo, *Max/MSP/Jitter for Music: A Practical Guide to Developing Interactive Music Systems for Education and More* (Oxford University Press, 2016).
2. T. Winkler, *Composing Interactive Music: Techniques and Ideas Using Max* (Cambridge, MA: MIT Press, 2001).
3. https://www.instructables.com/id/Intro-to-MaxMSP/.
4. https://www.kadenze.com/courses/programming-max-structuring-interactive-software-for-digital-arts-i/info. (This course is free to take as an observer, and certificates are available with a premium membership price of $20/month.)
5. Here is a helpful link: https://www.youtube.com/watch?v=aGrifWA5gq4.
6. Those who have experience with traditional programming languages such as C++ and Java may notice a discrepancy in the way that some terms are used in *Max*. In other languages, the term "object" usually refers to variable values and quantities (called "messages" in *Max*), whereas "functions" are actions performed by a computer (called "objects" in *Max*). However, in object-oriented

programming, the approach that was used to create *Max*, the word "object" refers to the predefined functions from which a program is constructed.

7. The sequence in which messages are received is explained in this *Max* tutorial: https://docs.cycling74.com/max8/tutorials/basicchapter05.
8. The idea for this tutorial was initially inspired by V. J. Manzo, "Introduction to Max," in *Max/MSP/Jitter for Music*.
9. In programming languages, *arguments* (also called parameters) are values that provide important information to functions as they run; arguments are specific types of variables that help define how functions work.
10. More background information about this aspect of *Max* implementation can be found at https://cycling74.com/forums/max-message-semantics.
11. For this reason, in the early years of the twenty-first century, many video game manufacturers stopped integrating MIDI sound platforms and hardware synthesizers into game consoles, and instead started using richer-sounding recordings through digital audio playback.
12. Also known as continuous controller ("CC") messages, these include sustain pedal (0/1 up/down), volume pedal, and data from external sensor devices such as the Eigenharp Pico https://www.youtube.com/watch?v=TVaTDXQdXkY.
13. Here are two helpful resources on MIDI for self-learners: P. D. Lehrman and T. Tully, *MIDI for the Professional* (New York: Amsco, 1993); and D. B. Williams and P. R. Webster, *Experiencing Music Technology*, 4th ed. (New York: Oxford University Press, 2022).
14. See Rick Wakeman's 1978 keyboard setup here: http://www.progarchives.com/forum/forum_posts.asp?TID=98771.
15. More useful information can be found at https://support.apple.com/guide/audio-midi-setup/set-up-midi-devices-ams875bae1e0/mac.
16. https://coolsoft.altervista.org/en/virtualmidisynth.
17. Unfortunately, one shortcoming of pneumatic player pianos was that they could not be synchronized with other instruments. This caused a real problem for composer George Antheil, whose composition *Ballet Mécanique* required sixteen player pianos to all play in time with each other while accompanying a film. Antheil ruminated for years about this issue after a disastrous performance at Carnegie Hall in 1927; a 1942 patent on radio frequency hopping that he coauthored with Hedy Lamarr represented an attempt to solve this issue. Ultimately, Antheil's synchronization problem was solved in the 1990s by a team including Paul Lehrman, representatives from the G. Schirmer publishing company, and Yamaha (manufacturers of the Disklavier digital piano).
18. The MIDI data provided in Mario.mid was originally sequenced by Neoguizmo in a copyrighted file posted on MuseScore.com: https://musescore.com/user/2072681/scores/2601926.
19. There is a great deal of important information about digital audio that is beyond the scope of this introductory tutorial. For those who would like to better understand the fundamentals, I recommend an excellent resource called "How Digital Audio Works," available for free from Cycling '74 at https://docs.cycling74.com/max8/tutorials/02_mspdigitalaudio. There is also a comprehensive and widely used digital audio textbook that, like this book, uses *Max* patches to apply and reinforce theoretical information: A. Cipriani and M. Giri, *Electronic Music and Sound Design: Theory and Practice with Max* (Rome: ConTempoNet, 2019).
20. The term "samples" here refers to individual amplitude values—snapshots of the waveform in very tiny increments of time. These samples are larger in size than MIDI messages and therefore require greater bandwidth; individual audio samples are often encoded using 16 bits, much larger than a MIDI 7-bit value. Audio transmission rates also have to take into account the typical doubling of data throughput because of the need for two channels (Left and Right) in stereo signals.
21. Physical interactions with digital music systems have been explored since the 1960s. Beginning in 2001, the annual International Conference on New Interfaces for Musical Expression (https://www.nime.org) has been gathering musicians and researchers who work on the design

of new interfaces for music, human-computer interaction, and the live performance of computer music.

Chapter 2

1. Audacity® is a widely used, free, cross-platform, open-source application for audio editing and recording, originally developed and distributed by Dominic Mazzoni and Roger Dannenberg at Carnegie Mellon University (https://www.audacityteam.org).
2. It can be accessed at: https://musiclab.chromeexperiments.com/Spectrogram.
3. While it is disputable whether we can hear the sounds of our own nervous systems, Cage certainly could listen to his own breathing and heart beating in the anechoic chamber. Kirk McElhearn, "John Cage and the Anechoic Chamber," January 16, 2016, https://kirkville.com/john-cage-and-the-anechoic-chamber/.
4. John Cage, *I–VI.: Questions and Answers* (Cambridge, MA: Harvard University Press, 1990), 26.
5. Pauline Oliveros, "The Difference between Hearing and Listening," TEDxIndianapolis, November 12, 2015, https://youtu.be/_QHfOuRrJB8.
6. Murray Campbell and Clive Greated, "Loudness," in *Grove Music Online (Oxford Music Online)* (2001), doi: 10.1093/gmo/9781561592630.article.17030.
7. Unequal perceptions of loudness across the audible frequency range have been studied for many years. Early work on this topic quantified the range of human hearing in "isophonic" or "equal-loudness" contour graphs. Harvey Fletcher and Wilden A. Munson, "Loudness, Its Definition, Measurement and Calculation," *Bell System Technical Journal* 12, no. 4 (1933): 377–430.
8. This aspect aligns with the activation or intensity component of emotional responses described in James Russell's Circumplex model of affect, which will be explored further in section 2.6. James A. Russell, "A Circumplex Model of Affect," *Journal of Personality and Social Psychology* 39, no. 6 (1980): 1161–1178, doi: 10.1037/h0077714.
9. Matthias Thiemel, "Dynamics," in *Grove Music Online (Oxford Music Online)* (2001), doi: 10.1093/gmo/9781561592630.article.08458.
10. Charles Taylor and Murray Campbell, "Sound," in *Grove Music Online (Oxford Music Online)* (2001), doi: 10.1093/gmo/9781561592630.article.26289.
11. Clive Greated, "Decibel," in *Grove Music Online (Oxford Music Online)* (2001), doi: 10.1093/gmo/9781561592630.article.07362.
12. Intensity is proportional to the square of the amplitude in a sound wave (or any type of wave). Clive Greated, "Intensity," in *Grove Music Online (Oxford Music Online)* (2001), doi: 10.1093/gmo/9781561592630.article.13825.
13. Geoffrey Chew, "Articulation and Phrasing," in *Grove Music Online (Oxford Music Online)* (2001), doi: 10.1093/gmo/9781561592630.article.40952.
14. Alessandro Cipriani and Maurizio Giri, *Electronic Music and Sound Design: Theory and Practice with Max 8*, 4th ed. (Rome: ConTempoNet, 2019).
15. Some expert sources connect this lub-dub heartbeat pattern to the "iambic foot" (an unstressed syllable followed by a stressed syllable), a component of the "iambic pentameter" metrical pattern used in English poetry.
16. The score provided in this salsa example was adapted from a public domain source that has a Creative Commons 1.0 Universal license: Cody Stumpo, "Latin Rhythms," Musescore, October 30, 2012, https://musescore.com/user/49768/scores/69780.
17. Ethan Hein, "Groove Pizza," NYU Music Experience Lab, v2.4.1, https://apps.musedlab.org/groovepizza.

18. Ethan Hein and Sumanth Srinivasan, "The Groove Pizza: A Study in Music and HCI," in *New Directions in Music and Human-Computer Interaction*, ed. Simon Holland et al. (Germany: Springer International, 2019), 71–94.
19. Fabrice B. R. Parmentier et al., "Why Are Auditory Novels Distracting? Contrasting the Roles of Novelty, Violation of Expectation and Stimulus Change," *Cognition* 119, no. 3 (2011): 374–380, doi: 10.1016/j.cognition.2011.02.001.
20. James Russell proposed a Circumplex model of affect in which emotions can be characterized using two descriptors: valence (positive or negative associations) and intensity (also called activation or arousal, referenced in endnote 8, above). These two components can be represented as variables on a two-dimensional plane and used to study how humans respond to a wide range of experiences. In section 2.4 "Intensity" above, we connected the intensity component to loudness in music; here in section 2.6, we are connecting the valence component to qualitative judgments about sound associated with terms such as consonance and dissonance, harmoniousness and discordance, etc. The structured approach presented in this book for characterizing how musical variables convey emotional associations is influenced by the work of Rosalind Picard and the field of Affective Computing.

    James A. Russell, "A Circumplex Model of Affect," *Journal of Personality and Social Psychology* 39, no. 6 (1980): 1161–1178, doi: 10.1037/h0077714.

    Vera Shuman, David Sander, and Klaus R. Scherer, "Levels of Valence," *Frontiers in Psychology* 4 (2013): 261, doi: 10.3389/fpsyg.2013.00261; Rosalind W. Picard, *Affective Computing* (Cambridge, MA: MIT Press, 1997).
21. Morwaread Farbood, "A Parametric, Temporal Model of Musical Tension," *Music Perception* 29, no. 4 (2012): 387–428.
22. Paul Hegarty, "Noise," in *Grove Music Online (Oxford Music Online)* (2001), doi: 10.1093/gmo/9781561592630.article.A2292545.
23. John Cage, *Silence: Lectures and Writings* (Middletown, CT: Wesleyan University Press, 1961; repr. 2012), 3. John Blacking, *How Musical Is Man?* (Seattle: University of Washington Press, 1974), 12.
24. As part of this discussion about how we label sounds as inherently musical or noisy, it is important to acknowledge the influence of cultural biases that frame the way we perceive what we hear. In particular, common assumptions about "high" (classical) and "low" (popular) music traditions play a role in the interpretation or "valencing" of noisy content. While the ideas of John Cage have been embraced warmly by the academic music community, popular artists in genres such as hip-hop have not yet been sufficiently recognized or represented in scholarship and curricula.
25. In this example, both notes share the same letter name; this will be explained further in section 3.2 "Name a Note." However, the lower note is located in the bottom half of the 88-note piano keyboard, whereas the upper one is located in the top half of the keyboard. The interval between these two notes is thought to be highly consonant; it is called an octave. Details about octaves will be explained in sections 3.2 "Name a Note" and 3.3 "Make an Interval."
26. In this example, the upper note is E5 and the lower note is A4. The interval between them is a perfect fifth, considered highly consonant. (Interval names will be explained in section 3.4.) Observant readers may notice that the frequency of E5 in common usage is not 660, however; it is 659.255 Hertz. This discrepancy is due to tuning systems, which we will discuss in Chapter 5.
27. Claude V. Palisca and Brian C. J. Moore, "Consonance," in *Grove Music Online (Oxford Music Online)* (2001), doi: 10.1093/gmo/9781561592630.article.06316.
28. "Dissonance," in *Grove Music Online (Oxford Music Online)* (2001), doi: 10.1093/gmo/9781561592630.article.07851.
29. Dissonant intervals may also be characterized by the speed with which their combined waveforms repeat; lower-numbered ratios repeat quickly, whereas higher-numbered ratios repeat more slowly due to the complexity of their combined waves. "It may be that the ear and brain find this

complicated sequence much more difficult to cope with than the simple rapid alteration that occurs with [lower-numbered ratios]." Taylor and Campbell, "Sound," in *Grove Music Online*.
30. Although less commonly discussed than the standard vertical pitch-based idea of dissonance, there is a corresponding horizontal concept called "metrical dissonance." Metrical dissonance can occur between different layers of motion through misalignments either of grouping (incongruent layers of different kinds of durations) or of displacement (similarly congruent layers that are not aligned in time). Harald Krebs, *Fantasy Pieces: Metrical Dissonance in the Music of Robert Schumann* (New York: Oxford University Press, 1999).

Chapter 3

1. Fred Lerdahl, *Tonal Pitch Space* (New York: Oxford University Press, 2001).
2. In German-speaking regions, the letter H is used for B♮, whereas the letter B by itself is used for B♭.
3. This seemingly redundant note-naming convention arose for historical reasons. Before the equal temperament tuning system was widely adopted, C♯ and D♭ had noticeably different frequencies and were considered to be distinctly different notes. Tuning systems are described in greater detail in Chapter 5.
4. William Drabkin, "Register," in *Grove Music Online (Oxford Music Online)* (2001), doi: 10.1093/gmo/9781561592630.article.23072.
5. The name half step likely comes from the fact that five out of the seven intervals that span adjacent letter-named notes are whole steps, consisting of two semitones. In the majority of cases where adjacent letter names are whole steps apart, the intervening semitone is represented by an upper key note on the piano keyboard. There are several established musical genres that commonly use sub-semitones and microtones, including the Hindustani and Carnatic traditions in India and Indonesian Gamelan music.
6. The concept of enharmonic equivalency in music is analogous to the idea of the "homophone" in language; homophones are words that sound the same but have different spellings or meanings.
7. There is some disagreement among experts about the consonance of the 4:3 ratio that defines the interval of the perfect fourth. The sound generated by this interval is often perceived by modern listeners to be dissonant and in need of resolution. The interval of a fourth is included among the perfect consonances because it is strongly related to the 3:2 ratio of the perfect fifth. Fourths and fifths are considered to be interval inverses of each other; this topic will be covered in section 3.3 "Make an Interval."
8. The concept of interval inversion resembles the mathematical concept of additive inverses, where two numbers sum to the additive identity of 0. (In music, the octave serves as a form of additive identity.)
9. Frank Jackson, "Epiphenomenal Qualia," *Philosophical Quarterly* 32 (1982): 127–136, doi: 10.2307/2960077.
10. Several musical examples of qualia have been addressed in recent music theory literature: Benjamin Hansberry, "What Are Scale-degree Qualia?," *Music Theory Spectrum* 39, no. 2 (2017): 182–199; Andrea Schiavio and Dylan van der Schyff, "Beyond Musical Qualia: Reflecting on the Concept of Experience," *Psychomusicology: Music, Mind, and Brain* 26, no. 4 (2016): 366; Piotr Podlipniak, "Tonal Qualia and the Evolution of Music," *AVANT: Pismo Awangardy Filozoficzno-Naukowej* 1 (2017): 33–44.
11. We should also acknowledge here that *Max* and other MIDI-based music software packages don't usually incorporate interval spelling rules. This is because MIDI treats each pitch as a pure number, without associated letter names or accidentals. When moving between a MIDI-based representation of pitch and a letter-based representation of pitch, a translation mechanism is needed that

takes context into account. *Max* lacks such a mechanism; for this reason, it will sometimes incorrectly spell notes and intervals using enharmonically equivalent note names. It can be helpful to include a "library" such as EAMIR by V. J. Manzo to correctly display note and interval names. (See endnote 20 for more information.) *Max* offers several useful libraries in a collection called the Package Manager.

12. Randomized interval identification activities such as the one presented in patch 3.4a are not typically used as a starting place for those who are new to ear training. If you are a beginner, it can help to simplify this task by starting with smaller interval sizes (seconds and thirds) and progressively adding larger ones. (Other common strategies include restricting the available intervals to just those that fit within a major scale and relying on familiar tunes to serve as mnemonic devices.) The code in this patch can be customized for beginning, intermediate, and advanced students. Limit the intervals to seconds and thirds by modifying just one variable in edit mode: locate the red random object in edit mode and change its argument from 13 to 5.

13. Zoltán Kodály, *The Selected Writings of Zoltán Kodály* (London: Boosey & Hawkes, 1974).

14. A memorable implementation of this idea was created for a class project by Jillian Verblaauw, TCNJ music education major and 2017 graduate of the College of New Jersey. While we cannot include her patch here due to copyright restrictions on the music files, you can create your own personalized interval ear training patch linking to your own favorite music recordings online. (This should be for your own personal practice; not for public distribution.) See if you can identify at least one song for each interval type, and try to include both ascending and descending forms.

15. There are some issues with these note spellings because the MIDI display format used in number boxes only uses sharps to spell accidentals. When converting from MIDI note numbers to the standard note naming convention (letter plus accidental), some errors can occur. Notes with flat accidentals have been removed from all the umenu objects on this patch because spellings in the number objects do not match. In the current patch, B♯ and E♯ are displayed in number objects using their enharmonic equivalents (C and F).

16. Nicolas Meeùs, "Scale, polifonia, armonia," in *Enciclopedia della musica (vol. 2, Il sapere musicale)*, ed. Jean-Jacques Nattiez (Torino: Einaudi, 2002), 84.

17. Alexander L. Ringer, "Melody," in *Grove Music Online (Oxford Music Online)* (2001), doi: 10.1093/gmo/9781561592630.article.18357.

18. "Notes and Neurons: In Search of the Common Chorus," World Science Festival, June 12, 2009, https://youtu.be/S0kCUss0g9Q.

19. "Musical Keyboard" (section on Size and historical variation), Wikimedia Foundation, updated December 8, 2022, https://en.wikipedia.org/wiki/Musical_keyboard#Size_and_historical_variation.

20. The infamous Stonehenge scene from the movie *Spinal Tap* provides a great example of modal mixture. Also, Sinatra's "Fly Me to the Moon" features a well-known passage in natural minor followed by harmonic minor in a descending melodic sequence.

21. V. J. Manzo's EAMIR Software Development Kit (SDK) is also available in the Package Manager section of the *Max* programming environment; it provides a library of interactive tools that handle different scale types. EAMIR stands for Electro-Acoustic Musically Interactive Room; it was originally created to help individuals with physical limitations enjoy creating and shaping musical performances using larger movements than might typically be needed to play musical instruments.

22. Dominant seventh chords used in the blues often feature a characteristic tuning that is sometimes referred to as a "blue note" or a "blues seven." In this style, the 7th above the root note is tuned differently from the conventional Western tuning, featuring a ratio of 7:4. Tuning systems will be covered in Chapter 5. For more information, please see "Blues," Wikimedia Foundation, updated January 5, 2023, https://en.wikipedia.org/wiki/Blues; "Dominant seventh chord," Wikimedia Foundation, updated July 2, 2022, https://en.wikipedia.org/wiki/Dominant_seventh_chord.

23. Brian Hyer, "Key (i)," in *Grove Music Online (Oxford Music Online)* (2001), doi: 10.1093/gmo/9781561592630.article.14942.
24. There are many great examples of composers who combine synesthesia and music, including Scriabin's color organ and "Prometheus Poem of Fire," as well as modern examples. Oliver Sacks, *Musicophilia: Tales of Music and the Brain* (Toronto: Vintage Canada, 2010); Richard E. Cytowic, *Synesthesia: A Union of the Senses*. (Cambridge, MA: MIT Press, 2002).

Chapter 4

1. T. M. Nakra, Y. Ivanov, P. Smaragdis, and C. Ault, "The UBS Virtual Maestro: An Interactive Conducting System," *Proceedings of the International Conference on New Interfaces for Musical Expression* (2009): 250–255. International Conference on New Interfaces for Musical Expression, Carnegie Mellon University. http://doi.org/10.5281/zenodo.1177637; E. Lee, T. Karrer, and J. Borchers, "Toward a Framework for Interactive Systems to Conduct Digital Audio and Video Streams," *Computer Music Journal* 30, no. 1 (Spring 2006): 21–36.
2. For information on why people like to "speed-listen" to podcasts and audio books, see: https://www.theatlantic.com/technology/archive/2015/06/the-rise-of-speed-listening/396740/. Researchers have conducted studies on this phenomenon: S. Vemuri, P. DeCamp, W. Bender, and C. Schmandt, "Improving Speech Playback Using Time-Compression and Speech Recognition," *Proceedings of the SIGCHI Conference on Human Factors in Computing Systems* (2004): 295–302. Association for Computing Machinery (ACM) SIGCHI. https://doi.org/10.1145/985692.985730
3. D. Epstein, "Beyond Orpheus: Studies in Musical Structure," *Journal of Aesthetics and Art Criticism* 38, no. 4 (1980): 480–482.
4. Martin F. McKinney et al., "Evaluation of Audio Beat Tracking and Music Tempo Extraction Algorithms," *Journal of New Music Research* 36, no. 1 (2007): 1–16; Daniel P. W. Ellis, "Beat Tracking by Dynamic Programming," *Journal of New Music Research* 36, no. 1 (2007): 51–60.
5. E. Lapidaki, "Young People's and Adults' Large-Scale Timing in Music Listening," *Proceedings of the Sixth International Conference on Music Perception and Cognition* (2000). Department of Psychology. Staffordshire, England: Keele University.
6. A rare exception can be found in Vijay S. Iyer, "Microstructures of Feel, Macrostructures of Sound: Embodied Cognition in West African and African-American Musics" (1998), 1323–1323. [Unpublished doctoral dissertation]. Berkeley: University of California. ("[M]usic perception and cognition are embodied, situated activities. This means that they depend crucially on the physical constraints and enablings of our sensorimotor apparatus, and also on the ecological and sociocultural environment in which our music-listening and -producing capacities come into being. I argue that rhythm perception and production involve a complex, whole-body experience, and that much of the musical structure found in rhythm-based music incorporates an awareness of the embodied, situated role of the participant."). https://scholar.harvard.edu/vijayiyer/publications/microstructures-feel-macrostructures-sound-embodied-cognition-west-african https://www.academia.edu/20277280/Microstructures_of_Feel_Macrostructures_of_Sound_Embodied_Cognition_in_West_African_and_African_American_Musics_1998_
7. From https://www.masterclass.com/articles/music-101-what-is-tempo-how-is-tempo-used-in-music#what-are-the-basic-tempo-markings.
8. B. Ramos de Pareia, *Musica practica* (Bologna, 1482/R); Eng. trans., MSD, xliv (1993). [from London, J. Rhythm. *Grove Music Online*. Retrieved March 24, 2022, https://www.oxfordmusiconline.com/grovemusic/view/10.1093/gmo/9781561592630.001.0001/omo-9781561592630-e-0000045963].

9. F. Gaffurius: *Practica musice* (Milan, 1496/R); Eng. trans., MSD, xx (1969). [from London, J. Rhythm. *Grove Music Online*. Retrieved March 24, 2022, https://www.oxfordmusiconline.com/grovemusic/view/10.1093/gmo/9781561592630.001.0001/omo-9781561592630-e-0000045963].
10. H. Buchner, *Fundamentum* (MS, c1520); ed. in *VMw*, 5 (1889), 1–192. [from London, J. Rhythm. *Grove Music Online*. Retrieved March 24, 2022, https://www.oxfordmusiconline.com/grovemusic/view/10.1093/gmo/9781561592630.001.0001/omo-9781561592630-e-0000045963].
11. T. M. Nakra and B. F. Busha, "Synchronous Sympathy at the Symphony: Conductor and Audience Accord," *Music Perception: An Interdisciplinary Journal* 32, no. 2 (December 2014): 109–124.
12. https://www.scientificamerican.com/article/how-music-can-literally-heal-the-heart/.
13. Hyperscore was first developed by Morwaread Farbood and Egon Pasztor in the Opera of the Future research group at the MIT Media Lab, in collaboration with Kevin Jennings at Trinity College Dublin. It is now distributed by New Harmony Line, Inc.
14. G. Chaffee, *Rhythm & Meter Patterns* (Miami: Alfred Music Publishing, 1994).
15. A. Ringer, "Melody," in *Grove Music Online* (2001). Retrieved January 19, 2021, https://www.oxfordmusiconline.com/grovemusic/view/10.1093/gmo/9781561592630.001.0001/omo-9781561592630-e-0000018357.
16. J. J. Fux and J. Edmunds, *The Study of Counterpoint from Johann Joseph Fux's Gradus ad Parnassum* (No. 277) (New York: W. W. Norton, 1965).
17. This list represents a compilation of rules adopted from Professor David Lewin's Counterpoint (Music 155) course notes at Harvard University (1991–1992), Professor Robert Young McMahan's Musicianship I (MUS 261) course at the College of New Jersey (2005–2020), Fux's method, and a standard college-level music theory text: Stefan Kostka and Dorothy Payne, *Tonal Harmony*, 8th ed. (New York: McGraw-Hill Higher Education, 2017). It's worth noting that Professor David Lewin distributed a caveat at the beginning of a year-long course, explaining that following the counterpoint rules does not always yield a "musical" result: "The following scenario must play itself out a hundred times a year. The instructor of a course in species counterpoint transmits to the students an elaborate set of rules for two-part exercises in first species. A student hands in an exercise which obeys those rules perfectly, only to be met by the instructor's criticism that the result is 'not musical.' 'Unfair,' cries the student loudly or, what is worse, silently. The instructor, in turn, feels profoundly uneasy at having to enforce strict obedience to a set of somewhat arbitrary rules while also applying an undefined criterion of 'musicality' to a melody comprising ten or twelve wholenotes." [from An Interesting Global Rule for Species Counterpoint].
18. A. I. Miller, *The Artist in the Machine: The World of AI-Powered Creativity* (Cambridge, MA: MIT Press, 2019).
19. *Grove Music Online*, https://doi.org/10.1093/gmo/9781561592630.article.27789.
20. https://jeffreychappell.com/pianist/what-is-character-in-music/.
21. Other examples of Leitmotiv theme & variations can be found in the Pixar film *Up* (2009), scored by composer Michael Giacchino (winner of the 2010 Academy Award for Best Original Score).
22. https://musiclab.chromeexperiments.com/Arpeggios/.
23. This patch alludes to an image on page 105 in Stefan Kostka, Dorothy Payne, and Byron Almen, *Tonal Harmony*, 7th ed. (New York: McGraw-Hill Higher Education, 2012), located in Chapter 7: Harmonic Progression and the Sequence.
24. https://www.microsoft.com/en-us/research/project/songsmith-2/.

Chapter 5

1. The reason why systems of pitch and tuning generally standardized on twelve subdivisions per octave was probably somewhat arbitrary, although the number 12 has many symbolic associations and

works well for several lower-numbered ratios. It takes twelve upward leaps of a perfect fifth to end up exactly at the same note you started from; those twelve steps comprise the twelve pitch classes. (You can verify this using patch 3.7 "Circle of Fifths.") Alternate systems such as microtonal music provide different ways to carve up the octave, and composer Wendy Carlos has invented her own scales with different octave subdivisions: https://www.wendycarlos.com/resources/pitch.html.
2. https://www.kylegann.com/histune.html.
3. https://www.kylegann.com/histune.html.
4. J. Swafford, "The Wolf at Our Heels," *Slate*, 2010, http://www.slate.com/articles/arts/music_box/2010/04/the_wolf_at_our_heels.html.
5. https://www.kylegann.com/histune.html#hist2.

Chapter 6

1. https://mymodernmet.com/robert-levin-mozart-pianoforte/.
2. The NBC Symphony's television sound stage, prized for its acoustics, currently serves as the production and performance location for NBC's *Saturday Night Live* in the building now known as "30 Rock" (30 Rockefeller Plaza) or the Comcast Building, originally called the RCA Building.
3. Dave Molk and Michelle Ohnona, "Promoting Equity: Developing an Antiracist Music Theory Classroom," *New Music Box*, January 29, 2020, https://nmbx.newmusicusa.org/promoting-equity-developing-an-antiracist-music-theory-classroom/.
4. Tod Machover, "Postlude: Music, Mind, and Marvin Minsky" (2014), https://www.musicmindandmeaning.org.

Glossary

!- (Max object)   reverses the subtraction process by subtracting the value received in its left inlet from the one received its right inlet

*~ (Max object)   multiplies (combines) two audio signals together

a cappella   unaccompanied singing

abs (Max object)   calculates the absolute value (non-negative value) for any input number

absolute tempo   the ability to recall or recreate precise tempo (BPM) values without any external references

absolute value   the non-negative value of a number

abstraction   a concept borrowed from computer science that explains how we use levels (or layers) of generalization or simplification to more efficiently manage complexity

accent   strong emphasis given to a note by an increase in volume or intensity

accidental   a symbol placed after a note letter name that preserves the letter while adjusting its pitch to an adjacent piano key; ♯ ("sharp") indicates that a note is raised in pitch by shifting it to the right by one key, while ♭ ("flat") indicates that a note is lowered in pitch by shifting it one key to the left. Using ♯ or x ("double sharp") shifts the note two keys to the right, ♭♭ ("double flat") shifts two keys to the left, and ♮ erases the effect of any previous accidental.

acoustic   an adjective describing either a property of sound or an unamplified performance or physical space

acoustic beats   unpleasant volume fluctuations or interference patterns that conflict with each other and create a sense of "roughness." They occur when misaligned frequencies combine and affect each other's amplitudes, resulting in quickly alternating moments of higher intensity (constructive interference) and lower intensity (destructive interference).

acoustics (musical)   an interdisciplinary area of scientific study that addresses the properties of sound; it includes aspects of fields such as physics, music, psychology, physiology, and signal processing

Aeolian mode   a modal scale that starts on the sixth scale degree of the diatonic scale pattern; also known as the natural minor scale

alankara   a segment of prepared melodic improvisational material in the Hindustani music tradition that can be connected and combined with other phrases

algorithm   a sequence of instructions that tell a computer how to accomplish a task (such as generate sound, as in algorithmic music); step-by-step procedures or recipes for handling data

algorithmic composition   the method of encoding rules and heuristics into algorithms to create music. It is a field of growing interest with the use of AI and Machine Learning to develop musical materials for compositions.

allegro   a quick tempo indication ("cheerful" in Italian)

amplitude   the height of the peaks in an audio waveform; the higher these peaks get, the louder they seem to us. (Also, the amount of change in an audio signal over one cycle of vibration, or the maximum displacement of air molecules from their equilibrium position as the sound pressure wave passes through them.)

amplitude envelope   the amplitude (loudness) level of an individual note, following the outer contour of the peak amplitude in a waveform. Amplitude envelopes typically have four phases: attack, decay, sustain, and release (abbreviated as ADSR).

aperiodic sound   an auditory waveform that has a random or non-repeating pattern. No part of the waveform pattern of this sound oscillates or vibrates at regular intervals.

argument   in programming languages, arguments (also called parameters) are values that provide important information to functions as they run; they are specific types of variables that comprise the definitions of functions. In *Max*, arguments are listed within the object box itself, following the object name.

arithmetic symbols (Max objects + – / *) arithmetic operators in *Max* that perform addition, subtraction, multiplication, and division operations on numbers and output the result

arpeggiator a hardware or software system that encodes rules, variables, and procedures to create arpeggio patterns with electronic sounds

arpeggio a "broken" chord in which the individual notes are played non-synchronously, using "melodic" (sequential) rather than "harmonic" (simultaneous) intervals. Arpeggios are sequences of notes that combine the horizontal aspects of melodies (range, contour, ascending/descending intervals) with the vertical structures of chords.

arrangement (arranging) a variation on a musical composition, usually for a different set of instruments or sounds from those used in the original version

articulation the way in which notes are shaped and separated from each other, for example: legato (connected, elongated), staccato (short), slurs, portato, tenuto, marcato, and accents. Analogous to the concept of amplitude envelope (above).

Artificial Intelligence (AI) the ability for software or computers to simulate or demonstrate the ability to reason or express themselves in a manner that seems similar to human capacities

aspect ratio the relationship between width and height in a rectangular graphical object

attack the beginning of a note, starting with an increase of amplitude from silence; the first phase of an amplitude envelope

augmented (interval quality) an extra-large interval; an increase of one semitone from a perfect or major interval

augmented triad (chord) a three-note chord containing two stacked major thirds

aural skills a component of traditional music theory curricula focused on the identification, production, and notation of specific notes, intervals, and other basic musical structures using auditory perception, dictation, and solo singing

Auto-Tune a proprietary audio processing software plug-in manufactured by Antares Audio Technologies that determines the real-time pitch of a sound and alters it either to correct the output or add a characteristic distortion to the sound

backbeat a beat that usually occurs on the second or fourth beat of a measure (less commonly on subdivisions of those beats); in styles such as rock and roll, soul, and funk, the snare drum backbeat is the loudest beat in the measure and the one that clearly delineates metrical grouping boundaries.

bandish a traditional fixed composition in the Hindustani music tradition, associated with poetic texts that impart additional cultural or emotional meaning

bang message (Max) a trigger command that causes actions to be initiated immediately

beat a pulse, or moment of strong emphasis, lined up in a regular, repeating sequence, evenly spaced apart. (see also: acoustic beats)

beat matching a technique used by DJs to adjust the tempo (and sometimes pitch) of adjacent musical tracks so that the two recordings align and preserve a consistent dance beat; this minimizes any jarring transitions between songs

beats per minute (BPM) a measure of tempo or playback speed that quantifies the number of beats per unit time

Bhairav both a thaat and a raga in the Hindustani music tradition, composed of notes consisting of two stacked harmonic tetrachords

Boolean value a type of variable described as binary because it has two possible values that represent true and false conditions, usually encoded in software as 1 and 0

bucket (Max object) an object that passes values one at a time to the next location on the right, as firefighters in earlier ages might have passed a water bucket in a "bucket brigade"

buffer~ (Max object) stores audio samples in a memory buffer for quick access by other objects

button (Max object) a human interface object that blinks and sends a bang message when clicked

cadence a sequence of chords that concludes a section of music and serves as a form of harmonic punctuation

Carnatic music the classical music tradition of South India

cent a unit of measurement quantifying the frequency distance between semitones; 1/100 of a semitone

chalan the order in which notes can be sequenced in a raga

character a way of performing music that can convey subtle qualities and nuances of musical emotions through musical expression techniques, such as varying timbre and dynamics. These precise shades of mood are often associated with human personality traits and can be thought of as expressions of personal temperament or identity.

chord a label or description of the simultaneous sounding of two or more notes together

chroma also called pitch class or harmonic pitch class profile; used by software systems to automatically estimate key and harmonic features from audio recordings

chromatic alteration accidental

chromatic scale a scale containing all twelve semitones per octave

circle of fifths a sequence of twelve consecutive adjacent perfect fifths that can be used to generate all twelve pitch classes and demonstrate how key relationships work. It is usually displayed in a circular arrangement; in recent years, it has also been described as a spiral.

Circumplex model of affect James Russell's influential theory that emotions can be characterized using two descriptors: *valence* and *intensity*. These components can be represented as variables on a two-dimensional plane and used to study how people respond to a wide range of experiences. This book connects the intensity component to interval size and loudness in music, and the valence component to qualitative judgments about sound such as consonance and dissonance. This approach is influenced by the work of Rosalind Picard and the field of Affective Computing.

click track an audible pulse train that is used to synchronize audio recordings and performances; often, musicians will listen to a click track on headphones while performing in a studio recording session in order for their parts to align perfectly in time with the other tracks

coherence a sense of a consistent, unified identity or message in a passage of music

coll (Max object) allows you to store, edit, and retrieve many lines of data using an index system

comment (Max object) a visual box in a *Max* patch that displays written text, labels, and instructions

common practice period a period of time defined by music theorists and associated primarily with European classical music written in the eighteenth and nineteenth centuries

common time a standard metrical pattern or method for organizing time where beats are grouped in units of four per measure

compound interval a pitch interval larger than an octave

compound meter metrical patterns where each measure contains five or more beats; these compound measures are often "subdivided" into multiple smaller units of two, three, or four beats

compression the tight packing together of molecules in a sound pressure wave; a moment of high sound pressure (as distinguished from audio compression algorithms and plug-ins)

conditional statement a coding structure that makes decisions using if/then/else statements; it uses Boolean values to evaluate whether conditions are true or false (used in the "if" object listed below)

conjunct "stepwise" melodic motion between notes, comprising a major or minor second interval

consonance attractive or comfortable combinations of sounds; any two notes are generally considered to be "perfectly" consonant if the ratio between them contains numbers of four or lower, including 1:1, 2:1, 2:2, 3:1, 3:2, 3:3, 4:1, 4:2, 4:3, and 4:4.

Constructionism Seymour Papert's philosophy of learning that built upon the work of Jean Piaget and incorporated creative technology. It describes how students actively construct knowledge by making things in the world and places the individual at the center of the knowledge creation process. Constructionism focuses on the process of "learning to learn," emphasizing the conversation-like steps that learners undertake when making things. It explains how these experiences facilitate the construction of new knowledge.

constructive interference an audio phenomenon that occurs when multiple audio signals have the same phase and combine together in the same acoustic environment; the resulting amplitude is equivalent to the sum of all the individual amplitudes, and the overall loudness is increased

continuous a variable where the measurable values can occur arbitrarily close together along a range (as compared to a discrete variable that has distinct, countable values)

contour the shape or outline that notes make in a melody, including the kind of movement in between notes (e.g., more gentle or more angular) this term can also describe the way that an amplitude envelope follows the contour of a waveform's peak amplitude

counter (Max object) receives and counts bang messages with different settings, including forward, backward, and "palindrome" (up followed by down). Two arguments represent the lowest and highest numbers in the loop.

counterpoint combinations and interactions between independent melodic lines

cycle~ (Max object) generates sine wave oscillations at fixed frequencies

dac~ (Max object) serves as a digital to analog converter and sends any signal inputs to the audio hardware on the computer for playback

daisy chain a configuration for connecting electrical or digital objects together in a chain or ring, resembling the way one might tie flowers together

data structure a way of formatting data that helps organize, store, process, or retrieve it

decay the second of four phases of an amplitude envelope; it follows the attack and is usually characterized by a brief decrease in amplitude (the *decay* phase)

decibel (dB) a standard unit of measurement used to quantify sound intensity levels, named for Alexander Graham Bell, the inventor of the telephone. A 1 dB difference in intensity level between two sounds is the smallest change detectable by human hearing, and an increase of 10 dB in audio intensity level corresponds to a doubling of perceived loudness and an increase of approximately one step in dynamic level (such as going from mezzo-forte to forte).

degree of resolution level of detail in a digital signal. In engineering terms, resolution is the smallest measurable quantity on a device; it is the smallest unit of measure. In digital audio (and MIDI) signals, this idea is expressed as "bit depth," or the number of digital bits used to encode each instantaneous sample value. A "high degree of resolution" means that a large number of bits have been used to encode each value, and therefore the level of detail is high.

destructive interference an audio phenomenon that occurs when multiple audio signals have different phases and combine together in the same acoustic environment; the resulting amplitude is equivalent to the combined value of all the individual amplitudes, and the overall loudness is decreased

dial (Max object) an interface object that outputs numbers based on user rotation of the dial setting

diatonic chords the standard set of chords that structurally occur on the scale degrees in any key. Roman numerals can be used to identify these chords according to their relationship to the tonic, with uppercase for major and lowercase for minor.

diatonic pattern a specific configuration of seven notes that fit within an octave and have interval spacings of five major seconds and two minor seconds. (This pattern is also defined by the separation of the minor seconds as far as possible from one another – in one case with two whole steps in between, in the other case, with three whole steps.)

diatonic system all intervals, scales, and chords that fit within the twelve keys, and the relationships between them

dictation a component of ear training and aural skills training in music theory classes, this activity strengthens one's ability to correctly identify notes, intervals, melodies, chords, and other musical structures by listening to them and writing them down. Regular dictation practice can help develop a student's sense of inner hearing and discernment of structure from sound.

digital audio workstation (DAW) music production software that allows users to record and edit multitrack MIDI or audio data, and mix, master, and produce their own recordings

diminished (interval quality) an extra-small interval; a decrease of one semitone from a perfect or minor interval

diminished 7th chord A chord consisting of a diminished triad and a seventh interval above the root note. If the seventh has a minor quality, then the chord is a half-diminished 7th chord; if the seventh has a diminished quality, then the chord is a fully diminished 7th chord.

diminished triad (chord) a three-note chord with a minor 3rd forming the bottom interval and a minor 3rd on the top

discordance (see "dissonance")

discrete a variable that has distinct, countable values (as compared to a continuous variable, where the measurable values can occur arbitrarily close together along a range)

disjunct motion "leaps," or melodic intervals greater than a major second

dissonance any two notes are considered to be dissonant if the ratio between them contains numbers higher than four, especially above seven (e.g., 8:7, 9:8, 10:9, etc.).

distribution a set of statistical probabilities across a range of possible outcomes

dominant (scale degree) the fifth scale degree (notated $\hat{5}$), second only to the tonic in its importance within the tonal framework

dominant 7th chord see major-minor 7th chord

Dorian mode a modal scale that starts on the second scale degree of the diatonic scale pattern; also known as the Dorian minor scale

drone an extended sound that sustains through a long musical passage

duple meter a metrical pattern where each measure contains two beats

duration length of time

dynamics characterizations of levels of audio intensity that often use Italian terms such as "forte" (strong) to represent loud sounds and "piano" (floor, level) for quiet, soft sounds. Italian prefixes and suffixes provide gradations: "mezzo" for medium, and "-issimo" for "very."

ear training the development of audio recognition skills, sometimes called "inner hearing," to identify intervals using minimal sound clues

edit mode (Max) when a *Max* patch is unlocked; you can move objects around and make changes

EDM (Electronic Dance Music) a style of music composed for dancing at nightclubs, often featuring a steady beat, sampling, and loops; EDM has been around since the 1980s, and is particularly popular in Europe

eighth note the ½ subdivision of a quarter note beat duration

enharmonic equivalency notes that share the same pitch number but have different "spellings," or intervals that share the same number of semitones but are named differently

equal temperament a tuning system in general use today that was first adopted in Europe about 400 years ago and evolved in parallel with the modern piano keyboard, although it was documented in China much earlier. The equal temperament system maintains a 2:1 frequency ratio for each octave and carves octaves up into twelve basic subdivisions; these twelve steps are said to be "equal" because they share the same frequency ratio, called the *twelfth root of two*. (As a result of using this ratio, adjacent semitones are separated by varying frequency distances that increase as the pitch increases.)

equals (==) (Max object) compares two numbers; outputs a 1 if they are equal and a 0 if they are not

ethnomusicology the study of historical, social, and cultural aspects of music in regions across the world, involving interdisciplinary connections to anthropology and other fields

"everyday tonality" a term coined by Philip Tagg to describe the general tonal framework shared by a wide range of musical traditions, purposefully including many styles beyond the European canon

expr (Max object) an object that computes simple mathematical expressions including arithmetic, Boolean operators, and other common functions

ezdac~ (Max object) audio output button; toggles the sound system on and off

Fandango a folk dance from Spain in triple meter

fiddle~ (Max external object) an object originally created by Miller Puckette in 1999 for pitch tracking violin sounds in real time. It is a well-known example of an "external" object, or an object developed by a third party to be used in *Max*. Although fiddle~ has been optimized to recognize notes created with string instrument timbres, it also works quite well on a range of instruments and voices.

fifth (chord) the third element in a chord, located an interval of a fifth above the root note when the chord is in root position

fifth (interval) an interval that spans five adjacent letter names; fifths are considered to be consonant intervals and come in three standard forms: perfect (seven semitones), augmented (eight semitones), and diminished (six semitones)

first inversion when the third of a chord occupies the lowest pitch in a chord voicing

floating-point numbers numbers that use a decimal point and decimal place values

flonum (Max object) a number object that handles floating-point (decimal place) values

flush (Max object) after receiving a bang message, the flush object outputs note-off messages for any notes it has received that have not yet been turned off

fourth (interval) an interval that spans four adjacent letter names; fourths are considered to be consonant intervals and come in three standard forms: perfect, augmented, and diminished

fpic (Max object) displays image files in formats such as JPG or PNG

frequency the speed with which pressure waves oscillate between opposite states of compression and rarefaction

frequency domain the vertical dimension of music, associated with pitch

frequency ratio the relationship between the frequencies of two notes, expressed as a ratio of proportion between the two.

ftom (Max object) converts a frequency number to a MIDI note number

fully diminished 7th chord see diminished 7th chord

fundamental frequency the primary, steady frequency of vibration in a note

gain~ (Max object) a slider that scales (adjusts) the loudness of an audio signal

General MIDI (GM) a technical specification maintained by the MIDI Association (https://www.midi.org) that defines specific features of MIDI synthesizers to ensure that MIDI files can be played using interchangeable sound sets, using a shared set of program numbers and names. (Two versions are maintained: GM 1 and GM 2.)

glissando sliding from one note to another; on the piano, sliding a finger over the keys of the keyboard (different methods are used on different instruments)

greater than (>) (Max object) compares the number arriving in its left inlet with its argument (or the number most recently received in its right inlet). If the left-inlet number exceeds the other number, > sends a value of 1; otherwise, it sends a 0.

groove specific combinations of elements such as timing and emphasis (loudness, attack) in a rhythmic pattern, adding intensity, variety, and recognizable features to the rhythm that can be associated with a style, genre, or an individual performer

groove~ (Max object) plays back digital audio files from a buffer~ object, with features including variable playback speed, reverse, and looping capabilities

gswitch (Max object) an object that selects between multiple pathways of incoming data. At the top of gswitch are two (or more) inlets where data streams in, and a control inlet that determines which of the streams gets to move through. You can think of this function a bit like switching trains in a train yard; when one train is moving onto the track, the other train has to halt and wait.

gswitch2 (Max object) similar to the gswitch object, except that gswitch has multiple inlets and one outlet, whereas gswitch2 has one inlet and multiple outlets

guru-shishya parampara the traditional teaching method in Hindustani classical music, where the teacher instructs the student by slowly elucidating the notes of a raga with increasing melodic expansion and variation

half-diminished 7th chord a chord consisting of a diminished triad and a minor seventh interval above the root note

half note a 2× multiple of a quarter note beat duration

half step see "semitone"

harmonic interval an interval where the two notes are played simultaneously

harmonic minor scale also called the Hijaz; a pattern of seven intervals stacked above a tonic in this sequence: M2 m2 M2 M2 m2 A2 m2. It is composed of a minor tetrachord on the bottom and a harmonic tetrachord on the top.

harmonic progression a set of chords in a specific sequence; harmonic progressions create a sense of momentum that propels the musical energy forward by modulating the amounts of tension and resolution at different moments in time

harmonic series a set of overtones or "harmonics"; components of a sound that occur above the fundamental frequency, whose frequencies are related by whole number (integer) ratios

harmonicity a quality of sound that indicates the presence of a fundamental frequency accompanied by a set of regular, orderly, periodic frequencies (acoustic components) called overtones or harmonics, related to the fundamental by whole number ratios

harmoniousness (see consonance)

harmony the system we use to describe the all the many ways in which simultaneous notes can relate to each other along the vertical dimension of music

Hertz (Hz) units of vibration, measured in oscillations/vibrations per second

hide on lock (Max) a feature in *Max* that allows you to select objects and have them disappear in patching mode

Hijaz a scale pattern that is ubiquitous in the Middle East and North Africa, also known as the harmonic minor scale

Hindustani music the classical music tradition of North India

homophony musical texture featuring melody with accompaniment

if (Max object) provides a conditional statement in if/then/else form and evaluates inputs based on the structure of the statement

imperfect authentic cadence a cadence where a first-inversion leading tone (vii°) chord substitutes in place of the dominant chord and progresses directly to the tonic chord (I)

imperfect consonance thirds and sixths; intervals that are defined as dissonances because their frequencies have ratios containing numbers above 4, but which most music theorists also consider to sound consonant

inclusive counting a method of counting that incorporates both the endpoints in the final count; used in music to determine the number of an interval by including the lower and upper notes

inharmonicity a quality of sound that indicates the presence of inharmonic oscillating components (overtones that are not perfect integer multiples of the fundamental frequency), non-oscillating components, or irregular components

inlet (Max) a virtual input port located on top of a *Max* object that allows the object to receive data from another source; inlets can also serve independently as objects that receive messages from outside the patch

inner hearing the ability to audiate and perceive intervals silently before producing them

Inspector tool (Max) a toolbar that can be used to edit or set the attributes of *Max* objects; a separate Patcher Inspector, available under the View menu, allows the user to set global settings for the whole patch

int (Max object) stores and outputs one integer value at a time. Updating a value in its right inlet sets the value without outputting it; updating a value in the left inlet sets and outputs the value. A bang message received in its left inlet outputs the current value without changing it.

integer whole number

intensity a measure of perceived loudness, musical "dynamic" indications, acoustic power, or signal amplitude. (Also: the vertical axis on Russell's *Circumplex model of affect*, referring to activation, energy level, or physiological arousal.)

interactivity flexibility or responsiveness to user input

interface (Max object) a subcategory of objects that allow user input and control via specialized interactive interfaces

interonset interval the spacing distance between two adjacent note onset times (attacks), usually measured in milliseconds

interval the difference in pitch between two notes, identified using two variables: the number of steps, and the quality (perfect, major, minor, diminished, augmented)

interval inversion the concept that intervals can be matched up with their complementary mirror-image within an octave, such as seconds and sevenths. Stacking two inverse intervals together creates an octave.

inversion (chord) when adjacent notes in a chord are swapped around to different registral placements, and chord tones other than the root occupy the lowest note position

Ionian mode a modal scale that starts on the first scale degree of the diatonic scale pattern; also known as the major scale

itable (Max object) an object that stores and displays a table of data; it can be used to keep track of a probability distribution or any other list of values

jitter variations in the timing of regularly occurring events

just intonation a tuning system in which intervals are tuned using whole number frequency ratios derived from the overtone system

key the orientation of all pitch-based musical structures (notes, intervals, scales, and chords) around a local tonic that serves as a metaphorical "home" (also: an element on a keyboard that enables a note to be played)

key (Max object) an object that reports the ASCII number of any key that is pressed on the local computer keyboard

key signature the list of accidentals associated with a key

keyup (Max object) an object that reports the ASCII number of any key as it is released on the local computer keyboard

kHz common abbreviation for kilohertz, or 1000 Hertz (cycles per second)

kräftig a tempo indication that is used to encourage a performance that is not too fast but vigorous or forceful in character ("powerful" in German)

kslider (Max object) an interface object that displays a customizable keyboard layout and outputs MIDI pitch and velocity information when any of its keys are activated

Glossary

leading tone the higher form of the seventh scale degree (notated $\hat{7}$); it is found in scales where the seventh step of the scale has an interval of a major seventh from the tonic, and functions as a strong tendency tone to the tonic

Leitmotiv a musical identity or theme that is assigned to a character in a story, containing embedded structures and variables that reflect aspects of the characters' personalities or actions. The purpose of a Leitmotiv is to help the audiences subconsciously recognize characters and bind emotional attachments and empathies to them in order to evoke specific feelings when they are played.

less than (<) (Max object) compares the number arriving in its left inlet with its argument (or the number most recently received in its right inlet). If the left-inlet number is less than the other number, < sends a value of 1; otherwise, it sends a 0.

letter notation the conventional system of referring to individual notes using letter names

live.button (Max object) an object that resembles a small indicator light; it lights up and sends a bang message when it receives any message (color selectable via the object Inspector)

live.gain~ (Max object) provides similar volume control as the gain~ object, and also indicates the current audio intensity level in decibels

loadbang (Max object) outputs a bang message when the patch is opened

loadmess (Max object) sends a message when the patch is opened

Locrian mode a modal scale that starts on the seventh scale degree of the diatonic scale pattern; the least used of the modes, due to the unusual tritone interval above its tonic

loop (coding) a sequence of events that repeats until a specific condition is reached or changed

loop (musical) a specific amount of sonic material that is intended to repeat for some time (noun), or the act of repeating, sometimes with a predetermined number of times, a selection of audio material (verb)

Lydian mode a modal scale that starts on the fourth scale degree of the diatonic scale pattern

major (interval quality) – for all non-perfect intervals, "major" (capitalized when abbreviated, as in M2 for major 2nd) refers to the larger of their two forms—seconds of exactly two semitones, thirds of exactly four semitones, sixths of exactly nine semitones, and sevenths of exactly eleven semitones

major scale a pattern of seven stacked intervals above a tonic that follows this exact sequence: M2 M2 m2 M2 M2 M2 m2. Or, using the whole step (W) and half step (H) convention, W W H W W W H. In MIDI, the pattern is numerical: 2 2 1 2 2 2 1.

major 7th chord also known as the major-major seventh chord, it consists of a major triad plus a major seventh interval above the root note

major-minor 7th chord also known as the dominant seventh chord because of its association with the dominant scale degree, it consists of a major triad plus a minor seventh interval above the root note

major triad (chord) a three-note chord with a major third forming the bottom interval and minor third on the top

Makey Makey a commercially available educational kit that was designed in 2012 by Jay Silver and Eric Rosenbaum. Each kit consists of a circuit board, alligator clip cables, tinned jumper wires, and a USB cable. The circuit board serves as a "keyboard emulator" by allowing electrical connections to directly control computer key and mouse commands. Kits can be purchased at https://makeymakey.com and elsewhere online.

marcato an articulation mark or instruction indicating that a note should be played in a more forceful manner, louder than a regular accent

mashup a form of musical composition that is created by blending together two or more prerecorded songs, often by overlaying the vocal track of one song seamlessly over the instrumental track of another

meantone tuning a tuning system that provided a middle ground between the mathematically equal intervals of equal temperament and the sweeter, purer intervals of just intonation during the eighteenth and nineteenth centuries

measure (also called a "bar") a regular unit of musical duration that contains groups of beats; it functions like a frame that repeats and loops many times. Measures can be combined together in larger groups to create musical structures and forms.

mediant (scale degree) the third scale degree (notated 3̂), named to indicate its location midway between the tonic and the fifth scale degree, the two most important scale elements

melodic interval sounding two notes in sequence (one after the other)

melodic minor scale A variation of the natural minor scale that combines two different scale patterns: one ascending, and one descending. The ascending form features a pattern of seven intervals stacked above the tonic in this sequence: M2 m2 M2 M2 M2 M2 m2. (It contains a minor tetrachord on the bottom and a major tetrachord on the top.) The descending form shares the same intervals and tetrachords as natural minor.

melody a sequence of notes that lasts approximately the length of a single breath and functions like a sentence. Melodies are usually complete musical utterances that have a beginning, middle, and end—much like a narrative arc.

message (Max object) stores and sends alphanumeric data (text)

meter the system of organizing short groups of beats into regular, repeating units called measures

meter~ (Max object) serves as a peak amplitude level indicator, visualizing the maximum amplitude of the signal that it receives

metro (Max object) a *Max* object that acts like a metronome, outputting bang messages at regular time intervals after it receives a start (1) command; the interval can be set as an argument or updated in real-time through the right inlet

metronome devices that were first invented around 1815 to generate steady reference tempos and help practicing musicians learn passages by gradually bringing them "up to speed"; while earlier metronomes used mechanical pendula, modern ones are available as mobile phone apps

microtone an interval or pitch measurement smaller than a semitone

middle C the fourth C in an 88-key piano keyboard when counting from the left side; it is the first note in the fourth full octave, also called C4, with a MIDI pitch number of 60. Middle C usually ends up in the center of the sequence of 88 keys.

MIDI "Musical Instrument Digital Interface," a technical standard that was created in 1981 by a consortium of musical instrument manufacturers and computer music researchers. The MIDI specification is a serial communications protocol that handles musical data. It ensures the interoperability of MIDI devices, such as keyboards, synthesizers, and controllers.

MIDI controller a physical or software interface that sends and receives MIDI messages; examples include keyboards, pad controllers, DJ-style interfaces, wind controllers, and other experimental devices (see https://www.nime.org/ for cutting-edge examples of musical interface design)

MIDI keyboard an electronic musical keyboard that resembles a piano and includes built-in MIDI functions. Many MIDI keyboards also feature assignable knobs, buttons, sliders, and pads; they usually connect to computers using a USB port.

midiflush (Max object) keeps track of all MIDI messages that pass through it, and when it receives a bang message, sends note-off messages for all hanging note-ons

midiin (Max object) monitors a specified MIDI port and outputs all raw MIDI data received

midiout (Max object) transmits MIDI data to a specified MIDI port

midiparse (Max object) receives incoming MIDI data and splits it out into component message types, including note-on, note-off, polyphonic pressure, control change, program change, aftertouch, pitch bend, and channel information

millisecond one thousandth of a second

minor (interval quality) – for all non-perfect intervals, "minor" refers to the smaller of the two standard forms – seconds of exactly one semitone, thirds of exactly three semitones, sixths of exactly eight semitones, and sevenths of exactly ten semitones

minor scale a pattern of seven stacked intervals above a tonic that features a minor third interval between tonic and mediant notes. There are a few different types, including natural, harmonic (also called the Hijaz), melodic, Dorian, and Phrygian.

minor 7th chord also known as the minor-minor seventh chord, it consists of a minor triad and a minor seventh interval above the root note

minor triad (chord) a three-note chord with a minor 3rd forming the bottom interval and major 3rd on the top

Mixolydian mode a modal scale that starts on the fifth scale degree of the diatonic scale pattern

modal mixture combining multiple modes while retaining the same tonic; swapping in "borrowed chords" from other modes (e.g., using a chord from Dorian mode in the context of a major key)

modes (modal scales) also called the diatonic modes, church modes, or Gregorian modes, modes are scales that share the same diatonic pattern with the major scale. They contain seven distinct pitch classes and are constructed by rotating the diatonic pattern.

modes of vibration the different resonant frequencies at which objects vibrate when activated by acoustic energy

modulo ("%") (Max object) inputs two numbers, divides the left value by the right value, and outputs a remainder

monophony music played by a single source (instrument, voice, etc.), one note at a time. (see also: texture)

motive a brief musical idea; the shortest component of a theme or phrase that still is identifiable as a unique idea. Motives provide bits of melodic material that can be combined together with other linking materials to create full melodies.

moving average a technique whereby a series of data points is processed to provide a constantly updating average value over a fixed number of previous values; it serves as a form of low-pass filter that smooths out the jaggedness of higher-frequency (noisy) events in the data

music defined by John Blacking as "humanly organized sound." John Blacking, *How Musical Is Man?* (Seattle: University of Washington Press, 1974), 12.

Music Information Retrieval (MIR) "a field that aims at developing computational tools for processing, searching, organizing, and accessing music-related data," as defined by the International Society for Music Information Retrieval at https://www.ismir.net

natural the natural (♮) symbol refers to an unmodified note, or erases any earlier sharp or flat and returns it back to its unmodified state

natural minor scale a pattern of seven intervals stacked above a tonic in this sequence: M2 m2 M2 M2 m2 M2 M2. The natural minor scale is composed of a minor tetrachord on the bottom and a Phrygian (upper minor) tetrachord on the top.

noise non-musical sound

note a sound containing a single instance of the element of pitch, combined with values for volume, duration, and timbre

object (Max) a visual block in a *Max* patch that performs actions and functions

octatonic scale a seven-note scale that is constructed using alternating whole steps and half steps. It is often associated with Russian composers of the late nineteenth and early twentieth centuries who were trying to create music that was both emotionally expressive and strikingly modern.

octave an interval that spans eight letter names, abbreviated P8. Octaves can have the quality of perfect, augmented, or diminished. The two notes in an octave share the same letter name and accidental, but they do not share the same pitch; instead, they span an interval of twelve semitones.

octave equivalence the perception that notes an octave or multiple octaves apart seem "the same," much like a unison

operating system an essential computer program that a user interacts with when accessing information on a computer or digital device; it manages all the basic software and hardware functions and services. Examples include macOS, Microsoft Windows, Linux, Android, and iOS.

orchestration arranging notes of different timbres to create interesting combinations that blend well together

order of operations a deterministic code pathway through which commands move and are interpreted

outlet (Max) a virtual output port located on the bottom of a *Max* object that allows the object to send data to another source; outlets can also serve independently as objects that send messages to locations outside the patch

overtones additional simultaneous frequencies that occur when a note is produced; these typically occur in regular sets called the overtone series or harmonic series (see "harmonic series")

pakad characteristic melodic pattern associated with a specific raga

panel (Max object) the panel object creates shapes such as rectangles, squares, circles, triangles, and arrows that can be used as interface elements in patching mode; these can be designed and customized with features such as transparency, borders, color, shadows, and gradients

patch (patcher) the object-oriented visual development environment within which *Max* code runs; a patch functions as a metaphorical blank canvas, into which objects and patch cords can be placed and connected together. *Max* patches are the basic file formats in the *Max* programming environment – they allow users to interact directly with code blocks on the screen and move them around on a two-dimensional surface.

patch cord (Max) virtual wires in a *Max* patch that connect objects together and allow data to flow in one direction: the outlet on the bottom of a sending object connects to the inlet on the top of a receiving object

patching mode (Max) when a *Max* patch is locked; the objects perform their intended functions and can receive user input commands

pedal point a note held for a long time that provides a sustained reference for other moving lines of music; usually in the lower registers

pentatonic scales scale patterns that contain five notes; six if you include both tonics. They belong to a class of scales sometimes described as "gapped" or "incomplete," containing at least one adjacent interval larger than a second. The most commonly used type is called the major pentatonic scale.

perfect a type of interval quality indicating a high degree of consonance (simple frequency ratios and significant overtone overlap), associated with unisons, octaves, fifths of exactly seven semitones, and fourths where the upper note is exactly five semitones above the bottom note

perfect authentic cadence a cadence where the dominant chord (V) moves to the tonic chord (I), with both chords in root position and the top note in the I chord landing on the tonic note

perfect consonance an interval ratio containing only numbers of four or lower

perfect pitch (absolute pitch) the special ability of a small number of individuals (approximately 0.01% of the population) to hear a frequency and identify its pitch. Perfect pitch usually develops by about age seven or so, when the brain centers for language development are most active.

periodic an event or movement that repeats in a regular cycle, as in an oscillation

pgmout (Max object) an object that can send program change messages to update the instrument timbre or "patch" on a MIDI-controllable synthesizer

phase vocoder a type of algorithm that analyzes an audio signal using a Fast-Fourier Transform (FFT), determines its frequency components, and reassembles them into an output sound, usually with some variations such as time-stretching or pitch modulation. (In the phase vocoder, the phase of each frequency component is shifted to avoid noise artifacts caused by constructive and destructive interference.)

Phrygian mode a modal scale that starts on the third scale degree of the diatonic scale pattern; also known as the Phrygian minor scale

pipe (Max object) serves as a delay that can hold data before releasing it at a specific fixed or variable interval

pitch the perceived "height" of a musical sound determined by its speed of vibration (frequency), or its placement within the range of possible note values. Commonly identified by name using letters, as in A, B, C, etc. In MIDI, there are 128 individual pitch values. Pitch is associated with the "vertical" dimension of sound, also called the "frequency domain."

pitch bend the ability to continuously adjust the frequency of a note on a synthesizer; also called portamento. The MIDI specification implements pitch bend as a 14-bit number, allowing for 16,384 possible values from low to high.

pitch class the letter name of a note (plus any accidental), without the octave register number included. Notes that share the same pitch class have the same name and therefore the same bindings and associations within a tonal structure and context. (Also called "chroma" or harmonic pitch class profile.)

playback speed the rate at which an audio file is played, affecting its tempo; determined by the ratio of the intended playback speed divided by the original speed of the source recording

playlist~ (Max object) organizes, displays, and plays sets of audio files

polyphony music in which multiple independent parts or sounds play together simultaneously (see also: texture)

polyrhythm simultaneous overlapping playback of multiple rhythms or metrical patterns

portato an articulation technique for string instruments where one continuous draw of the bow is modulated by occasional moments of emphasis, produced by the weight of the hand, that provide a sense of pulse or rhythm

pow (Max object) computes the value received in its left inlet to the power of an exponent listed as an argument or received in its right inlet

prepend (Max object) adds a pre-stored message to the beginning of any new message arriving in its inlet and then sends out the combined result

Presentation mode (Max) a top-level viewing layer for displaying the objects in a patch, allowing the user to choose where to place and resize objects independently of their position in patching mode. Presentation mode helps manage complexity by placing items "under the hood" and out of the way so they don't overly complicate the user's field of view.

psychoacoustics the study of how humans respond psychologically to sound, how they perceive sound, and how the mechanisms of hearing work – including the limits of human hearing

pulse an individual moment of strong emphasis; a beat. Pulses are instants in time that are set apart from other moments around them by the delineation of short sounds with a clear attack and release. Musical pulses are analogous to the arterial pulses that move blood throughout our cardiovascular systems.

pulse train a steady sequence of beats or pulses, each having the same duration of time between them

quadruple meter a metrical pattern where each measure contains four beats

qualia intrinsic qualities of subjective experience associated with specific sensory events, such as the blueness of blue, or the "sameness" of unisons and octaves

quality the type of an interval (perfect, major, minor, diminished, augmented) or a chord (major, minor, diminished, augmented, dominant, etc.)

Glossary

quantization the process of taking notes that have been performed by a human musician and adjusting their note onsets to align with a grid of beats and beat subdivisions; this is usually accomplished using features in digital audio workstation software. The original timing data can contain errors or jitter that are fixed through this process, as well stylistic groove information that is lost in the quantization process.

quartal harmony a style of harmony that uses chords constructed with intervals of a fourth

quarter note the standard unit of beat duration

radiogroup (Max object) an interface object that allows users to click on and select options from a list

raga, raag scales used in the Hindustani music system of North India

random (Max object) generates a random number between 0 and one less than the value of its argument

rarefaction the spreading out of molecules in the low-pressure phase of a sound pressure wave; a moment of low sound pressure representing a reduction of density

ratio a relationship between two values expressed as one value divided by the other

register the relative pitch height (highness or lowness) of a note or group of notes, often using an octave number. A variable that can be used to provide a sense of contrast in musical structure.

relative minor/major scale a major and minor scale that share the same notes (and key) but have a different tonic

release the fourth phase of an amplitude envelope, representing the end of a note, initiated by a decrease of amplitude from the sustain phase to fade out to silence

remainder the amount left over after a division computation

remix a compositional form in which songs are sampled and altered from their original state by adding, removing, or changing components; DJ dance remixes popularized the form, and artists such as Björk and Nine Inch Nails sanctioned and encouraged the creation of new works by combining or editing their original tracks

resolution (musical) a concomitant response that can follow moments of musical tension; after a build-up of intensity, complexity, or dissonance, the music tends to settle back to established or expected default conditions of calm, simplicity, and consonance. (see also: tension)

rhythm the way that notes relate to each other in time

root the bottom note of a chord

root position the basic arrangement of a chord with the root at the bottom

round (Max object) rounds up a floating-point number to the next integer

rubato the "stealing" of time internally by speeding up and slowing down locally in a way that balances out and returns (restores) back to the overall tempo of the piece

salsa a popular style of dance music that arose in New York City and Puerto Rico in the mid-twentieth century; it represents an amalgamation of Cuban, Puerto Rican, West African, Spanish, and American elements. It is associated with energetic rhythms produced by a collection of Cuban percussion instruments, especially bongos, congas, timbales, claves, maracas, and guiro.

sample (1) short audio recording

sample (2) individual amplitude values – snapshots of an audio waveform in very tiny increments of time

saptak name for the diatonic pattern in the Hindustani music system

scale a structured set of intervals that spans an octave, bounded on either end by a lower and upper note called the tonic

scale degree names or numbers that represent how individual notes are associated with the intervallic structures of the scale

scientific pitch notation the system of naming notes where numbers are assigned that indicate the octave register in which the note belongs

search path the specific list of nested folders and subfolders in which a file resides on a computer filesystem or hard drive

second (interval) an interval that spans two adjacent letter names and comes in two standard forms: minor and major. (A minor second is also called a half step or semitone, and a major second is also called a whole step.) Seconds are considered to be dissonant intervals.

second inversion when the fifth of a chord occupies the lowest pitch in a chord voicing

select (Max object) compares all incoming messages to its list of arguments; it sends a bang out of the outlet corresponding to any matching argument (or a bang out of its rightmost outlet if there is no match)

semitone also called a "half step" – the basic unit of pitch measurement; the smallest granularity of a note

sequencer an electronic device that records and plays back sequences of notes in a particular order

seventh an interval that spans seven adjacent letter names; sevenths are considered to be dissonant intervals and come in two standard forms: minor and major

seventh chord common chords that contain four notes and feature intervals above the root of a third, fifth, and seventh

shift register a venerable method for storing and moving data that has been used in computers for many decades

shrutis microtones used to create melodic variety and expression in the Hindustani music tradition

shuddh swaras the standard set of "pure" (correct) notes in the Hindustani music system

sig~ (Max object) converts a number into an audio-rate signal

sight-singing also called "prima vista" singing, this is the activity of viewing notated music and immediately vocalizing the indicated notes. Often combined with solfège (see below), it is a component of aural skills training in college-level musicianship courses.

signal in the field of signal processing, a signal is a sequence of analog or digital values that carry information; an audio signal is a signal composed of sound information, either recorded using a microphone (or a similar transducer), or created by a synthesizer

signal flow the sequential passage of audio data between stages (in *Max*, between objects via patch cords), often being modified or transformed at each step along the path

simple interval a pitch interval of an octave or smaller

simple meter a metrical pattern where each measure contains four or fewer beats

sixteenth note the ¼ subdivision of a quarter note beat duration

sixth an interval that spans six adjacent letter names; sixths are considered to be imperfectly consonant intervals and come in two standard forms: minor and major

slider (Max object) an interface object that resembles other sliding controls you might see in the real world, such as lighting dimmers or faders on sound mixing boards. Slider objects output numbers within a specific numerical range, shaped by a bottom number ("output minimum") and a scaling factor ("output multiplier"); these and other settings for the slider object are specified in its object Inspector.

slur a form of articulation that groups sequences of notes together and indicates that they should all be played with unified, smooth, continuous phrasing connecting from one to the other

solfège the Western classical music education system that assigns specific syllables to scale degrees ("moveable do") or pitch letter names ("fixed do"). Standard syllable names include Do, Re, Mi, Fa, Sol, La, and Ti; adjustments can be made to indicate accidentals that modify the syllable from its standard form in the diatonic pattern. (Similar to the system of "sargam" syllables in the Hindustani music of North India.)

sound spectrum the combined collection of all the frequency components in a sound (fundamental plus overtones), along with their amplitude levels

spectrogram a visual depiction of the frequencies in an audio signal; a sound signal displayed in frequency domain format, with the vertical axis representing frequency and the horizontal axis representing time. Spectrograms display the amount of energy contained at individual frequency values over specific intervals of time. They allow you to observe how frequencies change as the music flows by.

spectroscope~ (Max object) an interface object that receives an audio signal in its left inlet and displays a real-time spectrogram

spelling identifying notes by letter name and accidental, or using note spelling information to identify intervals by number and quality

Stradella Bass System the series of buttons that are arranged in columns on the left side of an accordion and used to trigger chord playback

style (musical) a distinctive quality of a piece of music that gives it a characteristic expression associated with a specific composer or performer, time period, geographic location, emotional effect, or social context. In Western classical music, styles are often associated with historical periods such as Baroque, Classical, Romantic, and Modern; in popular music styles, we use descriptors such as jazz, blues, swing, rock and roll, gospel, rhythm & blues, Motown, funk, soul, disco, rap, and hip-hop.

subdivision (beat) proportional divisions of musical time; a shorter duration that fits within an individual beat, typically occurring in groups of two, three, four, or sometimes more per beat. Two subdivisions per beat are each ½-beat in duration; three subdivisions per beat are each ⅓-beat in duration, and four subdivisions per beat are each ¼-beat in duration.

subdominant (scale degree) the fourth scale degree (notated $\hat{4}$)

submediant (scale degree) the sixth scale degree (notated $\hat{6}$)

subtonic (scale degree) the lower form of the seventh scale degree (notated $\hat{7}$), found in scales where the seventh step of the scale forms an interval of a minor seventh with the tonic below

"suitcase word" a term coined by Marvin Minsky in *The Emotion Machine* to describe short words that contain many complex sub-components. Suitcase words exist at too high a level of abstraction, masking a jumble of interrelated but unresolved relationships of meaning that remain to be clarified one day with more precise language. Musical terms seem to frequently serve as suitcase words.

supertonic (scale degree) the second scale degree (notated $\hat{2}$)

sustain the middle section of a note that holds a somewhat steady amplitude level for an arbitrary length; the third phase of an amplitude envelope

syncopation when different types of beat subdivisions are grouped together in irregular ways that extend across beats into longer, fractional durations

syntax rules in a spoken or written language about how to group words together in phrases and sentences to create meaning

tala the metrical system used to measure time in the South Asian musical traditions of Hindustani and Carnatic music

tap tempo a technique for calculating beats per minute (BPM) values by physically tapping out beats on an interface and dividing the total number of beats by a specific unit of time

tempo the speed of a musical section, quantified using the number of beats per minute (BPM)

tendency tones notes that have a strong sense of gravitational pull toward other adjacent notes

tension (musical) a commonly shared concept in tonal music that certain sequences of elements can cause a perception of increased intensity in listeners. Often, tension is built by raising the level of dissonance or complexity in the musical structure, or when a performer emphasizes and intensifies specific expressive features. Simple, consonant structures and relaxed expressions establish and reinforce a sense of comfort, stability, and normalcy;

changes to those default conditions, especially unusual or unexpected choices, can cause tension to build up. Novel patterns of tension and resolution in music can cause increased engagement in listeners.

tenuto   an articulation instruction that means "held" in Italian; it indicates that notes should be sustained for their full duration

tetrachord   a set of four notes that spans the interval of a perfect fourth and contributes to the formation of scales. The four basic types include major, minor (Dorian), Phrygian (upper minor), and harmonic.

texture   the way in which different musical elements are combined to create a uniform density of layers, usually categorized as monophonic (solo line), homophonic (melody with accompaniment), or polyphonic (multiple independent parts)

thaat   Hindustani scale family

theme   musical material that provides a sense of identity, usually with a recognizable melody and perceivable as a complete musical expression in itself

third (chord)   the second element in a chord, located an interval of a third above the root note when the chord is in root position

third (interval)   an interval that spans three adjacent letter names; thirds are considered to be imperfectly consonant intervals and come in two standard forms: minor and major

thirty-second note   the 1/8 subdivision of a quarter note beat duration

thispatcher (Max object)   receives messages that cause it to modify aspects of a patcher window while the patch is running

timbre   the specific tone quality or "color" of a sound, usually associated with a particular instrument or synthesis algorithm that created the sound

time domain   the horizontal dimension of music, associated with time. (In twentieth-century communications system engineering, the phrase "time domain" came to refer to changes in signals with respect to time.)

time unit box system (TUBS)   a system of rhythmic notation that uses rows of boxes to represent units of time, with checks in the boxes where sounds should be played

timer (Max object)   like a stopwatch, the timer object receives bang (trigger) messages and reports back the time difference between them in milliseconds

togedge (Max object)   receives values of 0 or 1 (often from a toggle object) and reports when they change. At the "rising edge," when going from 0 to 1, togedge sends a bang out its left outlet; at the "falling edge," when 1 changes to 0, it sends a bang out its right outlet.

toggle (Max object)   an interface object that outputs only Boolean values of 0 or 1. These values can be used like regular integers, or they can be applied in a variety of contexts to simulate conditions such as "true" and "false."

"tonal pitch space"   a term used by Fred Lerdahl in a 2001 book to frame and describe the conditions that define stable tonal relationships between structures such as notes and chords, characterizing those relationships using spatial concepts such as distance

tonal system (tonality)   the complex system of relationships between notes and note groupings in a scale or key that help to define the functions of each note

tonic (scale degree)   the foundational starting pitch of a scale

transposition   changing the starting pitch of a collection of notes (including scale patterns), and thereby raising or lowering all the notes by the same amount

triad   a chord with three pitch classes

triple meter   a metrical pattern where each measure contains three beats

triplet   a three-note group whose rhythmic pattern subdivides a larger duration into three equal parts

tritone   an interval that contains three whole steps and represents a perfect bisection of the octave. Tritones are considered to be highly dissonant.

Glossary

tuning the alignment of notes in the frequency domain so they sound good together

tuning system a tuning system sets the exact frequencies for all notes, providing a common framework so that different instruments and voices can play harmoniously together without needing to negotiate the terms

twelfth root of two the semitone ratio used in equal temperament to convert frequencies to pitch numbers: $2^{1/12}$, generally approximated as 1.059463.

ubutton (Max object) a transparent version of the button object that defines a clickable region on the screen. Place a ubutton over text, images, or other visual elements to define an area within which you can click to send a trigger or make a selection.

umenu (Max object) an interface object that displays a selectable menu of options; once a user clicks on an item to select it, the umenu object outputs the number and text associated with that item (the item number is sent out the left outlet; the item text is sent out the middle outlet)

"under the hood" the internal workings of complex systems. This book occasionally defers detailed discussions of technical issues in order to focus on a limited set of features. Simplifying an area of investigation by relegating certain topics to remain "under the hood" can be a practical way to support learning and problem-solving by initially reducing unnecessary complexities. This resembles how many of us drive cars and use mobile phones without knowing all the details of how they work.

unison an interval where there is no difference between two notes; they share the same pitch and are named identically. Unisons can have the quality of perfect, augmented, or diminished.

unpack (Max object) receives a list of alpha-numeric characters (numbers and letters) and splits it into its elements

valence positive or negative associations; used to quantify the relative amount of positivity or negativity in an emotional experience. The concept of valence connects to qualities of pleasantness and likability in sound; you can think about valence as a variable value along a continuum of positive and negative responses to music.

variable representation of a piece of data that has a changeable value. Variables allow us to remember (store) quantities and change them over time.

volume the perceived loudness of a sound

waveform (also, waveshape) an image of a sound displaying moment-to-moment, instantaneous loudness values on the vertical dimension and time on the horizontal dimension

whole note the 4× multiple of a quarter note beat duration, or a duration that fills a whole measure

whole step an interval of a major second

whole-tone scale a six-note scale with adjacent notes each a M2 apart. It gained some popularity in the early twentieth century among European composers who were interested in experimenting with "orientalist" and exotic sounds.

wolf interval a dissonant interval that results from using variable interval ratios in tuning systems such as Pythagorean and different forms of meantone temperament

Index

For the benefit of digital users, indexed terms that span two pages (e.g., 52–53) may, on occasion, appear on only one of those pages.

Tables and figures are indicated by *t* and *f* following the page number

a cappella, 173
Ableton, 3, 12, 17, 52, 69
absolute pitch. *See* perfect pitch
absolute tempo (perfect tempo), 146–47
absolute value, 83, 86, 159
abstraction (layers, levels), 9–10, 70, 75–76, 96–97, 118, 133–34, 163
accent, 77–78, 80
accidental (chromatic alteration), 99, 100, 103–4, 105, 131
acoustic (acoustics), 39, 41, 66, 75–76, 89, 90–91, 94, 138, 139
acoustic beats, 91–92, 93, 171, 175
acoustic power. *See* gain
ADSR, 77
Aeolian mode, 124*t*, 133
Affective Computing (Rosalind Picard), 191n.20
Afrofuturism, 182
alankara, 128
alchemy, 2
algorithm, 37, 140, 185–86
algorithmic composition, 156, 159, 185–86
allegro, 139
amplitude, 62–63, 74, 76–78, 79, 94, 138
amplitude envelope, 77–78, 94
Antheil, George, 88, 180
anticipation, 147, 161
aperiodic sound, 89–90
appoggiatura, 159
Arduino, 57–58, 184–85
argument (Max), 25–26, 30, 34, 37, 39, 41–42, 49, 52, 54–55, 59, 69, 78, 113, 134, 135, 145, 157–59, 161
arithmetic symbols (Max objects), 29–30, 34, 35, 41, 116–17, 134, 135, 159
arpeggiator, 162–64
arpeggio, 138, 162–66, 169
Arrange menu, 22, 23
arrangement (arranging), 48, 57–58, 94, 182
articulation, 77–78, 160, 180
Artificial Intelligence (AI), 2, 156, 183–84
aspect ratio, 70
atonal (atonality), 8–9

attack (component of an amplitude envelope), 77, 79, 94–95
Audacity® software, 62–63, 66, 76, 77
Audio MIDI setup driver, 44–47, 55–56
audio signal processing. *See* signal processing
augmented (interval quality), 102, 103–5, 106, 108, 110–11, 114, 117, 120–21, 128, 155
augmented triad (chord), 130–31
aural skills, 111
Auto-Tune, 170

Babbitt, Milton, 181–82
Bach, Johann Sebastian, 173
backbeat, 149–50
bandish, 128
bang message, 20–21, 23, 42, 50, 56, 59, 117, 157, 158, 161
Beach Boys, 130–31
beat, 26, 79, 80–81, 82–84, 86–87, 139, 142, 143, 147, 148, 149–51, 152, 157–59, 160
beat matching, 141
beat subdivision. *See* subdivision
Beatles, The, 125, 130–31
beats per minute (BPM), 25–26, 141–46, 148, 157
Bell Telephone Laboratories (Bell Labs), 181–82
Berry, Chuck, 130–31
Bhairav (raga), 128
Blue Öyster Cult, 39
blues, 8–9, 91, 120, 131, 169
boolean value (data type, operator, logic), 32, 35, 143, 148, 185–86
Boulez, Pierre, 109–10
button object (Max), 19–27, 32–33, 34, 42, 59, 71, 142, 178

cadence, 131, 167–68, 169
Cage, John, 64–65, 88
Carnatic music, 126–27
cent (tuning), 72–73, 176
chalan, 127, 128
character (musical), 119, 127–28, 139, 141, 149, 160–61
chemistry, 2, 7–8

chord, 57–58, 91, 129–32, 133, 136–37, 162–69, 173
chord progression (harmonic progression), 91, 129, 166–69
chroma. *See* pitch class
chromatic alteration. *See* accidental
chromatic scale, 114, 175
Chrome Music Lab (Google), 63, 64*f*, 164–65, 166*f*
ChucK, 12
circle of fifths, 135, 164–65, 167
Circumplex model of affect (James Russell), 108, 153
click track, 26, 141
coding (creative coding), 2–3, 4–6, 7–8, 10, 11–13, 16–27, 57, 169, 179, 184–86
coherence, 7–8, 77–78, 80, 86, 87, 118, 130, 133, 136–37, 149, 152–53
Coldplay, 125
comment object (Max), 17, 27, 33–34, 35, 42, 65, 89–90, 167–68
common practice period, 8–9, 130
common time, 26, 149, 150*f*
composers, 12, 88, 119, 121, 126, 133, 141, 152–53, 155, 161, 166, 168–69, 173, 180
composition (musical), 6–7, 63, 64, 88, 99–100, 127–28, 183
compound interval, 102, 107
compound meter, 150–52
compression, 66, 70
computer science, 8, 9, 11
conditional statement, 158
conjunct motion (stepwise), 153
consonance (harmoniousness), 62, 72, 87, 90–93, 96, 102, 104–5, 106, 108, 152–53, 166, 170, 171, 172
Constructionism, 8, 184–85
constructive interference, 91–92
continuous variables, 4, 46, 71–73, 138, 140, 170, 176
contour, 76–77, 78, 121, 153–54, 155, 157, 159, 160–61, 162
counter, 34–35, 34*f*, 152
counterpoint, 6, 180
cowbell (never enough), 39, 40*f*
Csound, 12
Cycling '74, 11–13, 16–17, 68–69, 113, 176

daisy chain, 82–83, 154–55
data (data types), 12–13, 14, 17–19, 22–23, 24, 27–28, 29–30, 31–32, 35–36, 41–42, 43–44, 48, 52, 53, 54, 55, 58, 62–63, 79, 82, 86, 101, 126, 129, 143–44, 145, 161, 163, 185–86
data structure, 163, 185–86
Debussy, Claude, 126
decay (component of an amplitude envelope), 77

decibel (dB), 75–76, 78
degree of resolution, 36, 71–73, 101, 170, 177
Derks, Dan, 13
destructive interference, 91–92
diatonic chords, 136, 137, 166, 167
diatonic collection, 127
diatonic pattern, 122–25, 133
diatonic system, 136–37
dictation, 111
digital audio, 16, 53–56, 59, 61, 62–63, 81–82, 97, 138, 140–41, 145, 181–82, 185–86
digital audio interface, 15
digital audio workstation (DAW), 4, 17, 47–48, 50–51, 53, 77, 114, 139, 162–63, 170
digital music protocol, 43–44, 48, 52, 53
diminished (interval quality), 102, 103–5, 106, 108, 110–11
diminished seventh chord (fully diminished 7th chord), 131
diminished triad (chord), 130, 131, 136
disco, 8–9
discordance. *See* dissonance
discrete variables, 58, 72, 99–100, 102, 138
disjunct motion (interval), 153
dissonance (discordance), 62, 87, 90–93, 96, 108, 130–31, 152–53, 160–61, 166, 170, 171, 172
distribution (statistical), 157, 168
dominant (scale degree), 118–19, 124–25
dominant seventh chord (major-minor 7th chord), 120–21, 131, 136, 166, 167
doo-wop, 181–82
Dorian mode, 117, 120, 123, 124*t*, 124–25, 133, 162
Dorian tetrachord. *See* minor tetrachord
double flat (accidental, chromatic alteration, ♭♭), 99, 101, 103, 105, 106
double sharp (accidental, chromatic alteration, 𝄪), 99, 101, 104, 106, 130–31
drone, 176–77
DrumGenius, 141
duple meter, 149–52
duration, 4, 7–8, 24, 27, 36, 37, 38, 39–41, 42, 53, 55, 59, 62, 67–68, 70, 74, 77, 79–87, 93, 94, 96, 97, 98, 138, 139–40, 141, 142–43, 148, 149, 150, 153, 154–55, 157–58, 160
dynamics, 74–75, 75*t*, 78, 160

ear training, 6, 65–66, 111, 112, 113–14, 157
edit mode (Max), 21, 32, 68, 69–70, 81–82
Egozy, Eran, 48
eighth note, 80–82, 86, 149, 150–51, 154, 157–58
Electronic Dance Music (EDM), 26, 83, 141–42, 182
enharmonic equivalency, 103, 104, 110–11, 116
envelope. *See* amplitude envelope

Index

equal temperament, 72–73, 172–76
escape tone, 159
ethnomusicology, 90–91
Eurythmics, the, 162–63
"everyday tonality" (Philip Tagg), 9, 129, 133, 172–73
external object (Max), 12–13, 60, 113, 176, 177, 185–86
ezdac~ (Max object), 71, 72–73

Fandango, 149–50
fiddle~ (Max external object), 113, 177
fifth (chord element), 129–31, 132, 162, 163
fifth (interval), 104–5, 106, 107, 113–14, 119, 122, 124–25, 130–31, 134, 153, 173
filename, 20, 54–55, 116–17, 157
Finale software, 84–85
first inversion, 130, 131, 167
flat (accidental, chromatic alteration, ♭), 99, 116, 127, 133–34, 135
floating-point number (value), 28–29, 30, 31*f*, 31, 35, 71–72, 139–40, 143, 173, 177–78
fourth (interval), 102, 104–5, 106, 113–14, 117, 132, 153, 155, 158–59, 160–61
Franklin, Aretha ("Respect"), 25–26
frequency, 62–63, 66–67, 70–74, 78, 87, 89–90, 91–93, 94–95, 96, 98, 100, 102, 103, 104–5, 107, 108, 153, 162–63, 170–77
frequency domain, 62–63, 87, 94, 96, 170
frequency ratio, 72–73, 91, 104–5, 107, 172–74
fully diminished seventh chord. *See* diminished seventh chord
fundamental frequency, 70, 89–90
funk, 8–9, 120, 123, 149, 150
Fux, Johann, 155

gain (acoustic power), 71, 73, 74, 78
gain~ (Max object), 55–56, 65, 69, 71, 78
General MIDI (GM), 39, 41, 42, 43, 46–47, 50, 51, 52, 81–82, 96, 158
Gershwin, George, 88
Giugno, Giuseppe Di, 12
glissando, 38–39
gospel, 8–9
GROOVE (Bell Labs music synthesis system), 12
groove (rhythmic style), 83, 141, 150, 169
Groove Pizza (Ethan Hein), 85, 85*f*
groove~ (Max object), 54, 55, 56, 65, 68, 140–41
gswitch (Max object), 82–83, 86, 113, 117–18, 128–29, 134, 135, 154–55, 158
Guitar Hero, 48
guru-shishya parampara, 128

half-diminished seventh chord, 131
half note, 80–81, 149

half step. *See* semitone
harmonic interval, 171
harmonic minor scale, 120–21, 128
harmonic pitch class profile. *See* pitch class
harmonic progression. *See* chord progression
harmonic series. *See* overtones
harmonic tetrachord, 117, 120–21, 128
harmonicity, 89–90
harmoniousness. *See* consonance
harmony, 129, 132, 168–69
heart rate ("heart rate tempo"), 147
Hertz (Hz), 70, 71, 73, 74, 89–90, 91–92, 107, 171, 172, 173, 174–75
"hide on lock" feature (Max), 27, 51, 52, 72–73, 109
Hijaz (scale), 120
Hindustani music, 126–28
hip-hop, 8–9, 26, 88
homophony (homophonic), 94
Huynh, Everett, 164
Hyperscore software, 149, 150*f*, 150–51, 151*f*

imperfect authentic cadence, 167
imperfect consonance, 91, 104, 105, 106
inclusive counting, 101–2, 106
inharmonicity (inharmonic), 89–90, 93
inlet (Max), 12–13, 18, 22–23, 27, 29–30, 31–32, 35, 37–39, 41–42, 49, 55, 71, 78, 82, 86, 97, 117–18, 128–29, 134, 135, 142, 143, 157, 158, 161, 173–74
inner hearing, 112–13, 176–77
Inspector tool (for Max objects), 20, 21–22, 27, 28, 33–34, 35, 41, 42, 49, 55, 70, 71–73, 74, 97, 98, 109, 111, 126, 129, 140–41, 157
integer (whole number), 28, 29, 29*f*, 30, 32, 35, 71–72, 89–90, 91, 134–35, 142, 143, 161, 171, 173, 177–78
intensity (emotional), 75, 92, 108, 118, 119, 120–21, 147, 153
intensity (loudness, volume), 69, 74–80, 91–92, 183–84
interactivity (interactive), 6, 7, 11, 12, 13, 14, 16, 17, 47–48, 51, 142, 181–82
Interactive Music Programming (course), 6
interactive music systems, 180, 185–86
interface object (Max), 20, 32, 42, 49, 52, 56, 72–73, 82–83, 86, 161, 163
interonset interval, 142–43, 145, 146*f*, 151–52, 154, 157
interval, 91, 101–14, 115, 116–17, 118, 119, 120, 121–22, 123, 124*t*, 125, 127, 128, 129, 130–32, 134, 153, 157, 158–59, 160–61, 166, 171–72, 173–74, 175
interval inversion, 106, 119
interval spelling. *See* letter notation

inversion (chord), 130, 131, 167
Ionian mode, 124t, 133
IRCAM (Institute for Research and Coordination in Acoustics/Music), 12, 109–10
Ives, Charles, 126

jazz, 6–7, 8–9, 91, 120, 128, 181–82
jitter (signal), 143
Jitter software, 12, 17
just intonation, 170–73, 175, 176

key (musical), 131, 132–37, 155, 158, 160–61, 167
key signature, 133–34
keyboard shortcuts, 19–20, 21–22, 27, 35
kilohertz (kHz), 176
Kondo, Koji, 48–49
kräftig, 139
Kraftwerk, 163

Labelle, 182
"launchbrowser" command, 27, 113–14
leading tone (scale degree), 118–19, 120–21, 125, 131, 136, 166, 167
Legend of Zelda, 125
Lego bricks, 3, 8, 62, 97, 117, 138–39, 172–73
Leitmotiv, 127–28, 160–61, 162
letter notation, 98, 99–100, 101, 110–13
lexicon, 19
Lincoln Logs, 8
LittleBits, 184–85
Little Richard, 131
"Lo, How a Rose E'er Blooming" (Michael Praetorius), 57–58
Locrian mode, 124t, 124–25
Logic Pro X software, 4, 5f, 48, 50–51, 162–63
Logo (programming language), 184
loop (musical, coding), 6, 23–24, 25–26, 27, 34–35, 49, 50, 54, 56, 82–83, 85, 100, 123, 124, 134, 149, 152, 154–55, 166–67
Lydian mode, 124t, 124–25

Mac Operating System (MacOS), 13–14, 19–20, 22–23, 31, 33, 44–47, 50, 51, 52, 56
machine learning, 9, 156
major (interval quality), 102, 104, 105, 106, 108, 110–11, 113–14, 117, 119, 121–22, 123, 130–31, 153, 172, 175
major key, 133, 135, 137, 158, 167
major scale (mode), 115–17, 118, 119, 120, 121, 122–23, 125, 127, 128, 133, 137, 158
major seventh chord (major-major 7th chord), 131
major-minor seventh chord. See dominant seventh chord

major tetrachord, 117, 118, 121, 124–25
major triad (chord), 130, 131, 136, 163, 164–65
Makey Makey, 56–61, 97, 100–1, 115–16, 126, 184–85
Malloy, Dan, 57–58
Manzo, V.J., 17
marcato, 77–78
mashup, 141
Mathews, Max V., 12, 181–82
Max console window, 19–20
meantone tuning (temperament), 173
measure (bar), 34–35, 149–52, 169
mediant (scale degree, chord), 118–19, 131, 136, 137
melodic interval, 96, 102–3, 153, 155
melodic minor scale, 114–15, 120, 121
melody, 59–60, 137, 152–62
message object (Max), 30–33, 34, 35, 42, 49–51, 54–55, 65, 113–14, 135, 165, 171
Messiaen, Olivier, 180
meter (musical), 26, 85–86, 138, 148–52
meter (audio level), 55, 65, 79
metronome, 19, 26, 86–87, 141, 148, 157
microtone (microtonal), 72–73, 127, 169, 176
middle C, 39–41, 100, 101, 116, 134–35, 173–74, 175
MIDI (Musical Instrument Digital Interface), 5f, 15, 16–17, 35–52, 53, 54, 59, 61, 70, 72–73, 77–78, 81–82, 83, 96, 97, 98, 99–100, 101, 115, 116, 120, 122, 134–35, 145, 151–52, 154–55, 157, 158, 163, 170, 173–75, 177, 178, 185–86
MIDI Association, 17, 42, 44
MIDI keyboard (MIDI controller), 15, 43–44, 45–47, 60, 97
MIDI message (types), 36, 37
millisecond, 24, 25–26, 27, 37, 39–41, 78, 81–82, 86, 93, 109, 135, 142–43, 148, 151–52, 157, 158
Minecraft, 8, 184–85
minor (interval quality), 102, 104, 105, 106, 108, 110–11, 113–14, 120, 121–22, 123, 130, 131, 153, 175
minor key, 160–61, 162
minor scale (modal scales, Hijaz, natural, harmonic, melodic), 114–15, 120–21, 123, 125, 128, 133
minor seventh chord (minor-minor 7th chord), 131
minor tetrachord (Dorian tetrachord), 117, 120–21, 124–25
minor triad (chord, 7th chord), 130, 131, 136, 164–65
Minsky, Marvin, 2, 184

Mixolydian mode, 124*t*, 124–25
modal mixture, 125
modes (modal scales), 120, 122–25, 124*t*, 133
modes of vibration. *See* vibration
modulation (musical), 131
modulo, 134, 135, 137
monophony, 94, 162, 176
motive, 160
Motown, 8–9, 182
moving average, 143, 144*f*, 144, 145
Mozart, W.A., 180
MTS-ESP, 170
Muscle Shoals Rhythm Section, 26
Musescore software, 4, 5*f*, 48, 51–52
MUSIC I–V, 12
Music Information Retrieval (MIR), 135
music notation, 4–6, 11, 39–41, 43, 47–48, 51, 84–85, 138, 182–83
music theory (fundamentals), 2–6, 7–8, 11–12, 15, 62, 91, 111, 133–34, 138, 155, 182, 185–86
Musique concrète, 88

natural (accidental, chromatic alteration, ♮), 99, 133
natural minor scale, 120–21, 123, 125
"New Tonality" (John Harbison), 8–9
New Wave, 162–63
Nintendo, 48–49
noise, 62, 64, 67, 87, 88–90, 92–93
non-chord tone, 159
note (definition), 96–98
'note on' message (MIDI), 35, 36–38, 42, 52, 96

Obenauer, Emily, 111
object (Max, definition), 12–13, 20
octatonic scale, 126
octave, 99, 100, 101, 102, 103–4, 105, 106–8, 114, 115, 119, 122–23, 134–35, 153, 158–59, 163, 171, 172–75
octave equivalence, 107
Ondes Martenot, 180
Opcode Systems, 12
operating system, 12, 44–46
orchestration, 94, 160–61
order of operations, 18
ordinal numbers, 102
outlet (Max), 12–13, 22–23, 27, 29, 31–32, 34–35, 37–38, 49–50, 52, 54–55, 59, 60, 71, 117–18, 128–29, 134, 143–44, 158, 161
overtones (overtone series), 62, 70, 89–90, 91–93, 94–95, 102, 103–4, 107, 108, 135, 171, 173

pakad, 127, 128
Palestrina, Giovanni Pierluigi da, 180

Papert, Seymour, 184, 185
passing tones, 159
patch (patcher), 12–14, 16–17, 18–20, 21–23, 25, 26–27, 28–32, 33–35, 37–42, 45–46, 48, 49–52, 53–55, 56, 57–58, 59–60, 61, 65, 68–72, 79, 81–82, 91, 97, 100–1, 103, 109, 111, 112, 113–14, 116–17, 118, 126, 128, 129, 132, 134, 135, 137, 140–41, 142, 143, 145, 151–52, 156–57, 159, 161, 163, 164, 167, 168–69, 170, 171, 176–77
patch cord, 12–13, 17–18, 20, 22–23, 24–25, 26, 27, 29, 31, 33–35, 37–39, 41–42, 50, 52, 54–55, 56, 68, 71, 135, 142, 143, 154–55
Patcher (predecessor to Max), 12
patching mode (Max), 21, 32, 68, 74, 83, 126
Pd (software language), 12
pedal point, 176–77
pentatonic scale(s), 114, 121–22
peripheral devices, 15
perfect (interval quality), 102, 103–5, 108, 113–14, 117, 122, 124–25, 130, 134, 135, 172, 173
perfect authentic cadence, 167
perfect consonance, 91, 102, 106, 171
perfect pitch (absolute pitch), 73, 107, 133, 146–47, 176–77
period (periodic), 89, 141–42, 147
Periodic Table, 2
phase, 77, 94
phase vocoder, 140
Philadelphia Sound, the, 182
Phrygian mode (Phrygian minor scale), 120, 124*t*, 124–25
Phrygian tetrachord (upper minor tetrachord), 117, 120, 121, 124–25
physiology (physiological), 1, 107, 147
Piaget, Jean, 184
piano keyboard, 11, 15, 38–41, 72–73, 99–100, 102, 122–23, 134, 172–73
pipe object, 24–26, 27, 37, 81–83, 109, 134, 135, 145, 154–55, 158
pitch, 4, 7–8, 11, 36, 37–38, 39–41, 50, 53, 57–58, 59–60, 62–63, 66–67, 70, 72–74, 79, 81–82, 83, 89, 93, 94–95, 96–137, 138, 140–41, 142, 152, 154–55, 158, 163, 170, 171, 172–73, 174–75, 176–77, 178, 183–84
pitch bend, 36, 170
pitch class (chroma, harmonic pitch class profile), 94, 100, 108, 115, 118, 122, 123, 129, 133, 134–35, 136, 137
pitch tracking, 113, 177*f*, 177
playback speed, 48, 51, 139–41, 145–46, 154
Ploskonka, Thomas, 167
polyphony (polyphonic), 94, 162, 180
polyrhythm, 86–87

pop (popular music), 4, 6–7, 8–9, 11, 25–26, 109–10, 120, 121–22, 123, 130–31, 141, 162–63, 166–67, 182
portato, 77–78
Praetorius, Michael, 75
Presentation mode (Max), 68–70, 78, 81–83, 99, 100–1, 117–18, 126, 132, 140–41, 157, 167–68
Pro Tools software, 162–63
Processing (computer language), 184–85
programming, 11, 12–13, 16–17, 19, 27–28, 158, 184–86
progressive cadence, 167
progressive rock (prog rock), 44
protocol, 43–44, 48, 52, 53
psychoacoustics, 74, 90–91
psychology, 87
Puckette, Miller S., 12, 53, 113, 177
pulse (pulse train), 79, 82–83, 139, 141–42, 147, 148, 157
Pythagoras, 91–92

quadruple meter, 150, 151–52
qualia, 107
quality (interval, chord), 101, 102–4, 107, 109–10, 129, 130, 131, 163, 164
quantization, 83, 141
quartal harmony, 132
quarter note, 80–82, 149, 157–58

Rachmaninoff, Sergei, 126
raga (raag), 126–28
rap, 8–9, 182
rarefaction, 66, 70
Raspberry Pi, 184–85
ratio (frequency ratios, interval ratios, playback speed ratios, etc.), 72–73, 76, 82–83, 89, 91–93, 102, 104–5, 107, 108, 139–41, 145–46, 154, 170–74, 176
RCA Corporation, 181–82
Redding, Otis, 25–26
Reference Tool (Max), 20
register, 39–41, 100, 134, 160–61, 173–74, 177
relative minor/major scale, 120, 133
release (component of an amplitude envelope), 77, 79
release velocity, 36–37
remainder, 134–35, 137
remix, 2–3, 7, 13, 88, 152
resolution (musical), 62, 87, 90, 92, 93, 105, 118, 119, 128, 130–31, 147, 152–53, 161, 166, 167, 169
reverberation (reverb), 64, 66, 180
rhythm, 11, 26, 79–87, 125, 131, 147, 148, 152, 155, 157–58, 160, 163, 183–84

rhythm & blues (R&B), 8–9, 25–26, 123, 181–82
Rimsky-Korsakov, Nikolai, 126
Roberts, Rebecca, 57–58
Roblox, 8, 184–85
rock and roll, 8–9, 121–22, 125, 131, 149, 181–82
Rock Band (game), 48
root (root note), 129–31, 136, 162, 163–64
root position, 129, 130, 131, 167
Route Patch Cords (Max setting), 23
rubato, 139, 160
Russolo, Luigi, 88

salsa (rhythmic pattern), 83–85
sample (audio file, individual amplitude value), 53–54, 55
sample code (sample patches), 13, 14, 15, 16–17, 19, 20, 25, 33–35, 39, 48–49, 56, 58, 60, 65, 68, 81–82, 83, 91, 94–95, 102–3, 106, 108, 110, 111, 122, 126, 151–52, 154–55, 156, 164, 165, 166, 167
saptak, 127
scale, 59–60, 98, 114–29, 133, 136–37, 153, 155, 158, 160–61, 162, 175
scale degree, 118–19, 120–21, 123, 125, 131, 133
scientific pitch notation, 100
Scratch (programming language), 8, 11, 57, 184–85
Scriabin, Alexander, 126
search path, 49, 54–55
second (interval), 102, 104, 105, 106, 108, 110–11, 113–14, 117, 119, 120–22, 123, 128, 153, 155, 158–59, 175
second inversion, 130
segmented patch cords, 23
semitone (half step), 72–73, 100–5, 106, 109, 112–13, 115, 116–17, 120–21, 122, 123, 124–25, 126, 127, 131, 133, 134, 171, 172–75, 176, 177–78
sequence (musical), 49, 79, 80, 98, 115, 120, 122–23, 124, 127, 134, 135, 136, 138, 141–42, 148, 152–53, 154, 163, 166–67, 168, 175
sequencer, 49
Seurat, Georges, 162–63
"seven plus five" keyboard layout, 123
seventh (interval), 102, 105, 106, 131, 158–59, 162
seventh chord (7th chord), 131–32, 169
sharp (accidental, chromatic alteration, ♯), 99, 116, 133, 134, 135
Sheehan, Kyle, 57–58
shift register, 143–44
shruti, 127
shuddh swara, 127, 128
sight-singing, 111

signal (audio, acoustic, electrical, digital, musical), 11, 19, 36, 44, 53, 54, 55–56, 62–63, 65, 66–67, 71, 73, 74, 76–77, 78, 79, 91–93, 94, 121, 138, 139–40, 143, 147, 176
signal flow, 18, 185–86
signal processing (audio signal processing), 12, 53, 56, 62–63, 95, 143
simple interval, 102, 105
simple meter, 151–52
sixteenth note, 80–81, 86, 149, 154
sixth (interval), 105, 106, 107, 130, 158–59
slur, 77–78
solfège, 111
Songsmith, 168–69
Sonic Pi, 12
soul music, 8–9, 149
Soundtrap software, 114, 115*f*
sound library (sample library), 48, 55
sound intensity level (SIL), 75–76, 78
sound pressure level (SPL), 66–67, 76
sound spectrum, 94–95
spectrogram, 62–63, 89–90, 93, 94–95
spelling intervals. *See* letter notation
Star Wars, 113–14, 160–61
state (computing), 32–33, 77, 135, 185–86
STEM, 4–6, 9, 10, 11, 184
STEAM, 11, 57
Stradella Bass System, 132
Stravinsky, Igor, 126
style (musical), 4, 8–9, 26, 83–84, 141–42, 166, 169, 175–76
subdivision (beat), 80–81, 82–83, 86, 149, 150–51
subdominant (scale degree, chord), 118–19, 131, 136, 166
submediant (scale degree, chord), 118–19, 120, 131, 136, 166, 167
subtonic (scale degree, chord), 118–19, 120–21, 125
"suitcase word," 10, 96–97, 183
Sun Ra's Arkestra, 182
Supercollider, 12
supertonic (scale degree, chord), 118–19, 131, 136, 137, 166
Super Mario Bros. (video game), 48–49
suspense, 147, 161
suspensions (musical), 159
sustain (component of an amplitude envelope), 77, 80
swing, 8–9, 181–82
syncopation, 81
syntax, 18
synesthesia, 133

Tagg, Philip, 9
tala, 152
tap tempo, 142, 144–45
tempo, 26, 52, 80, 85–86, 138, 139–48, 152, 157, 158, 160, 163, 164–65
tendency tone, 105, 118–19, 155, 159
tension, 62, 87, 90, 91–92, 93, 118, 119, 120–21, 147, 152–53, 155, 161, 166, 167, 169
tenuto, 77–78
tetrachord, 117–18, 120–21, 124–25, 128, 129
texture, 94, 109–10, 160, 162–63, 183–84
thaat, 127–28
The College of New Jersey (TCNJ), 6, 57–58, 111, 164, 167
theme, 48–49, 50–51, 113–14, 160–61
Theremin, 180, 181–82
third (chord element), 129–30, 162
third (interval), 102, 104, 106, 107, 110–11, 119, 129, 130–31, 132, 153, 158–59
thirty-second note, 80–81
timbre, 36, 37, 39, 41–42, 59–60, 70, 82, 93–95, 96, 97, 98, 113, 158, 160, 183–84
time domain, 62–63, 66, 138, 153
time unit box system (TUBS), 83–85
Tinker Toys, 8
"tonal pitch space" (Fred Lerdahl), 96
tonal system (tonality, tonal music, tonal framework, organization, structure), 8–9, 100, 103–4, 108, 129, 133, 134–35, 136–37, 172–73
tonic (scale degree, chord), 114, 115, 116, 117, 118–19, 121–22, 123, 124–25, 126, 128, 131, 133–34, 136–37, 153, 155, 157, 158, 159, 166, 167, 168, 169, 171, 175
transposition (transpose), 114, 115*f*, 116–17, 172, 173
triad, 129–32, 163
triple meter, 149–50, 151–52
triplet, 80–81, 83, 150–51
tritone, 104–5, 124–25, 130
tuning (tuning systems), 8, 11, 48, 72, 92–93, 101, 127, 170, 171, 172–73, 175–76
twelfth root of two, 173–75
twelve-tone tuning system. *See* equal temperament

ubutton object (Max), 27, 42, 97, 98, 109, 111, 113–14, 117, 135
"under the hood," 10, 38, 43, 44, 49, 51, 52, 53, 62–63, 66–67, 68, 72, 78, 81, 82, 99, 100–1, 108, 132, 135, 157
unison, 103, 104, 107, 110–11, 158–59
upper minor tetrachord. *See* Phrygian tetrachord
USB port, 15, 58

valence, 87–93, 183–84

variable, 18–19, 24, 25–26, 36–37, 41–42, 50, 68, 72, 74, 80, 94, 99–100, 102, 108, 114, 116–17, 123, 139, 141–42, 143, 153, 162
vibration (frequency, cycle, modes of vibration), 66–67, 70, 71–72, 74, 76, 89, 91, 96
volume, 18–19, 36–37, 39–41, 50, 53, 59, 65, 66, 69, 70, 71, 74, 75, 78, 81–82, 89, 91–92, 94, 96, 97, 98, 108, 113, 119, 149, 164, 171, 180

Wang, Jonathan, 57–58
watt, 75–76
waveform (waveshape), 62–63, 66–67, 68–69, 76–77, 94–95, 138
Well-Tempered Clavier, The (J.S. Bach), 173

whole note, 80–81, 149
whole step, 104–5, 112–13, 115, 118–19, 120–21, 123, 124, 125, 126, 133
whole-tone scale, 126
Williams, John, 160–61
Windows operating system, 13–14, 19–20, 21, 22–23, 24–25, 45–46, 50, 52
Winkler, Todd, 17
wolf interval, 173
Wright, Matt, 17

YouTube, 7, 16–17, 25–26, 27, 54, 113–14, 140–41

Zimmer, Hans, 147